Recollecting Our Lives

Recollecting Our Lives

Women's Experience Of Childhood Sexual Abuse

Women's Research Centre

PRESS GANG PUBLISHERS
VANCOUVER

CANADIAN CATALOGUING IN PUBLICATION DATA
    Recollecting our lives

        Includes bibliographic references.
        ISBN 0-88974-019-4

        1. Adult child sexual abuse victims. I. Women's
    Research Centre (Vancouver, B.C.)
    HQ71.R42   1989   362.7'044   C89-091462-1

The Women's Reasearch Centre acknowledges the financial assistance of Health and Welfare Canada's Victims of Violence Programme and the Women's Programme of the Department of the Secretary of State of Canada.

First Printing November 1989
1   2   3   4   5   92   91   90   89

Edited by Penny Goldsmith and Megan Ellis
Indexed by Robin Van Heck
Design, typesetting and production by Val Speidel
Editor for the Press: Barbara Kuhne
Type produced by The Typeworks
Printed by Gagné Printing
Printed and bound in Canada

Press Gang Publishers
603 Powell Street
Vancouver, B.C. V6A 1H2   Canada

Recollecting Our Lives is the result of a collaborative effort by Pamela Sleeth, Jan Barnsley, and Megan Ellis who, along with the Women's Research Centre, are responsible for its content.

Written by: Pamela Sleeth and Jan Barnsley.

Interviewers: Megan Ellis, Margaret Jones, and Pamela Sleeth.

Researchers: Nadine Allen, Jan Barnsley, Megan Ellis, Margaret Jones, and Pamela Sleeth, with literature review assistance from Jan Forde.

Acknowledgements

We at the Women's Research Centre are grateful to the women interviewed for this project. Your honesty, your willingness and your courage made this book possible. We dedicate *Recollecting Our Lives* to you and to all women who, by telling their stories, break the silence and affirm women's survival.

We also thank the women who worked on the project. We acknowledge in particular Pamela Sleeth's work in developing the Survivor's Cycle and the concept of "exits from the cycle," which frame our discussion of the consequences of child sexual abuse and the ways women and children break free. Thanks, too, to Diana Ellis, who initiated the Centre's research on this issue (urged on by Pam); to Jeannie McIntosh and Jennifer Ellis for their skill and perseverance in word processing; and to Lisa Price, Shelley Rivkin, Diana Ellis, and the women we interviewed who read the manuscript and provided such useful suggestions. Finally, special thanks to Megan and Pam for their staying power, and to Jan for holding it all together.

—Women's Research Centre

There are many people who have helped and enabled me in this work. My friends Lisa Price and Martha Royea supported and encouraged me from the beginning; my brother, Jim, passed on his computer and held my hand as I overcame my computer phobia; my friends tolerated my absence with only gentle complaints. I also want to acknowledge the women who have worked with me over the years in my private practice. You continue to challenge, teach and inspire me. My heartfelt appreciation also goes to Karlene Faith, Silva Tenenbein and Devorah Greenberg for their support and most useful criticism. My friend and co-writer, Jan Barnsley, has provided amazing faith, good sense, and goodwill in the face of all the obstacles presented through the course of this project. And finally, if I were to acknowledge any single person for enabling my work, it would be my mother, Phyllis Benedict. She has persisted in loving and encouraging me and my work throughout my unconventional life.

—Pamela Sleeth

I want to express my gratitude to the many women I've learned from: to the women who were interviewed for this book and whose stories renew my commitment to understand and to act; to the feminist groups whose work make action possible; to my co-workers for the countless discussions which informed and challenged me; and to Darlene Munro and Lorraine Mitchell, whose words so often echoed in my mind as I wrote.

I am particularly grateful to Lisa Price for her patience, support and wise counsel respectfully given; and to Barbara Kuhne, who pointed the way when the re-writing seemed impossible. I also thank my friends for their interest in this work as well as for reminding me to play tennis and walk on the beach. And special thanks to Andrée Buchanan for her insight, encouragement and understanding, and for regularly helping to restore my perspective.

—Jan Barnsley

Contents

Introduction

It was radical then—to sit talking and plotting the overthrow of a centuries-old secret. Seam by seam we unstitched the vestment of myth from a common but well-concealed truth: Children were regularly molested within the home as a matter of everyday living. (Armstrong 1985:10)

W OMEN who were sexually abused as children endured a range of assaults. Some were "just" fondled. Some were penetrated by fingers or objects. Some were raped. Some were tortured. For some children the abuse occurred as isolated incidents. For others it was a daily fact of life for years. It all had consequences.

Yet women survive. Adult survivors say that in time they can name what was done to them and come to understand the abuse was not their fault. Piece by piece they collect the fragments of their lives which were damaged, distorted or displaced by the abuse and they make sense of their experience.

Recollecting Our Lives is about women's experience of childhood sexual abuse. It is also about women and children's survival. This book is based on interviews with seventeen adult survivors and eight women whose children were sexually abused. We interviewed women because we know that women talking about their lives makes it possible to separate the truth from myths and theories. And unless we know the truth about childhood sexual abuse, we can't know how to stop it.

We have made the book as much as possible a dialogue among women. In the pages that follow we compare and contrast the experiences the women we interviewed described to us and we discuss the patterns that emerged for us from their accounts. We focus on the similarities and differences in what women told us, much as women would do talking together in a group, exchanging stories.

We believe that weaving together the patterns in women's experience of abuse will help survivors, as well as mothers of abused children, to develop perspective on their lives, to understand how and why the abuse was not their fault, to know they're not alone, and to learn more about how it is possible to survive.

Who We Are

The motivation to do the interviews which led to this book grew out of our participation in women's groups. Each of us involved in the Women's Research Centre's committee for this project has worked with women for many years in a variety of settings.

Three of us had worked with battered women in the early 1980s doing organizing, educational and support work and research through Vancouver Transition House, Battered Women's Support Services, and the Women's Research Centre. One of us is a long-time advocate and activist on issues that affect women who are raped and a founder of the Women Against Violence Against Women Rape Crisis Centre (WAVAW/RCC). Two of us, as members of the Working Group on Sexual Violence, had also worked on the issues of prostitution and pornography. Two of us had done years of child sexual abuse counselling work with adult survivors, children and mothers. Some of us are survivors ourselves and all of us have friends or lovers who are survivors.

We learned about child sexual abuse from our own experience and from talking with women. We learned that women talking together, breaking the silence which surrounds our lives, challenges women's subordination in our society. We learned also how essential it is to build our analysis and action on women's issues from the ground up, beginning with women's experience.

The Women's Research Centre has, from its inception in 1973, made interviews with women the cornerstone of its research and action on a range of issues from wife battering to sexual harassment in the workplace to economic issues. When women at the Centre decided to do research on childhood sexual abuse, there was no question but that it would be based on women's descriptions of their experience. The Centre's previous research on wife assault had shown that making visible women's lived experience of abuse revealed the truth so often obscured in what Louise Armstrong has referred to as the "problem management industry" which grows up to meet any newly identified social issue. (Armstrong 1985:28)

We also believed that women's descriptions would help us to understand more clearly the practical links among various aspects of violence against women—the symbiotic connections among rape, wife battering, pornography, prostitution, and child sexual abuse. And, most importantly, we believed that accounts of how women live with childhood sexual abuse would contain valuable lessons for their mothers, daughters, sisters and friends. From the start we knew we wanted to include the experience of mothers, the women who are so often blamed, accused of complicity, and ignored. Their perspective is essential if we are to understand the dynamics involved in child sexual abuse and to develop effective responses.

The researchers responsible for this book were guided by these beliefs and by insights gained from decades of work in the feminist movement. The research was done not from a distanced or detached stance but from a commitment to reveal the truth of women's lives and to work for fundamental change.

One of our first tasks as researchers was to declare to each other the assumptions we brought to the work. We did this because the kind of participant-observation research the Centre does includes a conscious acknowledgement of the researcher's interest and knowledge rather than denying they exist. Everyone, even a researcher, has a point of view, feelings, and opinions. Ignoring them and their influence means neglecting an important factor in the research process and makes for biased research.

We discussed our assumptions in order to understand each other's perspective and to clarify the research we would do. Out of these discussions we identified the questions to ask the women we interviewed. Our statement of assumptions and the interview guides outlining specific questions we asked women are in Appendices I and II.

To this information about what we think and who we are, we add that we are white women from middle class and working class families. Two of us are married, two of us have children, three of us are lesbians. Some of us have university degrees, some don't. Some of us had done research before this project, others had not. We are all between thirty and fifty years of age and live in Vancouver.

The Women We Interviewed

Most of the women we interviewed were referred to us by counsellors and therapists in the Greater Vancouver area or by the Women Against Violence Against Women Rape/Crisis Centre. A few women had simply heard about our research and independently indicated their willingness to be interviewed.

What we asked of these women was the will and, of course implicitly the strength, to tell us their stories and to allow us to use them as the basis for our work. Using referrals from counsellors and therapists restricted our interviews primarily to women who had the financial means and/or knowledge of such resources and services. This restriction was offset somewhat by referrals from WAVAW/RCC and by self-referrals.

The women we interviewed range in age from mid-twenties to early fifties, the majority being in their thirties. Some have attended university or college, others have not. They work in a range of occupations: bank worker, artist, teacher, counsellor, writer, full-time homemaker, film-maker, real estate agent, clerical worker, secretary, university student. The majority of the adult survivors are or have been married. Nine women told us they are lesbians.

Women said they had grown up in various types of communities ranging from rural parts of Britain, the United States and Canada, to large North American cities or their suburbs. One grew up on a Canadian air force base, another in a Norwegian farming community, another in a small British mining town, and another in a mining town in Ontario. Two are from the eastern United States, and several grew up in or near Vancouver. Several adult survivors said their families had moved from place to place when they were growing up. All of the children whose mothers we interviewed now live in Vancouver or the Lower Mainland of British Columbia.

Most of the women have more than one brother or sister—only two of the adult survivors and one of the children whose mothers we interviewed are only children. More than half of the adult survivors were the only girls in their families.

Five of the adult survivors lived with mothers who were separated, divorced or widowed. One spent most of her childhood in foster homes after her mother became ill and eventually died. Of the mothers we interviewed, all but one had separated from or divorced the fathers of their children. Several of these women referred to the economic difficulties inherent in being a single parent. They spoke of the strain of coping with financial constraints resulting in more restricted lifestyles, crowded housing, and limited funds for legal fees, therapy or recreational activities with their children.

About half of the adult survivors we interviewed said their mothers had not worked outside the home while their children were growing up. Of those mothers who did work, many worked full-time and either shared the role of breadwinner for the family, or bore that responsibility alone. Others had jobs or volunteer work which took them outside the home only part-time or sporadically. Several took employment only after their children entered school.

Most women, adult survivors and mothers alike, said the

families they grew up in were middle class, lower middle class, or comfortable financially. Several, however, indicated their parents did have to struggle to make ends meet and a few identified economic hardship as a serious problem at various times, if not consistently, in their early years.

The women we interviewed reflect a range of backgrounds in economic terms. We found no simple correlation between class and child sexual abuse nor between class and the resources available to a child to deal with the abuse.

The mothers and survivors in this book are with only one exception whites of Western-European heritage. The majority were born in Canada—one of Japanese-Canadian parents. One woman is physically disabled.

The accounts of childhood sexual abuse represent the experience of the women we interviewed. We do not presume to generalize or claim that their experience is broadly representative. We do believe there are many patterns and insights contained in their accounts which other women can relate to. But the relative ethno-cultural homogeneity of the women in this book underlines the importance of the work being done by women of colour, disabled women, and women of all cultural traditions to give voice to their experiences in their own ways and on their own terms. It's clear also that more support for such work is needed if we are ever to know the full range of women's experience.

What Women Told Us

Our interviews with women lasted an average of four hours each. Several said the interview marked a turning point for them: it was the first time they'd told their stories, or been asked to do so, to anyone other than a counsellor. For some women, doing the interview indicated a kind of liberation; it meant they'd made sense of their experience well enough to tell it to others. For others the telling itself illuminated pieces of their experience they hadn't recalled before.

When we asked women to talk about their family life, they described a range of circumstances. Some said their families seemed ordinary to them and they suspected that to outsiders they appeared to be no different than other families in their neighbourhoods. Yet the vast majority of these women had experienced or witnessed violence in their homes in addition to the sexual abuse. Many had seen their mothers physically and emotionally abused and raped by their fathers/stepfathers. Several women also said that they and their sisters and brothers were abused by these men. Given what we know about the incidence of woman battering and child abuse and how hidden a problem each has been until recently, it is hard to say whether these families are atypical. Women's descriptions of their childhoods are presented in Chapter I.

In answer to our questions about the abuse itself, women told us of the many forms of coercion abusers used, and they described in detail what the abuse consisted of. Chapter II focuses on their descriptions of the abuse, but here are some of the specifics from women's accounts.

The mothers we interviewed have a total of nineteen children—twelve girls and seven boys. Of these children eleven of the girls and four of the boys were sexually abused. Although the remaining girl and boys had not been sexually abused, they had been emotionally and/or physically abused. In addition, when we asked mothers whether they remember experiencing sexual abuse when they were children, six of the eight said yes and a seventh said she was raped as a teenager. Given that we had not set out with the intention of interviewing mothers who had themselves been abused, this figure is remarkably high. In the interviews several of these women provided us with information about their own histories of abuse. We include what they told us in talking about adult survivors' experience throughout this book.

All but one of these women had been abused before the age of four. Of their children, indications are nine had been sexually abused before the age of two—including two children for whom the abuse began at nine months. All had been abused before the age of eleven. The age of onset among adult survivors is very similar, ranging from infancy in two cases to age twelve—

including four who were abused before the age of two. Twelve of the seventeen adult survivors were less than six years of age at onset.

This contrasts with the findings in David Finkelhor's review of research on child sexual abuse. He notes that "in the literature the peak ages [at onset] tend to fall between 8 and 12." He does, however, acknowledge that younger children are abused and suggests that greater public awareness of this fact combined with more effective programmes for younger children would increase reporting and alter the statistics. (Finkelhor 1984:91, 233)

In addition, adult survivors' accounts indicate that children who are abused from a very young age and children whose attempts at disclosure are not heard have very little recourse but to try to block their memories of the abuse. In fact, many women said they had not remembered details of how and when the abuse began until quite recently. Some mothers began to remember only when their own children's abuse was disclosed. Several women received needed reassurance that we indeed believed what they told us; they had doubted themselves and worried that we would doubt them too. But there is no question about it— children are abused from infancy, as the mothers we interviewed can attest. And most often the abuser is the father who violates and betrays his child's trust and innocence.

With few exceptions the abusers were members of survivors' immediate family—fathers, stepfathers, or brothers. Of the total of thirty-nine survivors (including the mothers we interviewed), twenty-three were sexually abused by more than one offender. All but four of the abusers are male. Accordingly, throughout this book we use male personal pronouns to refer to abusers unless we are speaking specifically about abuse by a woman. And we use the female personal pronoun to refer to victims and survivors unless we are speaking directly about the abuse women told us their brothers or sons experienced.

We use the phrase child sexual abuse instead of the term incest. Incest is defined in the *Concise Oxford Dictionary* as "sexual intercourse between persons too closely related to marry each other." This definition leaves out the many forms of violation other than or in addition to sexual intercourse. It also veils the coercion involved in an adult's exploitation of a child. From what women told us about their own or their children's experience of child sexual abuse and using as a base the definition Sandra Butler developed in her research (Butler 1978:4-5), child sexual abuse is:

> any manual, oral or genital sexual contact or other explicit sexual behaviour that an older person imposes on a child, who is unable to alter or understand the abuser's behaviour because of her powerlessness in the family and or in society.

This definition reflects the fact that abusers are most often adult family members while encompassing the reality that a child is relatively powerless against abuse by an older brother or cousin, for example. We note, however, that the abuser of a disabled child need not be older than the child to be more powerful than she is. The definition also makes it clear that any imposed or exploitative sexual touching—even that which is commonly referred to as "fondling"—is not affectionate or loving but abusive.

Women told us, too, about the many consequences abuse has, reaching into all aspects of a survivor's life. They described the confusion, self-estrangement, entrapment and loss of a positive sense of self, as well as the range of survival skills they or their children developed to endure the abuse and its aftermath. In Chapter III we use Pamela Sleeth's Survivor's Cycle as a framework for understanding the myriad effects women and children contend with. The Cycle reflects what women told us about the distinctive but common experiences and beliefs about themselves they developed as a result of the abuse. We pay particular attention to how women's sense of their own sexuality was affected; to the effects of an abuser's victim blaming and his use of pornography; and to the lessons implicit in the abuse.

Understanding the consequences makes it possible to find ways to break free. In the chapter *Exits: Reclaiming Self*, we first describe how the mothers of this generation have acted courageously to stop the abuse and protect their children. Next we describe the strategies adult survivors have developed and used in recollecting their lives.

There are many lessons to learn from women's accounts. One is that sexually abused children do try to tell others about the abuse but they are often not understood or believed. Survivors and mothers demand we listen and ask for a child's disclosure and believe it when it comes. They also urge children, adult survivors and mothers to talk about their experience and not to keep the secret.

Language—what is said and how—is very significant for survivors. Many women told us vehemently that they hate the term "victim," which the *Concise Oxford Dictionary* defines as:

> living creature sacrificed to a deity or in performance of religious rite; person or thing injured or destroyed in seeking to attain an object, in gratification of a passion etc., or as result of event or circumstance; prey, dupe (the numerous victims of the confidence trick).

Part of women's abhorrence of the term is its implication of powerlessness and destruction. These women have survived and are proud of it and they want that recognized. The term "survivor" helps to give them the recognition they deserve. It means "one who outlives, is still alive, continues to exist in spite of" such evils as sexual abuse. They are due such recognition and the right to be called what they choose precisely because they have survived being injured, being preyed upon or tricked, and they have survived being sacrificed to the "deity" of male sexual demands. The term victim accurately denotes aspects of sexually abused children's experience and what was done to them. It is not an accurate term for what survivors achieve for themselves.

One woman we interviewed suggested the need for another term that goes beyond survival. She said she realizes she wants to do more than just continue to exist; she wants to live life fully. In the absence of a specific term which adequately reflects the strength and courage that takes, and the accomplishment inherent in it, we use survivor as a term to encompass the living women and children do—in all its richness, struggle, and diversity.

There are lessons also, and encouragement, in the differences between the experience of survivors and mothers of this generation and the last. There is greater public consciousness of child sexual abuse and there are more programmes, services, and sympathetic professionals in the social services and criminal justice systems. But there is still a long way to go.

From what women told us we must note a distinction between abuser and offender. "Offender" is the term women often used to refer to the people who sexually abused them. It is the commonly used term and it is an apt term since it connotes doing wrong and transgressing the law or rules of decency. However, although child sexual abuse is against the law, *none* of the offenders women referred to in our interviews had faced criminal prosecution. The only sanctions imposed against them were the result of mothers' determination to protect their children by restricting the fathers' access. These men are indeed abusers but, in the absence of successful criminal prosecution, they are not technically labelled as offenders by the criminal justice system. It is more than semantics, for the justice system's failure to prosecute means these men suffer few or no consequences. It means children continue to be at risk. And it calls into question the extent to which the system really sees child sexual abuse as a crime at all.

Women told us that the key to stopping child sexual abuse is stopping the abusers. They stated that the two primary explanations for why men so often get away with sexually abusing children are that children in our society are considered not to have rights and that the sexual abuse of children goes hand in hand with the subordination of women. In the chapter entitled *Beyond Survival* we discuss these and other challenges women see ahead for all of us.

Recollecting Our Lives

We chose the title of this book, *Recollecting Our Lives*, for several reasons. First and foremost, it sums up what adult survivors of child sexual abuse struggle to do, how they collect the pieces of their experience, reflect on them, try to fit the pieces together and come to an understanding of their lives.

Similarly, women whose children have been sexually abused told us how their children have had to build a sense of their own autonomy and rights. Survivors of whatever age have to reclaim their lives. For those who were abused in infancy—and there are many—it is a matter of developing an accurate sense of themselves for the first time.

The phrase recollecting our lives is also meant to remind us that, as women, we all struggle to own our lives, to reclaim them from the effects of male violence. Violence against women in all its aspects touches all women's lives directly or indirectly. As painful as it is to acknowledge, as much as we try to live around it, we must expose it. Violence against women defines our lives. It defines where we walk at night, what we wear, how we act. It prompts us to jump at an unexpected sound when we're out alone at night or waiting at a bus stop or going to our car in a parking lot, day or night. It puts us on guard in our relations with men where we work or in our homes. It defines our sexual practice whether we are heterosexual or lesbian. Male violence and men's definitions of sex have ruled and conditioned us, defined what's good or bad, acceptable or unacceptable. What women want has been defined in reaction to men's rules: men's definitions have been the starting point for our search for positive alternatives, for the work of finding new ways of relating which will better meet our needs as women. For all women, the struggle for our autonomy and integrity, the struggle to define and fulfill ourselves, involves dealing with the reality of male violence in our society.

So survivors of child sexual abuse are not different or other. We cannot afford to distance ourselves from their experience. Rather, by understanding women's experience of childhood sexual abuse, we can recognize the commonalities we share and respect the specific struggles each of us faces. We are all, as women, recollecting our lives, trying to believe and make sense of our experiences and live on.

The women we interviewed told us their stories, recollected their lives, in the hope that it will help women and children who are struggling to survive. In recognizing and respecting survivors' courage and strength we must not forget those women and children who are still trapped in the cycle, who struggle alone to hang on to their lives, and who may not believe they'll make it. As the women in this book stressed over and over again, survival is possible but it is a long and difficult journey. One survivor referred to it as a life-long process of gathering "grains of positiveness, grains of sand." She said, "each time you can love yourself and believe it," each time you find positive things in yourself, "it emanates from you back to the world and then you get it back. It's one of those grains of sand you collect to remind yourself" who you are and that it's possible to heal. She said it's the little grains you find that add up. She hoped this book would be, for women and children, one more grain of sand. We sincerely hope so too.

References

Armstrong, L. 1985. Making an Issue of Incest. *Northeast Magazine*. 3 February:10-29.

Butler, S. 1978. *Conspiracy of Silence*. San Francisco: New Glide Publications.

Finkelhor, D. 1984. *Child Sexual Abuse: New Theory and Research*. New York: The Free Press.

I

Childhood and the Family

C HILDHOOD is a crucial development period during which we get a grounding or base to build on for the rest of our lives. The family is the primary site of this base building. While few among us acquire the ideal quotient of physical, emotional and intellectual nourishment in childhood, it would seem safe to assume that children who are sexually abused must have particularly troubled childhoods. For the abuse to have occurred, survivors' families clearly must have been dysfunctional. Yet to survive sexual abuse these children must have had some special source of strength to draw on.

To understand the context in which children are abused and the resources survivors could draw on in dealing with the abuse we asked the women we interviewed to tell us about their childhoods. We asked them to describe how members of their families got along with each other, what the attitudes in their families were about affection, touching and sex, and what outside influences they recall. In the interviews with women whose children were sexually abused we asked about both their own and their children's early years.

From women's accounts of childhood and family life, it's clear that survivors' circumstances do not reflect the ideal of childhood or family life but neither are they extraordinary. Their accounts reveal a range and diversity of experience which sounded echoes of our own childhoods—for those of us who were abused and those of us who were not.

It's also clear that because the abuse began for so many at such an early age there is no "before and after" picture. Even for those women who were not abused until they were six or eight or older, the abuse dominates their recollections of childhood and family life.

In this chapter we present a picture of the atmosphere in which survivors grew up and the lessons inherent in it. Since the overwhelming majority of children were abused by members of their immediate families, we describe family life in detail. In doing so, we focus on what women told us about relationships with parents and about violence and authority in their homes as well as relations among brothers and sisters and sex-role divisions. Throughout the presentation of their accounts, and particularly in describing attitudes in their families regarding affection and sexuality, we pay close attention to what women's descriptions reveal about the resources that were or were not available to help them deal with the abuse.

Atmosphere in the Family

Economic stability is commonly considered to be an important factor of family life. However, comments from adult survivors we interviewed suggest it's important to avoid oversimplifying the influence of economic security or insecurity in childhood. For example, one woman who had experienced years of financial instability spoke about the downside of the stable life which her third stepfather offered. She said she began to trust her stepfather in large measure because

He offered me a type of stability such as three square meals a day on the table; bed time is at such and such; these are your school clothes, these are your play clothes, your allowance. All of that I'd never had. It felt like a home.

But in retrospect this woman identifies beginning to trust and beginning to allow herself to feel affection for her stepfather as the time "when it became unsafe." She describes herself as a child who was needy, "a sitting duck" for her stepfather who manipulated her need for love and security and sexually abused her "for his own selfish needs."

Another woman described one of the most economically deprived periods of her life as the happiest because she was with her mother with whom she had her "closest ties, like heart ties."

We were very poor. I would sell lemonade for pennies. I remember being in one room. I slept on a trunk in the hall, but it didn't matter to me as a child. That was the happiest time in my life.

Soon after this period her mother became terminally ill and she was shunted from one foster home to another, through a revolving door of insecurity and abuse.

It's clear from these examples that genuine affection and affirmation can be at least as important to children as are material comforts.

For many women we interviewed, their family's economic situation had not been a problem. Their parents were middle class, owned their own home and provided adequately for their children. Some women, however, were aware that their parents struggled to provide for them and others noted that money was a significant factor in their lives because of a parent's illness or because of the effects of alcoholism or divorce or simply because their parents worried about money. One woman recalled her father provided very well for his family but she felt vulnerable because he maintained that without him the family would starve. Another woman recalled that her father was frequently unemployed and it was her mother who bailed out the family financially.

Several of the mothers we interviewed alluded to financial

strains they experienced following separations from their husbands or partners. As single parents they had to contend with the extra costs of counsellors and lawyers to deal with the sexual abuse of their children.

Whatever their economic situations, many women noted that their sexually abusive fathers were particularly concerned about upholding a positive public image. They sought to be perceived as good neighbours, family men, good with children. In some cases these men held positions of leadership in the community such as city councilman, chaplain for a professional sports team, member of the chamber of commerce, or chief of the auxiliary police. Others were active in their churches. An abuser's public image as an upstanding, respected citizen made it especially difficult for his child to disclose the abuse for fear that her word would not carry as much weight as his. Furthermore, many abusive fathers preached what survivors referred to as "moralistic," conservative values, strict religious beliefs, and respect for adults' authority. These men constructed and maintained a convenient lie which served to shield themselves and their abuse from exposure and to prevent their victims from challenging their violation.

Women told us that the atmosphere in the home was clearly controlled by their fathers or husbands. Mothers and wives submitted, assented, or reacted. One mother recalls intervening when her husband punished their year-and-a-half-old daughter for not cleaning her room. Another woman was very upset by her husband's verbal abuse of their daughter but felt her only recourse was to try to persuade him to stop. Those women who protested vigorously against men's authority were forced to either give in or leave.

The self-esteem of the children as well as the mothers in such homes was undermined by their relative powerlessness. Several survivors recalled growing up with the sense they couldn't do anything right. Others referred to their childhoods as a particularly lonely time. Many described themselves as confused, bewildered, and uncertain about what was expected of them.

The fact that the same men who berated and abused their

children sometimes seemed to be good fathers only added to the children's confusion. One of the mothers we interviewed told us her husband rarely got angry but he called his daughter names like "stupid." Yet at times, she said that he and the little girl had a lot of fun together.

Other women described their children's fathers as emotionally disconnected and uninvolved in the children's care. One believes her husband saw her as "a pretty accessory for him to show off" and their daughters as "toys to parade around when he needed to impress someone." Some women noted they attempted to offset their husbands' attitudes by encouraging the children to think for themselves and value their abilities.

Most adult survivors recalled that any sense of being loved and cared for came from their mothers who tried to relate to the children's world, played games with them, and took them on outings. Several, however, noted their mothers were controlling, suffocating, demanding.

In almost all cases, survivors' positive relationships and experiences, through which they could have received support and caring and learned independence, autonomy and a sense of their strengths, were sabotaged by the abuser. In many instances, the offender deliberately undermined his daughter's relationship with her mother. As one woman said, "He basically taught me to hate her." She had a strained relationship with her mother, who was unquestionably an emotionally abusive woman, but their problems were exacerbated "because I believed a lot of what my father said about her."

Many of these men were a puzzle to their children—women described them as sometimes fair and gentle, at other times abusive. Indeed, the emotional atmosphere in most survivors' homes seems to have been confusing. Several characterized either or both parents as emotionally inept, indirect and aloof yet subject to dramatic and even violent outbursts.

Some women tried to understand and accept their parents' inconsistencies. For example, one woman said, "I don't feel I got my needs met... but I think they were doing what they thought they should be doing, being how parents should be."

Others spoke rather longingly about how families *should* be, about what they considered closeness in a family to be. Their comments reflect the very elements which were missing in their own lives. One said closeness means "some sort of affection, some sort of ease, at some basic level, knowing that person cared about you and wanted things to be good for you." Another defined a close family as "always being there for one another no matter how rough it is; really talking without being judgmental; supporting and meaning it." Some women referred to the need for loyalty and "some sense of responsibility if someone is in trouble."

None of the adult survivors we interviewed witnessed this kind of closeness between their parents. Although a few referred to some apparent affection, it was either short-lived or superficial. One woman said she'd thought her parents had a close relationship because they didn't fight. However, when she was a teenager, her parents separated as a result of her father's drinking and violent behaviour. The majority remembered "no love or positive feelings" between their parents, "no display of affection," and a lot of emotional distance. And one woman concluded, "There was never a chance for intimacy to implant, let alone flourish."

The atmosphere women described to us was one in which openness, trust, and aspirations were discouraged. For most of them the climate in which they grew up was, almost literally, stifling.

Relationship with Parents

Women's early experiences of emotional distance, put downs, and lack of communication produced conflicts and confusion in their relationships with their parents. Some noted that their mothers tried to be supportive and loving but even their best efforts were inadequate.

One adult survivor was caught in a struggle between her need to develop a sense of independence and autonomy on the one hand, and her need for protection against sexual abuse on the other. She said of her mother: "In a nutshell she was a nag, a worrywart, very smothering, but very, very warm and loving too." She resented what she considered to be her mother's nervousness and over-protectiveness.

> She was a wreck having kids anyway. She worried about us going out for a walk—we might get hit by a car. She felt like a detective on my back from the time I was even eight years old. It was a big production for me to sleep over at my friends'. My friends' mothers were more lenient. I saw that and resented it at my home.

She was frustrated, disappointed—and trapped—as she realized her mother "was smothering me but couldn't protect me. It was kinda daft—she didn't know how to protect me."

While this survivor needed both more independence and effective protection, another survivor's comments indicate her autonomy was an illusion that stood in the way of her getting the protection she desperately needed. Sexually abused by her father from the age of two, she described herself as "always very self-directed and independent," adding that her mother told her she'd been that way from age three or four on. In retrospect she challenges her mother's perceptions:

> She [mother] says "you were fine on your own. I could let you be, you were fine." I don't think that's true. I think I needed her.

She surely needed her, but she also indicated that her mother might not have been capable of providing her with the support and attention she sought. She told us her mother was prone to depression and had a nervous breakdown when the survivor was only six weeks old. Her father later started drinking and left the mother to cope on her own with two children.

A mother's inaccessibility due to illness was a difficulty for several women. They talked about a kind of role reversal between themselves and their mothers, whereby the children felt they had to take care of their mothers, in most cases because their mothers had physical or emotional problems.

In addition to distancing a child from her mother as a possible confidante or resource regarding the sexual abuse, a mother's illness also fostered insecurity. Survivors responded as children by being, in one woman's words, "a good girl who tried to please, tried to take care of everyone."

Another survivor said her mother "was prone to getting depressed, I would always spend time worrying and taking care of her emotionally." She added, "Our roles were reversed: I was Mom, not daughter." And for one woman her mother's illnesses, "migraine headaches, neck injuries, a lot of stuff," meant that, as a child, she had to do the cooking and laundry for the family. It also meant that each summer she and her brothers were sent to live with her aunt and the uncle who took advantage of her vulnerability and sexually abused her.

While many survivors' mothers were not available to them as protectors or as adults they could talk to about the abuse, their fathers were not resources they could call on either. One woman said her father "didn't play an important role at all, he didn't have any time for me... He used to beat my mother. When they got divorced I really didn't have a good image of him." Another woman described her father as an honest man, a man with integrity, but "he hit the kids. He wanted to hit her [his wife] but it was beneath him." One survivor, when we asked about her relationship with her father, said, "My first thought was good and then I thought non-existent." She has a sense that she "protected him in some way" she couldn't quite articulate. However, she did note that "he was more like one of the kids, more like a child than an adult"—a perception presumably derived from her father "always being passive, always defending himself" against her mother's anger at his behaviour.

> My mother was really angry at my father. She didn't like him very much. He was an alcoholic and drug addict and he was always bringing women home. My mom would find him in bed with other women... Because my mother always screamed a lot, I blamed her. I thought it was her fault.

Although the responsibility for protecting their children from sexual abuse and other harm is commonly ascribed to mothers, fathers and stepfathers cannot be exempted from this obligation. From what survivors told us, however, even those fathers who were not abusers abdicated their parental responsibility. Children who are being sexually abused would hardly turn for help or support to men they saw as distant, emotionally immature, alcoholic or violent. The fathers who paid little attention to their children (except perhaps to discipline them), or who beat their wives and children, compounded their children's isolation and powerlessness.

Violence

To understand the lessons these women learned as children, and the lack of means they had to deal with the abuse, it is important to examine the prominent role violence played in many of their families. Several adult survivors spoke about the physical and emotional abuse they suffered and/or witnessed in their families and about the effects of that violence. They named fear and uncertainty as major consequences for themselves and for other family members.

One woman referred to her father's drinking as a precipitating factor:

> We never knew if he was going to be a happy or a mad drunk. The majority of Saturday nights we had to get our uncle to stop Dad beating Mom. On Sunday we'd go for drives... Sometimes he would try to drive the car off the road just to scare us.

This man's assaults and threats against his children, as well as against his wife, kept them all in a state of fear.

> We each had our turn. None of us were okay. If not this week then next. It was like a cycle. Each of us took turns.

Other women also described living in fear. One said she lived in constant fear of both her parents who hit her regularly. Her father hit her mother "once, very violently and they stopped sleeping together after that." Another woman said she was "deathly afraid" of her father who beat his wife and also

> ... beat up my brothers a lot more than me... He used to get a new pair of slippers every Christmas and my brothers hated it 'cause that's what he'd use to beat them with. When the slippers were new, they were hard.

She said, "I didn't respect him at all... I think for the most part it was actual hatred... paradoxically, he was still my father and I'd do things to please him."

Similarly, a survivor whose mother was physically and sexually abusive talked about the uncertainty she felt and her efforts to control the situation by being good.

> It was scary to make mistakes or not meet her expectations. I remember being watchful of her moods. She was very explosive.

Another woman, whose father sexually abused her and whose mother was emotionally abusive, recalled a great deal of fear in her relationship with her father. In addition, she felt guilty about her parents' divorce. One of her early memories of the period before the divorce was of her parents yelling at each other. She described her response:

> I never disagreed with my father or my brothers. I was scared in some ways—I didn't want to "rock the boat." I was probably a nice little girl and nice little girls don't cause trouble.

Living in an environment of physical, sexual, and emotional violence produces, among other things, fear, watchfulness, and attempts to please and not "rock the boat." Children caught in such situations are obviously trying to control the uncontrollable, or at least to stem the unpredictable. They do this at no small cost to the fulfillment or even expression of their own needs, self-esteem, sense of identity and any possibility of assertiveness. Furthermore, the wife assault which was a feature of several women's families contributed to the atmosphere of fear and uncertainty; it also served to undercut *both* parents' potential as effective resources for the children.

The accounts of several of the mothers we interviewed illustrate these points. One woman described the terrifying behaviour of her ex-husband who sexually abused their daughter. She said he was verbally abusive and that he would also get physically violent. She cited the time "he put his fist through our door three times, saying that he wished it was my head." On this occasion, her husband "only" threatened and intimidated her. On other occasions, he'd say nice things to you and then all of a sudden he'd be saying bad things and pulling your hair and then he'd go back to saying nice things. It was like he'd turn on and off... It was so scary.

Obviously, neither this woman nor her infant daughter had control of this man's violence, and they lived in fear. Other women referred to their husbands' confusing "Jekyll and Hyde" behaviour.

One woman recounted incidents of physical, emotional and sexual assault by her husband. For example, when she was asleep after taking medication that made her very drowsy, her husband "thought it was funny to see how far he could go in intercourse before I woke up." Once when her husband was in a rage and berating her daughter, she called her parents for help. The woman stayed with her husband in the kitchen, literally between her daughter and her husband's fists, waiting for her parents to arrive.

I asked them to take her [the daughter] out of the house. I felt that hopefully he [the husband] would beat up on me and take his anger out on me and that as long as I didn't leave the house, he wouldn't go after them. But it didn't work. He went out.

Her husband knocked her seventy-year-old father down on the road and kicked him repeatedly, breaking his arm in three places and severely injuring his back. The little girl who witnessed this assault on her grandfather, not surprisingly, didn't want to see her stepfather anymore. The woman eventually managed to protect this child and her other daughter whom her husband sexually abused. But to do so she had to overcome the effects of persistent emotional abuse by her husband.

No matter what I did I would never be able to do anything properly. For example, if I did my art work or housework, I would be told I didn't spend enough time with the children. If I spent more time with the children I wasn't doing enough of my housework or my art work... I can remember saying to myself how stupid I was. I'd tried to be good but I thought "you just can't, you always just have to do something wrong."

She said that over time her husband tried to make both her

and her daughter feel that they were nothing, worth nothing, and couldn't do anything right. He succeeded in that "he began to be able to get control of my mind in a way where he'd be able to say 'you think this' and I'd believe I did. He'd tell me how I felt. I lost the sense of being able to think for myself, feel for myself." If she crossed her husband he threatened he'd take the children from her and try to prove she was an unfit mother.

Women in this kind of situation must be nothing short of heroic to be able to preserve themselves, let alone afford any kind of protection to their children.

Some survivors told us their mothers felt they could do little other than try to counteract the destructive effects of their husbands' behaviour. They did this by supporting and encouraging their children in the present and trying to instill hope that the future would be better. As one woman said, "Mom told us we didn't have to live like this and she hoped we would choose differently for ourselves." The mothers we interviewed eventually conquered the kind of fear and feelings of helplessness one woman articulated so well.

> I would feel helpless at times because I would feel in my daughter's eyes she was looking at me wanting me to help her. She didn't understand that if I helped her it would only make it worse for both of us, for her especially.

Many of these women walked a tightrope, desperately trying to maintain a balance between their allegiance to their children and the wishes of their husbands. Losing that balance often carried grave risks for themselves and for their children. For the women we interviewed as mothers of children who were sexually abused, the safety net was at least visible, if not secure; for the mothers of the last generation the abyss must have looked very deep indeed.

Authority

A battered woman's confidence in her ability to care for her children *and* her authority to do so are systematically undermined by her husband's violence. The recurring pattern of criticisms, insults, threats, slaps, punches, kicks, and rapes rob her of a sense of security or self-worth. She is told time and again that she can never do anything right, that she is stupid, ugly, useless, slovenly and a bad mother. She is told this by someone who has greater physical power, frequently backed up by economic control. Worse still, she is told this by someone she loves, or once loved, someone to whom she may be bound in the solemn vows of matrimony. If she stays she is told she is a failure; if she leaves she may well be told she has failed.

However, as society commonly gives men the authority to make the rules in marriage and the family, violence and the overt exercise of authority are not always necessary to maintain this control. Obedience can be secured in other ways. One such way is by reference to "higher authority" to justify the father's right to determine what goes on in the family. Some women described the use of religion in this way in their homes. One woman, for example, recalled that she was forced to go to church and, usually on Friday night, her father lectured the family about "confession, God, and how it was bad for brothers and sisters to fight or talk back to parents." For another survivor there was, in her family, "a lot of stress on moralistic values; honesty, truthfulness, respecting adults, respecting authority. Both parents were Christian, my mother especially. She taught respectfulness, truthfulness, not showing anger." These religious teachings, which demanded respectfulness and not talking back, enhanced the authority and control of the fathers and, in turn, helped to secure children's silence about the sexual abuse.

Some adult survivors described their mothers as the dominant parent in their families. In almost all such cases, however, their comments indicate that, in spite of this impression, their fathers had the ultimate authority. For example, one woman remembered that her father "always would tell us that my mom was the authority in the house and to listen to her." Her mother was labelled as the decision-maker in the family, although her decisions were always made with her husband in mind. But this woman also recalled witnessing her father rape her mother. At age three or four she took her breakfast into her parents' bedroom, and witnessed the following:

> My dad was on top of my mom and they were having sex, but my mom wanted him to stop and he was holding her down... My mom kept telling him to stop, but he wouldn't until he ejaculated, I guess. Then my mom, by that time was so upset with him that she was crying, but she was also angry with me because I had spilled my breakfast.

Another woman said her mother was dominating. She recalled her stepfather "just sat there. He did what she said." However, he undermined her mother's authority behind her back, criticizing her and calling her names. "When he was alone with us kids, he was like a kid but when she was home he stepped back and gave over to her... " Looking back, however, this woman sees her mother as "insecure... we always protect her, still."

In some cases, their parents' roles were clearly delineated or at least clear to their children.

> Mom would nag. Dad came in on the "big problems" like my brother quitting school in grade eleven... Mom would lay down the law to me and Dad would implement it. They might do it together. If it was [a] mild [discipline], she'd spank me; if it was serious, he'd spank me. He was the heavy; she appeared to run the show.

In other cases, survivors' comments indicate that they were ambivalent or confused about who was really in charge and they are still struggling to sort it out. One woman described her feelings of anger towards her father who was, on some levels, more loving and less violent and emotionally abusive than her mother. Nevertheless she thought he was responsible for many of the problems in her family.

> I see my father as kind of incompetent and having an insecure sense of himself and dealing with that in terms of using his daughter [by sexually abusing her]. I have anger still about that. I have a lot of feelings about the whole way it spiralled and affected the damage, affected the dynamics of the whole family.

It's important to note that, in the examples we've just cited, the fathers and stepfathers involved all sexually abused their daughters. As the survivor we quoted last points out, the sexual abuse distorted both the child's sense of the nature of relationships in the family and the relationships themselves. The children's relationships with the non-offending parents were also twisted and undermined; they were, in effect, contaminated by the dynamics of sexual abuse.

Many of the fathers/stepfathers who sexually abused their daughters were clearly authoritarian. Their very authority, whether or not they used violence to enforce it, intimidated their families into submission and effectively removed the mothers as sources of protection and comfort for their children. Other men were not—at least not obviously—dominant, but instead appeared to be, as some survivors put it, "wimps" who were, like their children, subject to the mother's authority. But in several cases, this appearance was falsely created by the offender to encourage the child to favour him over her mother and, thus, to gain the child's compliance and silence about the sexual abuse. These abusers attempted to secure the allegiance of their victims using the lure of being "Daddy's little girl" or "sharing our secret," setting up these children against their mothers, thus ensnaring their victims in a manner which prevented them from reaching out for help.

Setting up the impression of the mother as the authority, whether or not it was done intentionally, also served to obscure the offender's responsibility for the abuse and to place the blame for letting it happen on the mother. And, finally, by appearing to be a wimp or "one of the kids," the offender fostered a sense of guilt in his victim who would understandably come to believe she must have consented to the abuse, or at least failed to stand up to this apparently powerless man.

Relations with Siblings

Some survivors found a measure of comfort and support in their relationships with their siblings. One woman pointed out that she and her brothers were all very close: "we had to have camaraderie or we wouldn't have survived." She said they banded together against their mother who was very ill and often emotionally abusive. Another survivor recalled being close to her brother when they were both young. Significantly, she said she admired him because he seemed to be more assertive with their parents and he fought back.

One adult survivor, who was sexually abused by her father until she was nine years old, describes her eldest sister as her second mother. Although she didn't tell her sister about the abuse, she said:

> She was there when I needed her. She was more approachable than Mom. There wasn't as much age difference, she was seven years older than me. I could talk to her, share secrets... she was a great help.

Other survivors described taking care of or trying to protect brothers and sisters who were sick or "got treated badly." One woman said she was aware as a child that her brother, the last born, had been unwanted. She empathized with him and with his attempts to get attention by getting into trouble as much as possible: "I always felt sorry for him. I could see how the stuff he'd do would bring it on."

One survivor who was sexually abused by her grandfather, uncle and father, beginning when she was a year old, recalled taking care of her sick mother as well as her younger sister. She said, "I took care of my younger sister a lot, looked out for her, loved her a whole lot, I used to teach her things." Furthermore, this woman recalled trying to protect her mother against her older brother's violence.

> My brother grew up really hating/fighting with my mother, really aggressively. I used to side with my mother. He was really vicious verbally and physically. He used to call her all those women-hating names. She used to take it somehow.

Another woman remembered trying to talk two of her brothers out of committing suicide.

While taking on this kind of responsibility is something a child should not have to do, perhaps it at least had the effect of helping these children to feel better about themselves. In some cases it did seem to give them a sense of closeness and worth they lacked in the rest of their lives. However, one woman who was sexually abused by her stepfather apparently felt that the responsibility she had to assume for her stepsister and stepbrother had no redeeming value. She thinks that it distanced her from the members of her family.

> They were never my sister and brother; I was their mother. There wasn't much chance for them to be close to me. I was really bossy, always controlling them. I didn't get involved with anybody in my family. It's still that way, I back off.

And for many, no matter how close their bonds with their sisters and brothers, the abuse and the emotional distance that pervaded their families affected what they could both take from and give to these relationships. For example, one woman said:

> I was real close to my older sister, though I don't remember much. I remember she used to walk me to school holding my hand. I don't remember talking about personal stuff; I didn't have a language around emotional stuff. I sought her out for comfort and being in her physical presence made me feel better.

Without a language to talk about her feelings and what was happening to her, she was unable to take advantage of her closeness with her sister to even try to get the help she needed.

Differences in ages among siblings produced understandable tensions. One survivor, for example, saw herself as "a little sister getting on my brother's nerves" by "bugging" him, being a "copy-cat," following him around, and so on. Another said her older sister hated it that "I followed her around and always tried to be with her friends." Still another remembers being close to her older sister until her sister started going out with boys; "I got told not to tag along then and to leave her alone."

One woman talked about fighting a lot with her brother because of sibling rivalry.

> I think he really hated me because of the attention I got from my mother that he didn't get. I got away with a lot from my mother because I was a girl. I seemed to instigate a lot of trouble and blamed him for it. He hated me for that. [laughing] I wonder why!

In turn she was jealous that her brother got a lot of attention from their father that she didn't get. But she added that their parents' fighting with each other meant that in spite of the jealousy "there was some kind of a bond between us, because we had the same parents and we were living in the same chaos."

Still another woman, however, found it impossible to be close to her brothers. She not only didn't spend much time with them after her parents divorced, but one of her brothers simply "didn't listen to me, didn't take me seriously; he'd laugh at me." Undermined by her mother's emotional abuse and sexually abused by her father, her need to be taken seriously was particularly acute.

In some cases brothers were clearly abusive. One woman, who'd been sexually abused by her father and an uncle, was also physically and sexually abused by her oldest brother. This brother, in her words, "resented me being a girl, resented that I existed. He would go to great lengths *not* to have me—a girl— play with him." She recounted what happened to her on one occasion when he surprised her by asking her to join in his game.

> I thought it was strange he would invite me to play. I swung on the rope until it got caught on the hook: I was stuck and couldn't get down and he was shooting me with the BB gun while I was up there.

If we accept the adage that "children can be cruel," perhaps this boy's sadistic treatment of his sister might be considered a problem only in terms of the degree of cruelty involved. But it must have been a particularly devastating experience for this girl to be subjected to this kind of treatment by a brother who also sexually abused her.

Another woman was sexually abused by her father and also by one of her three brothers. Her two other brothers both "tried it." She described worshipping her eldest brother in spite of the fact that he was very much like her father, "explosive, with almost no sense of responsibility... plus an alcoholic like my father."

While several women did describe emotional connections with their siblings which provided some comfort and a partial antidote to the pain they experienced in the rest of their lives, they were still children together and thus, relatively powerless to change their situations.

Sex Roles in the Family

We asked women whether the girls and boys in their families were expected to behave differently or do different chores. Their answers indicate that there was a clear distinction between male and female chores and that it contributed to their problems in the family. Essentially it was the traditional split between indoor work such as housework, cleaning, cooking, laundry, which the girls were expected to do, and outdoor work of taking out the garbage, mowing the lawn and so on, which the boys were expected to do.

Only one woman got a clear, definite indication from her mother that boys and girls should do the same chores.

> My mother was quite adamant that everybody do chores so we rotated... everyone did dishes, garbage... although my stepfather did piss all! She definitely believed the boys shouldn't get out of doing dishes just because they were boys.

Sexual division of labour in families is very common. But it's important to be aware of its implications particularly in relation to childhood sexual abuse. Indoor chores take up more of a child's time largely because they consist of regular, daily tasks particularly related to meals—cooking, setting and clearing the table, doing dishes. Significantly, this work takes place inside the home, which for many children is the location of the sexual abuse. Outdoor chores, which are more marketable and readily valued, have at least the potential of taking the child who does them into the public world and often provide a source of income as well as recognition, which girls rarely receive for helping with housework.

As one woman pointed out, her three brothers "would go off and earn money shovelling sidewalks, cutting grass" leaving her to do their usual outside jobs around the home. She described herself as angry at the injustice of having to take on their work while they were out there earning money. The division in chores was not based on a notion of boys' greater strength. As one woman told us:

> It was okay for me to do everything, for example chop wood and carry water and do housework. But they couldn't clean. That wasn't considered man's work. There was no indoor plumbing so we carried water. There was a lot of physical work to do.

Not surprisingly, several women expressed resentment about their brothers' greater degree of independence, control, autonomy, and freedom. In short, they resented the male privilege they perceived in the sex roles within their families. One woman summed it up this way: "Boys can wander; girls are homebodies." Another said, "The boys had the freedom and the fun. They did different work. I was Cinderella—I would clean their rooms."

Differential treatment of girls and boys extended beyond specific chores. The girls were also expected to take more responsibility for other members of the family. Several of the women we interviewed described taking care of their mothers or brothers and sisters when they were sick and generally being the caretaker for the family. Some became surrogate mothers.

One woman recalled that from the age of eight or nine she always took care of her brother and sister and she gave us an account of a typical day in her life.

> I got up at 6:00, did breakfast, made the beds, did dishes, made lunches, took my brother to school with me, picked up my sister, made snacks, cleaned up, did supper, cleaned the house and put the kids to bed. Then I was alone. By then all the other kids were inside, so I went to my room and did things alone, read. My brother started playing with fire; I was to see that he didn't hurt anything or himself. I was really young for all this responsibility. Mom said, "if you're sick, call the doctor, make an appointment for yourself. If you have a problem, you handle it."

As she suggests, she was too young for all the responsibility. Though they were clearly expected to care for others, there is little in women's accounts that indicates their work was valued or appreciated. Indeed, some of them remembered receiving clear messages that their own needs, thoughts and ambitions simply didn't count as much as their brothers'. One woman said:

> I remember being very vocal about political things. There were definite messages from my mother discouraging that. My father was quite passive. He didn't say anything openly like my mother but he didn't encourage me either. There were definite messages from my mother that it was more important for my brothers to go to university...

Another woman concluded from the attitudes and comments of family members that she simply wasn't important.

> The boys were raised differently. For example, Mom would say "I'm willing to work to put the boys through college but you put yourself through." So I was told on the one hand girls don't go to school and on the other "we can't afford a big wedding for you either, do it yourself." So they really didn't support me in traditional female roles either. I simply wasn't important. My Grandpa said "I bought the farm so the boys would have a place"—again, there was no indication I should have a place.

Other women also cited confusing messages they received as children about their roles. They were encouraged to be "proper young ladies," to be passive, conforming, and dependent, and to be nice and not run around and play like their brothers. But they received little support or regard for conforming to the traditional female roles, and for some, being schooled in proper feminine behaviour included training in passive sexual roles which set them up for the role of "Daddy's little girl." As one woman recounted, "I was treated like a little girl with a lot of sexuality. I was encouraged to be cute, encouraged to be adorable, encouraged to be nice."

In her book, *The Silent Children: A Parent's Guide to the Prevention of Child Sexual Abuse*, Linda Tschirhart Sanford points out that the very traits most encouraged in little girls—to be ladylike, polite, accommodating, nurturing, entertaining, and helpful—are precisely what the offender seeks in a girl victim. She contends that sex-role stereotyping is a "bad habit" that "markedly contributes to our children's victimization." She argues that "it is worth our time and energy to assess and change our individual contributions to this habit." (Sanford 1982:23, 31)

There is some evidence that attitudes about sex-role stereotyping are changing. The mothers we interviewed were adamant about treating their sons and daughters the same. They maintained that "everybody in the family does everything" and expressed a strong belief in equality.

These mothers are clearly making an effort to change some of the more blatant forms of stereotyping. Even to do this, they indicated they sometimes had to counter the traditional views of their husbands and/or their children's grandparents, and, of course, the conventional images that still predominate in much of the rest of society. Some of the mothers alluded to efforts to change the more subtle, but fundamentally important aspects of sex roles, with the hope that their children would not be bound by the same invisible restrictions they had experienced. Perhaps their greatest challenge is to overcome the negative messages about the value of girls' and women's role which is inherent in the wife assault these children witnessed and the sexual abuse they experienced in their families.

Attitudes Towards Affection, Touching and Sex

What women told us specifically about the attitudes in their families regarding affection, sex, and touching is a crucial aspect of their childhood experience and of the context in which the child sexual abuse occurred.

Children need love, care, affection and tenderness. Indeed, David Finkelhor contends that children who receive little physical affection are particularly at risk of sexual abuse. For example, he suggests that "a child who is starved for physical affection from a father may be less able to discriminate between a genuine affectional interest on the part of an adult and a thinly disguised sexual one." (Finkelhor 1984:26) Finkelhor has compiled a Sexual Abuse Risk Factor Check List, designed to help identify children at risk for sexual victimization. Among the eight strongest independent predictors included in this checklist are "not close to mother" and "no physical affection from father."(Finkelhor 1984:28-29) These factors are not the cause of sexual abuse, but are aspects of children's upbringing which make them more vulnerable to sexual abuse.

Certainly the great majority of the adult survivors we interviewed indicated that affection within their families was the exception rather than the rule. It simply was not a part of ordinary interaction among family members. In this respect, their families seem to reflect cultural and societal norms of their generation.

One woman, for example, said her parents were never affectionate with each other or with her: "I don't recall them ever touching each other. There was no physical contact." Another said she couldn't recall her parents having "a real flow of affection: I remember my father coming home from work, hugging my mother and her recoiling." For one woman, the only memory of real affection was her grandmother's warmth towards all members of the family. Other women described their family interactions as "very reserved" or "pretty remote and intellectualized" or "sterile, I never saw anyone hug or kiss."

Two others referred to their mothers as uptight or "having a hangup about touching." One woman, however, said that her mother "used to apologize sometimes" for not being affectionate and that her father seemed "extremely uncomfortable, sort of repulsed" by touching. And another woman noted, "I never sat on my mother's knee, there was no squeezing and kissing, but we were very close [in spite of the fact that] there was no physical expression of emotion at all." Only one survivor referred to touching and hugging as common in her immediate and extended family.

The mothers we interviewed indicated that physical affection was much more common among their children and themselves than it had been in their own childhood homes. Perhaps parents of the '70s and '80s are generally less reserved about expressing their emotions through both words and touch. No doubt reticence is still not uncommon, and depends on family traditions, circumstances, cultural backgrounds, and the individual personalities involved. Although the more open display of affection in the families of the current generation clearly did not and could not provide protection from the abuse, it may have contributed to the children's ability to tell their mothers what was happening to them.

The lack of tenderness and caring in adult survivors' families underline what other aspects of family life conveyed to them: that their needs didn't count; that their feelings were not important. One woman was particularly clear about the messages she derived from the absence of affection in her family. She said, "It was like a stoic facade we were supposed to maintain or at least that's the feeling I got as a kid." She understood that "kids were supposed to be 'seen and not heard.' I never had the feeling that I could let my emotions loose at all and I never saw it with my brothers either." These messages taught this child that she was not supposed to express her reactions to what was happening to her—even her reactions to being sexually abused by her father and brother.

It is noteworthy that the absence of affection was a fact of life for the adult survivors we interviewed whether the sexual abuser was part of their nuclear family or outside it. As children, these women were all sexually abused and were, almost without exception, starved for affection. We might therefore assume they were less able to distinguish between genuine affection and abusive behaviour disguised as affection. While this is no doubt true for many survivors, several were very clear about the various kinds of touch and affection they experienced. For example, many dismissed as not real what one woman called a *pro forma* kind of affection. They referred to the traditional good-night kiss—"we got pats on the back, kisses on the cheek at sleep time," and "pecks on the cheek from Mom and Dad, saying hello, good-bye," or being tucked into bed. In one woman's words, "My general impression is that I wasn't cuddled enough, hugged enough."

Others talked about experiencing indirect affection through playing games with their parents.

The time that was most physical was in play—indirect affection. I remember Mom being part of that. That kind of touching was all there was.

When I was little my father used to play with us a lot. I remember sitting on his lap and stuff—he'd pick us up and play "Sasquatch" and "Monster" and stuff.

While in some cases this playing was innocent, in other cases it was sexualized or used as a front for abuse by the offender. One survivor's account illustrates how the absence of affection left her "longing for touch" and how this need was distorted and used by her father. She vividly remembers being touched only, it seems, when it was absolutely necessary:

I remember baths, chest colds and Vicks rubs, turpentine/lard plasters and having to hold the cloth on my chest. I also remember hair washing—I loved the touching and I hated the water in my face. My mom would get rough if I cried about it.

She found affection and positive touching for a time in her father's Sunday morning wrestling matches with her and her brothers: "He would get in bed and wrestle with us. We'd read the comics and play fight." However, at age ten, she "quit doing that" because "my father wanted to keep me in bed and 'teach me things.' He'd get the boys out. He trapped me, held me—I couldn't get away and the boys would leave." Her father's use of this playtime as a cover for abusing her not only destroyed one of her only opportunities for physical closeness, it also put up barriers between her and her brothers.

I remember the loss. I still feel sad now. It caused me to be alienated from the boys—they could still play, I couldn't.

Other survivors noted touching and affection in their families was sexual in nature rather than uncomplicated or straightforward. One said that her parents "touched a lot and I felt like it was always sexual in nature. It wasn't like they screwed right in front of us but. . . I guess affection in our house was quite sexual, between adults anyway."

Other survivors also found that the sexual abuse affected the giving and receiving of affection both with offenders and non-offenders. For one woman, being abused by her father made even the traditional good-night kiss from her mother repulsive.

> I shoved her away... I didn't want to kiss either of them—especially him.

Another woman's account suggests that the abuse was the only affection, however distorted, she knew in her family. She remembers her father was affectionate with all of the children in the family until she was five or six years old, but "then he withdrew." Significantly, this was about the time he stopped abusing her.

For some survivors it was not sexual abuse but their parents' physical violence that made expressions of affection problematic. One woman said she was close to her three brothers, and affectionate with the younger two, but that they were scared of their real mother, "she was the stick lady." Both her mother and father hit them when they were small. She noted the lasting impact of her parents' violence: "Now when they want to hug us, everyone backs up. It's confusing now."

Another woman said her father was verbally, emotionally, and physically violent towards her and her sisters. The violent atmosphere his behaviour created coupled with the fact that there was very little touching or warmth from either her mother or father resulted in distance between herself and her sisters. The only remotely positive touch took the form of fighting. She said, "My sister and I would fight, we'd sort of wham each other around a bit."

There were similar accounts in some of our interviews with mothers of children who'd been sexually abused. For example, one woman remarked on what she called "violent touch" between her children, "hitting and punching" that she spent considerable effort trying to stop. Another mother said that her husband, who sexually abused both their daughters and sexually assaulted her, never touched, cuddled, or hugged. She also remembered that her own father who had sexually abused her was cold and unaffectionate.

The first time I saw Dad show affection to my mother I was in grade five. I was shocked. Hugging him is like a piece of wood, there's nothing there.

Some mothers told us that relationships between themselves and their children, and among their children, became significantly more open and affectionate after the abuse was disclosed. This was a common result of the child's relief in naming the problem, and of the mother's efforts to protect the child from further abuse and to share the process of healing.

Attitudes Towards Sexuality

In most of these families, the lack of open expression of affection was accompanied by a similar reserve about bodies, about reproduction, and about sexuality. This extended even to the routine concealment of the body. Most adult survivors told us that nudity was simply unacceptable in their homes.

Nudity seemed to be particularly forbidden in homes where the abuser was in the nuclear family. To the question, "Was it all right to be seen naked?" several of the women who had been abused by family members simply answered "No." The attitude in one woman's family was that "wearing a one-piece swim suit was terrible. You should cover your arms. You should cover your legs." Another said that although her parents professed to be liberal people there was no nudity in the house.

Other women said one of their parents was more uncomfortable about nudity than the other. One survivor recalled her mother was comfortable with it but "my father would go out of his way to hide his body." She referred to herself as "extremely modest." She also told us her father abused her from the age of eighteen months, making her undress to be spanked and then touching her genitals. Another woman told us her mother was the one who insisted on everyone being clothed and thought nudity was rude and dirty. Her mother often told her she should be ashamed of herself, ashamed of her body, and even ashamed to be seen with bare arms or legs.

In some families the attitudes were more relaxed. Though being nude was not, as one woman put it, "the norm," children would sometimes bathe together, or family members would sometimes be seen undressed in the natural course of family life.

As bodies were hidden, so was information about their functions, particularly those associated with sexuality and reproduction. Several women said their mothers gave them books to read, or told them about the facts of life when they began their first menstrual periods. One said her mother gave her "basic information about how babies are made" but not much more. Another woman noted that when she started menstruating she "had to go—or at least I felt I had to go—to some friends to show me how to use the pad and the belt." Another said that she thought her mother had talked to her about menstruation, but she wasn't sure. She did remember that her older sister and friends had talked to her about it. One woman's mother "didn't discuss it at all" but her sister did: "She was practical, she told me about periods but it was all so hush, hush, secretive, because of the way she did it. She took me into her room so no one could hear."

Significantly, the mothers we interviewed are taking more initiative in educating their children positively about sex. Their efforts are both helped and hindered by the fact of the abuse. The abuse gave them increased motivation and opportunity, however tragically, to talk with their children about sex. However, it also made the task more complicated and very difficult and loaded for the children. For example, one woman said that she and her husband have taught their children that there's a distinction between loving touching and touching that's uncomfortable, and that "there's a time to say 'no.' " This teaching, coupled with an attitude that "sex is a natural thing that's part of a person's growth and development," and an openness about answering any questions their children have, stands in sharp contrast to this woman's experience in her own childhood.

> The reproductive section of the medical manual was ripped out... No information of any kind. After the age of four sexuality was never mentioned. I don't think I saw my father naked after age five. My mother I would see naked from time to time but I would not be naked in their presence.

One mother said she has made a point of teaching her children the correct terms for parts of their bodies and explaining where babies come from because she didn't want the children to be ashamed. The fact that neither she nor her husband had a "proper education" about their own sexuality made another woman particularly committed to talking openly and freely and answering any questions their children raised about sexuality.

As some women explained, their efforts to educate their children have been affected by the abuse. One woman told us that the disclosure has resulted in more openness in the family. She said there is lots of genuine affection, "a lot of touching, hugging, and kissing," but noted that her children are "nervous talking about sex." She said one child thinks it's "very disgusting" and the other giggles about it. Perhaps her children are just too young and not ready to talk about sex, or perhaps their discomfort is a result of their experience of sexual abuse. It may well be a combination of both.

This woman's children had recently told her that it had bothered them to see their father (who abused them and from whom she is divorced) walk around the house nude. She recognized that both these children were going through a time of wanting privacy and she is being more cautious about nudity herself. Another woman also reported there was increased caution about nudity in her family since the sexual abuse was disclosed. She said no one was self-conscious about being naked, but her child's non-offending father puts on his dressing gown more than he used to, and is a little more withdrawn about talking about sexuality.

In their efforts to be positive and open in educating their children about sex, these non-offending parents had a lot to overcome. They had to struggle to counteract the distortion of sexuality stemming from their children's experience of sexual abuse. And some had to repair the effects of a range of damaging behaviour and attitudes the children had witnessed in their families in the past. Yet their efforts clearly surpass those of most parents a generation earlier.

Secrecy and shame about bodies was reflected in many adult

survivors' families' attitudes about sexuality. In these families "sex" was a word which encompassed an entire set of prohibitions, a collection of matters about which one was to say as little as possible. Sometimes the subject was simply obliterated by a forbidding silence. Other times there were subtle mysterious messages that it was "rude," "dirty," "evil," "shameful." Some women were told that sex was "no good," certainly not before marriage, and even then that it was to be endured, or it was a woman's duty. Others were told that it was okay if you were married, or if you were in love. A few parents talked openly with their children about sex, telling them that sex was natural. A couple of parents clearly overstepped the bounds. They used their children as an audience for tales of their own sexual exploits.

How Children Learn About Sex

Undoubtedly children acquire sexual information in a variety of ways, only one of which is what their parents tell them. Information about reproduction and sexuality often comes in fragments, abstracted and distorted, and only rarely in a way in which children can make sense of it in terms of their own lives.

This presents particular problems for children who are sexually abused. For example, one survivor said that the impression her family gave about sex was that it didn't exist. Yet this woman was sexually abused by several people, including her father, from age four until she was fifteen. This experience, taken in combination with her ignorance about sex, suggests that she did not connect what she understood sex to be, with what was being done to her. Although we might assume that children who are sexually abused are knowledgeable about sex, several other survivors of sexual abuse also spoke about seeing sex as "a mystery" when they were young.

Many children who are sexually abused do not experience the sexual abuse as sex. It's wrong, therefore, to assume that experiencing the abuse means they have sexual knowledge. As children, the women we interviewed did not or could not link their experience of sex, in the form of abuse, with the understanding their families gave them about sex.

In part this was due to the ways in which offenders portrayed the abuse as a game or as sex education. In part it resulted from the distorted language the abusers used or the silence they invoked which blurred children's understanding of what was being done to them. It is also likely that these children assumed that sex was something which happened between adults, perhaps only married adults, and therefore something quite different from their experience of being sexually abused. Many families did not equip children with any words to describe what was happening to them. Most families were characterized by an atmosphere in which the children's experience of sex, in the form of sexual abuse, had to be suppressed or denied.

One implicit message women said they derived from their parents' attitudes was that "sex had a very big power." One woman said "homes got disrupted because of it," and she explained how her brother was actually left behind when she and her mother moved to another city to be with her mother's new partner. She saw her mother's sexual relationships taking precedence over everything else and deduced that sex was "this very big powerful thing." It is, therefore, not surprising she felt particularly vulnerable and trapped later when her stepfather began sexually abusing her.

Another woman recalled that there were "a lot of messages in the family about sex" that led her to associate sex with problems between her parents.

> I knew that there were a lot of problems between my mom and dad, a lot of marital problems. . . I felt that there was a big sexual problem between them and I wondered what that meant.

Some women indicated that they realized from an early age that men and women had different attitudes towards sex: their fathers wanted it, their mothers didn't or went along out of duty. One woman said, "I got the sense from my mother that she didn't enjoy being sexual with my father and it was something she endured." Her mother gave her the impression that "if you enjoyed being sexual, then there was something immoral about you." The understanding another woman grew up with was that sex was permissible after marriage: "There wasn't any sense of women's sexuality. It was a duty for women to have sex with their husbands." One woman remembers being in her room above her parents' bedroom and hearing "the sounds coming through the vents in the floor." What she heard was "my mother didn't want it, my father did" and, as a result, "my idea of sex was 'No!'"

From their perceptions of their parents' relationships this woman and others we interviewed got messages which would make resisting sexual abuse all but impossible. They learned that women and children have little if any choice but to accommodate men's sexual demands; that saying no doesn't work; and that sex is something a man does to a woman whether she wants it or not. These lessons could only confirm their sense that they had no right to complain and no right to be protected.

Sometimes a sense of fear or discomfort was passed on to these children in less direct ways. One woman recalled that her mother "tried to talk positively about sex but it was hard for her to do in a relaxed way." Another noted that, though her mother "told us the facts of life quite young," she was scared by sex because of her family's prohibitive attitude towards it.

The sense that sex was bad and dangerous was conveyed to one woman by the way her adoptive mother talked to her when she started her period at ten and a half.

> She laid this whole trip about how if I smiled at a boy, I'd be pregnant. She used to go on about how the same thing would happen to me that happened to my birth mother, having a child at sixteen.

Though the information this woman was given was more inaccurate and more frightening than most, much of the information about sexuality that women did receive directly was primarily aimed at avoiding pregnancy. Even so, this was in some cases limited to a clear emphasis that sex before marriage was wrong; only a few mentioned receiving practical birth control information. As one woman explained, the shame and misinformation which characterized the sketchy sex education she received left her ill-prepared to deal with an abuser's sexual advances.

> [Sex] wasn't talked about or dealt with. Mother tried to get me to learn by giving the babysitter a book and I was forced to read it for a half hour before bed. She gave me a box of Kotex sanitary pads and a belt. She was prepared, I wasn't. That's why it took me so long to clue in. [Her stepfather] was quite friendly to any woman in our house, when she wasn't around he made sexual gestures to them all.

One survivor remembers, as a teenager, a more positive conversation with her mother who spoke relatively openly from her own experience rather than coldly presenting facts or edicts.

> Mom said go easily, be careful. She liked my boyfriend. He and I had been together for five months. He was twenty and I was fifteen. He was the first one I went all the way with. I made light of it. Mom told me her story about being pregnant with my brother [before she was married]. I felt sad but I also liked the way she talked to me— like we were both adults. She said they were planning to get married anyway: "I think the Lord's forgiven me; I can forgive myself!" It's hard for religious people. Mom said she was glad for her marriage and for her kids.

Unfortunately, this young woman had previously been sexually abused by her father for years and had seen her mother simply as a prudish woman who thought sex was just bad.

Not all of the survivors perceived their mothers as merely dutiful or unwilling participants in sexual activity. Some women said their mothers had very positive attitudes towards sex. However, two of these daughters indicated they did not share their mothers' views. One woman, sexually abused by her cousin and a teacher starting at age twelve, recalled the period after her parents were divorced. She said:

> My mother was very promiscuous and when my parents divorced and we were quite poor, my mother and I would sleep in the same bed in the same room and my mother would masturbate in bed. I think she thought I was sleeping. And I remember thinking it was dirty and wishing she would stop. She was also a salesperson and

she would go on the road and I remember her sleeping with other salesmen. When we were poor she would be out late and I knew she was sleeping with some man. She must have told me and I used to be really mad at her for staying out late.

Even though this survivor is one of the few we interviewed who described her family as generally affectionate, positive and open about touching and nakedness, she developed a negative sense of sex. She clearly felt that her mother's attitude to her own sexuality was sometimes insensitive and intrusive, and at other times the cause of her absence. She saw her mother's sexual activity as a barrier between them. She now knows her mother was herself a victim of sexual abuse as a child, and she sees some of their difficulties as stemming from that experience.

The other survivor whose mother was particularly sexually active also said she felt lonely when her mother brought men home.

She slept with a lot of different men. I found it hard. I was lonely. I didn't know people. She wouldn't even know their last names. She slept in the living room and I would walk past her in bed with them. It was really damaging for me to see her.

She said, "I could ask mom anything I wanted to know" about sex and she would answer "forthrightly" and her impression was that when they were together her "mom and dad thought sex was really quite wonderful." However, it seems this young woman would have preferred less openness. Having been sexually abused by her father from the age of two she said she couldn't remember *not* knowing about sex. She remembers skipping health education class because it triggered too much in her and she didn't want to talk. She told us her sex education came from taking a class in sculpture and asking her mother questions. She was understandably trying to control what, and how much, information she received. Accordingly, she resented that her mother "always told me the details of her sex life" after her parents split up.

For other women, abusers' apparent openness or positive attitudes towards sexuality were accompanied by ulterior motives.

One woman explained how her father's liberal attitude about sex was self-interested.

> Dad was an offender. I could get pregnant and it would not really shock him. If he thought I was getting it on with someone else, it turned him on. Because if someone else had intercourse on me, then maybe he could.

Another survivor recalled that her father was "freer talking about sex than Mom was. He wanted us to think it was a natural, okay thing." Yet this man gave his daughter contradictory messages about sexuality, tinged with shame and a sense of ownership.

> My first impression [of sex] was when I was six. I took my pants down and boys tickled me with weeds. I remember the kids saying "you're in trouble." I had to sit on my dad's knee and tell him what happened. He was gravely serious: it was never to happen again.

His reprimand suggests that he had a particular definition of what was "natural" or "okay." Although this woman recalled the incident with the boys as harmless exploration between children, her father treated it as a serious transgression. However, he later used "sex education" as an excuse to abuse her—giving his own particular twist to his definition of what was "natural."

Another offender reportedly promoted sex to his children as "groovy, and he'd talk about it a lot. It was a natural thing, it was beautiful, there was nothing wrong with it." He told his children that their mother hated sex and was frigid. His daughter, whom he sexually abused, remembers him telling her, when she was as young as five or six, that she should live with somebody before she got married and that if she ever got in trouble, got pregnant, she could come to him.

Seen in the context of this man's abuse of his daughter, this open attitude about sex was clearly part of the set up for sexual abuse. In the apartment where he lived after he and his wife divorced, "he would cut out pictures of asses and breasts and frame them and put them on the walls and inside cupboard doors." He encouraged his daughter to look at them and to read the pornographic magazines he collected. He would also look through his binoculars into other people's apartments to see if he could see women undressing, and he included his children as participants in this voyeuristic practice.

—Pornography

For several survivors, pornography was a factor in learning about sex. Sometimes their fathers and/or brothers simply had it around. Though it was usually hidden, the children in the family had access to it. One woman said her brother "used to hide stuff under the covers" and she suspects her father/offender might have used pornography. Although in her words "he had a veneer of appearing really upstanding," she recalled him making "leering comments about photographs and he treated women like sex objects, on the street making comments and stuff."

Another survivor said her stepfather had *Playboy* and *Penthouse* magazines around the house all the time, though her mother wouldn't let him have a "pin-up" calendar where the children would be able to see it. She remembers:

> He showed me the pictures once. And he tried to show me a deck of playing cards with pictures on them of men and women having orgies. Mom brought the cards back from Japan for him. There was a man putting jam on a woman and licking it off and he said he wanted to do that to me.

Another woman, when we asked if anyone in the family used pornography, described photographs taken by her father and one of his friends.

> Dad took photos of me, really seductive, all looking under my dress. There are pictures taken by his friend—faces of me with a dress strap down; age three/four, wrapped in a curtain; ages two to seven are most of the pictures, shadowy; age five/six where the vagina is the centre of the picture.

This man also talked "openly" to his daughter about his sexual practices.

> He talked to me about Mom, all the women he had sexual relationships with—using whips and chains, all his perverted stuff. He

talked about us sleeping in the same room together. He was fixated on it. All his conversations had to do with sex.

These men, through words and pictures, initiated their daughters into the pornographic view of the world. Sometimes pornography was used in the course of the sexual abuse, perhaps partly for the offender's own stimulation, and certainly as a way of showing these children that such activities were a normal part of life. Even when offenders did not use pornography directly as part of the abuse, the verbal and visual images that these men pressed upon the children can only have compounded the confusion and shame they associated with sex and sexuality. Instead of being taught to look to adult women for support, these girls were taught that women were there for exploiting by men, that women were powerless and/or complicit in fulfilling men's sexual demands. These men presented images of womanhood which would have reinforced children's sense that there was never any way out.

In addition, many of the mothers we interviewed said the men who had sexually abused their children were consumers of pornography. Some of these men also used pornography in making demands on their wives. Several raped their wives, coerced them into unwanted sexual activities and/or subjected them to pornography. One woman talked about trying to refuse to go along with some of her ex-husband's range of sexual demands. She talked about putting up with activities she found painful and humiliating, "never [having] enough guts to say 'no.' " Her ex-husband, who sexually abused both their children, used to send her to the store to get XXX-rated videos and magazines, and to save arguments, she'd give in.

Another woman said she found it intimidating and degrading that her husband had pornographic magazines everywhere in the house, under the bed, in the bathroom, under the couch. She said her husband figured that she was closed-minded about it.

He wanted to take pictures of me, do a porno movie with me. He wanted me to be part of a threesome with him and some other guy. He seemed to believe everything he read—the stories of couples that do a threesome or things like that. He seemed to believe them and wanted me to be convinced that it would be really good and I would really like it... I was frightened by what he read in the magazines and wanted to do. He wanted me to be his sex slave. And there's just no way I would do that. I was too scared of what that would mean.

This woman told us of accompanying her husband to a film which featured bondage and sadism. Although they walked out of the film, when they returned home he wanted to tie her to the bed, something he had not previously tried. She refused, because "it seemed a frightening thing, he could do whatever he wanted. If you're tied up, how can you stop him?" This woman has since discovered from her three-year-old daughter's disclosure of sexual abuse that her husband had few qualms about exploiting someone who had even less power to refuse.

Women told us about efforts to confront offenders about their use of pornography. An adult survivor who had been encouraged by her father to read his *Playboy* magazines, told us that she had innocently told her mother a joke she'd read in one them. Her mother got very angry with her father, but he dismissed her rage: "His reaction was just to think she was a prude." Another woman told us she had felt queasy about the pornography her child's father used but, in spite of the discussions she had with him about it, nothing changed. After she separated from him she learned he had sexually abused their daughter. A third woman also told us her teenage son brought home pornography. "It was bondage, it was to do with children. It was violence towards women." She and her husband told him clearly and directly that it did not represent "real life," and they refused to permit him to have it in the house. They were, however, unsuccessful in dissuading him from using it, and later discovered that he was sexually abusing his younger stepsister and stepbrother.

Whether the children of these women were directly exposed to the pornography or not, the survivors' accounts of the impressions they got about sex suggest that children learn from the messages implicit in what they observe and overhear in their parents' relationships as well as from what they are specifically told or taught. Like the adult survivors, the children of the mothers we interviewed unfortunately had ample opportunity to learn very damaging lessons about men's definitions of women's sexuality and about women's relative powerlessness.

The sexual messages women received in their families ranged from denial and condemnation to an almost open display of sex. None of them reported receiving information which was geared towards their need to know, according to their level of development. Whether secret or explicit about sexual information, their parents determined this aspect of their children's education based either on their own inhibitions or on a wish to exhibit, rather than on their children's needs.

Children's effort to understand the meaning of sex is made all the more difficult when they are sexually abused, and when the messages they receive from their parents are confusing and contradictory. For example, what is a child to think when her father, in private, sexually abuses her under the guise of teaching her about sex, while when the rest of the family is around he seems prudish about nudity and makes a point of telling her and her brothers to put their clothes on? Or the child, sexually abused by both parents, whose mother indicates that enjoying sex is immoral but criticizes her daughter for not "dressing female enough" and suggests there "was somehow something wrong with me that I didn't care more about how I looked, about looking attractive." Such mixed messages leave these children in a quicksand of sex and sexuality, with no basis from which to deal with abusive behaviour.

Relationships Outside the Family

While family life is a major influence on children's early development, we thought that their relationships with people outside their families might either reinforce or counter the messages survivors had received and perhaps provide resources or role models to assist them to deal with their abusive experiences. We asked women if they had close friends their own age and how they thought their friends' lives were similar to or different from their own.

Many survivors told us they did not have close friends either because they moved around a lot and never went to the same school twice or because their friendships were primarily with brothers and sisters rather than outsiders. One woman said she wasn't allowed to have friends; her mother told her "they're not good enough for you" and made her come home and stay home at the end of her school day. Another woman described herself as lonely until she was fifteen when she finally developed friendships with two other girls.

Some survivors suggested that there were barriers between themselves and potential friends. As one said, she "always felt there was something to hide." Women felt responsible for not having friends but their comments, and those of other survivors who had problems in the friendships they did have, indicate that the major obstacle was the sexual abuse. For example, one woman recalled having one close friend but losing her because, "I initiated sexualized play, a tickling game with her and then I couldn't visit her anymore." In retrospect she sees her behaviour with her friend as a result of sexual abuse by her father from the age of two, and as one of the "many indicators there was something wrong." In this woman's case "acting out" the abuse she'd experienced meant she lost her only childhood friend.

In other cases, women said their friendships were a means of getting away from their abusive home lives. One woman said she and her friends wouldn't talk about feelings but they played together. Another woman said she and her friend were "similar in that we preferred to be away from our families and hang out with each other."

Of the survivors who had close friends, most were acutely aware of the differences rather than the similarities between them. The sexual abuse itself, as well as other forms of abuse and the emotional impoverishment that prevailed in their families, made the survivors we interviewed feel "different." One woman said simply, "Everyone was different from me." Another survivor cited her friends' interest in boys as something she couldn't relate to. One survivor said she felt she knew more than her friends, who seemed extremely naive.

One woman thought she was more passive than her friends "even though they were pretty conforming" and very feminine. In addition to lacking even the limited degree of self-esteem and assertiveness she saw in her friends, she also felt inadequate and isolated because her friends had hobbies and interests that she didn't have. Others referred to their friends as "more well-rounded" or more fortunate, with parents who "treated them like human beings."

Many of the women we interviewed commented on the greater closeness and warmth they saw in their friends' families, in comparison to their own. For some the absence of divorce among their friends' parents was notable. Others talked about cultural, social or economic differences and similarities. But what really stood out was the fact that their friends' families "didn't have the same kind of trauma and scenes"; "seemed closer, had a solidness"; "didn't seem quite as screwed up and seemed much pleasanter, more openly affectionate." One woman found it remarkable that the parents of her friend in the first grade hugged and kissed in front of them, and she described the differences she saw between her friends' families and her own.

> They had a close, supportive family [where] the kids were a unit and the parents a unit. In our family the kids were competing and the parents were separate.

Another woman's comments reflect the repression, demands and expectations she lived with: "Other families were more open generally in terms of feelings and you were more okay without having to perform." And another echoed this sense of not being valued for herself in her own family, saying that her friendships were with "only children or the last child left at home so there weren't other kids around for them and being friends with them meant that I was important to them." Survivors' comments about what they saw in some of their friends' families highlight the very things they sorely needed as children. These were things they rarely got from their parents: affection, support, openness, and a sense that their own needs as children mattered.

The School Experience

School provided an opportunity for survivors to begin to observe and interact with other adults and children. It was a place where adults paid attention to them. And most adult survivors remembered school as a place where they could, legitimately, spend time away from the abuser's sphere of control. One woman said:

> I liked parts of school. I was very involved in school life. On lots of teams, clubs, and all that stuff, which meant I spent a lot of time at school after school hours which was semi-deliberate I think.

Another woman recalled feeling free at school "because I didn't have parents around me. I could be myself." It was the only place she could develop friends because her mother was controlling and critical of her peers.

> I had friends at school, but [I] had to come home right away from school and I couldn't go out after I got home. So school was the only socializing I did... The only freedom I had was there.

Another survivor who described herself as being "not very good at school" nonetheless enjoyed her time there: "I liked school because I got to hang out with the other girls. I'd get the attention I didn't get at home. So I did like it, but not for... what I learned." For her school was a place to be with friends, a safe and friendly place where some of her emotional needs were met.

School contrasted favourably with one survivor's home life. Hers was an upper middle class family where no affection was displayed, where her brothers were "belted" regularly by their father, and the family as a whole was governed by her father who possessed absolute authority. This survivor was so impressed with her first teacher and with school itself that, while still in elementary school, she decided she would become a teacher.

Her first teacher was a fair-minded, gentle person. Not only was she patient, she also "kept a book about what was good and bad," a welcome orderliness for a confused child. School became the only place where she could feel good about herself: "I was good at it. I got lots of goodies. I got praise, attention, respect. It was ordered, predictable. I liked learning." School increasingly functioned as a "refuge" in her life. Her decision to become a teacher "was part of a commitment to myself, and at the same time a longing for something different in my life."

Another woman talked about teachers who were particularly helpful to her and helped to offset her extremely negative early school experiences. She recalled:

> I was chastised for being left-handed. It was this phenomenal sin. To be left-handed! I had my hands tied to my waist and behind me, or to the drawer in the desk. I failed grade one twice. I peed my pants in class and stuff like that...

Despite this bitter beginning, school later became a refuge when teachers took a personal interest in her well-being. Her fourth grade teacher, for example, cared enough to ensure that the child had meals when she was locked out of the house. She thrived and excelled under this attention and caring.

> I fell in love with her. My marks shot up. I'd have done anything for her. Crossing that desert was worth it to see the smile on her face... At least she was there to go to every day.

She said, "It felt so safe to think... it was so easy!" Although she later found school boring, it provided her with both a sanctuary and people who cared for her.

For another survivor elementary school was a very liberating and exciting time in her life. She liked it because of "the social aspects, the extra-curricular activities, sports and dances we used to organize, but also because of the competitive aspects of school work." Unfortunately, her high school years were not a positive time: at age sixteen she was sexually harassed by one teacher and blackmailed by another, who forced her to have intercourse with him.

For a time at least, school was a place where survivors began to meet the challenge of learning to make their own way as individuals. Free from the direct supervision of their parents, they were faced with the challenge of making independent choices as well as dealing with the direct consequences of those choices. They learned what was and what was not acceptable as they attempted to adapt to the social and academic requirements that faced them.

Because all children are required to attend school, it is also a potential detection and intervention point for children who are being sexually abused at home. School is the one place where a child regularly comes into contact with adult authorities who have power in relation to her life and within the community. It is a place, too, where adults can reach children with the kind of discussions which might encourage their disclosure of sexual abuse.

In the 1980s, society is beginning to recognize the prevalence of sexual abuse, the plight of children who are being sexually abused, and the damage caused by sexual abuse. Many survivors see school as "the only realistic intervention point" for many sexually abused children.

Women They Looked Up To

To try to get a sense of what visions survivors had of how women's lives might be, we asked them about women they looked up to or admired when they were children. They responded by talking about women who were independent, women who had interests, abilities, and an obvious sense of self-esteem. One survivor remembered older cousins, "independent women who were artists. I admired their independence, their creativity, competence and power." Others referred to "independent women in story books" or "my father's girlfriend who was a feminist of sorts" or "a friend of Mom's who was always doing stuff." Others recalled admiring women they knew who had careers; one survivor talked about her mother's sister who was a biochemist as "someone who was doing something different than my mother, something that was not centered on families."

As well as admiring independence, survivors valued the women who gave them support for thinking and for learning new things. These included the biochemist who took her niece to show her the lab where she worked, a grade four teacher who made it feel "so safe to think" and a first grade teacher who was "very important to me... I remember feeling good about myself."

For some survivors, older women they knew who travelled and were out in the world a lot were significant not only because they were self-sufficient but also because they had left their families. As one survivor said of her cousin, "She went away from home so I knew it was possible." Another woman has a vague memory of her aunt telling her that "one day I would be older and able to go places and do things... she was outgoing and excited about life. It made me think that there was another way to live."

In addition, many survivors indicated they valued the openness and warmth with which they were treated by adult women outside their families. This stood in stark contrast to the emotional distance and abusive behaviour that predominated in their families. They described warmth and patience, nurturing and caring from women teachers or from friends of their mothers who were "jolly and funny" or "just so loving with me; they were caring." One survivor described women in her neighbourhood who were "caring, warm, affectionate, hot chocolate givers" and who showed that they liked her. These women made a lasting impression on her: "To this day that is something I admire most in a person—they can be open—and what I see in those people is they were open towards me." She was also impressed by the orderliness and economic stability which they had and she lacked in her life.

Another survivor said one of her mother's friends was a particularly positive influence because "she would talk with us and treat us quite egalitarianly; she was in less of a parent role; she would talk with us about books, films and stuff."

Unfortunately, as valuable as these women were as role models of other ways to live, they were apparently unable to provide practical and immediate help in dealing with the childhood sexual abuse. As children, survivors could only struggle to live through what was happening to them in the hope that, as one said, "if I just waited, it would be okay."

Expectations and Hopes

When we asked the mothers we interviewed what they had hoped their lives would be like, their answers mirrored their own childhood experiences and those of other adult survivors. Not surprisingly, the word "safety" figured prominently. Their hopes and expectations for safety and security, to be loved and cared for, which several women spoke about, are not extraordinary, but they stand in stark contrast to the abuse and exploitation many experienced in childhood.

One woman said she wanted "the big Cinderella story"—to be taken care of and loved by someone with whom she could work towards the "common goal of security, health, and happiness." Others dreamed of an escape from the trauma of their childhood. One woman said she wanted "some emotional togetherness that didn't have strings attached." She definitely wanted to have children and expected that life "was going to be very exciting." Significantly, however, all her expectations involved "being far away and travelling a lot." Another saw marriage as a way out. "It would fix everything that was wrong." She also saw it as a way of fitting in, which was important to her since "I always felt different when I was growing up, different than anyone else." However, her efforts to realize her dreams, and the very fact that she had dreams, were derided by her husband, who abused both her and her children.

The lesson one woman's childhood taught her was to not think very much of herself. She never felt that she would amount to more than a wife and mother. From similar childhood experience another woman learned a somewhat different lesson: she developed a clear determination not to put up with the kind of relationship she'd seen between her parents.

I didn't think of marriage as very valuable because my parents had such a horrible relationship. I had high hopes that it would be workable, but if it didn't work I was not going to hang around spending my whole life waiting for the relationship to straighten out, as I saw my parents doing. I wanted children, but I didn't know what they needed from a father. I pulled through on what I wanted to do, but the men that I picked were absolute failures. And I did do what I said I would do: when it didn't work, I got out of it fast.

Looking back, one woman characterized her expectations as very unrealistic.

I wanted to marry this tall, dark, handsome fellow who would protect me, care for me and give me lots of physical affection. And live in a nice little house with a white picket fence. And have children who would love me for being me and I'd be the best mother going... And have a close family. A family of myself, my husband and children. I wanted to be a nurse and care for people.

She described the gaps between her dreams and how her life turned out. Instead of having the safety and security she wanted for herself, she ended up protecting herself and her children from abuse by their father.

The marriage didn't work out... Three days after we were married he started physically abusing me. I worked as a waitress rather than a nurse. I never lived in a nice little house. It was trailers and dumps. I do have three really nice children. And I spent my time giving them love and protecting them from their father.

These women wanted only what cultural images tell them should be every woman's dream. But "the happy family" is not most women's reality, as both the adult survivors and mothers we interviewed know too well. In fact, in families where there isn't child sexual abuse, there are elements which don't fit the myth of family life and which stand in the way of women's attainment of independence, self-confidence, and even safety. Women who were sexually abused in childhood must overcome the confusion, emotional deprivation, schooling in powerlessness and disdain for women and children inherent in the abuse. Their childhoods gave them few positive resources to draw on aside from the glimmering possibilities they saw in role models or in their dreams.

References

Finkelhor, D. 1984. *Child Sexual Abuse: New Theory and Research.* New York: The Free Press.

Sanford, L. 1982. *The Silent Children: A Parent's Guide to the Prevention of Child Sexual Abuse.* New York: McGraw Hill.

II

Description and Analysis
of the Abuse

The Acts and Consequences

I F we are to understand the reality of sexual abuse, its effects, and what to do about it, we must be clear and specific about what childhood sexual abuse actually is. Therefore, we asked adult survivors and mothers of children who'd been sexually abused to describe their experience of sexual abuse in their own words.

Their accounts are shocking and enraging. There is a tendency when confronted with this kind of information to shy away, to avert our eyes, to avoid knowing what offenders really do. Adult survivors told us about the discomfort and horror they've sensed in even close friends' reactions when they've tried to talk about what happened to them. Mothers admitted having to force themselves not to scream or turn away when their children disclosed the details of their experience. Women who do public education on sexual abuse have described the glazed eyes, the "tuning out" of their audiences and the outright hostility they've encountered when they try to communicate what sexual abuse is.

There is also a tendency, particularly among people who believe that in order to be effective helpers they must maintain a degree of detachment, to categorize acts of sexual violence using terms or phrases which allow some distance and safety by removing the sting and the pain inherent in victims' and survivors' words. Of course, those who live the experience cannot find distance and safety so easily, if at all.

Some people contend that presenting first person accounts of sexual abuse is sensationalism and even dangerous in that abusers and others reading such accounts may "get off on them." This is a valid, but regrettably an irresolvable concern, one which we debated in deciding how to write respectfully and honestly about women's and children's experience.

We decided to include what women told us about the abuse but to place it always in context. Rather than providing an isolated list of abusive acts, we have juxtaposed some of the consequences women and children suffered: the physical injuries and pain, the fears and the long-term damage. Although we discuss the consequences of child sexual abuse in detail in Chapter III, here we present examples of the consequences as part of the lists in order to make it difficult to ignore them. These reminders of the consequences will, we trust, not only serve to curb any inclination readers might have to objectify or minimize women's and children's experiences, but will also emphasize the connection between the abuse and its effects.

Another concern we considered is that listing examples of women's and children's sexual victimization reinforces the "victim stereotype," that women and children *are* victims. But we cannot and must not deny the reality of women's victimization. For it is only by saying what is happening that we can name sexual abuse and provide effective advocacy and support for each other. Indeed, one of the obstacles we face is that for too long women have been silenced by society with the result that issues, programmes and policies have been defined from an abstract or theoretical perspective, not from women's perspective.

To avert our eyes from the reality of women's and children's lived experience, to avoid realizing what offenders do, means a dangerous avoidance of the reality of childhood sexual abuse. In turn it means limiting our understanding, analysis and actions. We can't "tidy up" women's accounts and risk turning real-life experience into an abstract or speculative discussion.

Those of us who work with or are friends or relatives of victims and survivors must come to terms with our shock and discomfort and turn our outrage into action. Those of us who are survivors and victims need to know that we are not alone, that what has been done to us is not our own private nightmare but an assault others do know, recognize and survive.

The lists we present of acts and consequences consist of words and phrases from the interviews. In some cases, we have included children's words from their disclosure statements provided to us.

At age three or four, my father raped me. I remember him choking me, his hands on my throat. I was sodomized...
I felt different growing up, different than anyone else... It was agony to speak in school... I had anxiety attacks. I used to have convulsions... I remember running away at age seven...

Inserting pencils in her vagina, inserting his fingers in her vagina... She said he even asked her to pee on him.
Nightmares, refused to stay in her own bed... angry at Mommy for hurting Daddy—she said that if I didn't go back to him, she had to be the Mommy...

Oral sex with ejaculation... she said "tongue swollen up, Daddy took his pee-pee out. I had to swallow my spit. Daddy was hurt—he was saying oh! oh!"
Cut her own tongue with scissors; cut her hair and her sister's hair in big chunks. Threw dishes on the floor, wrecked furniture, ran in front of cars, walked up to strangers and hit them, played with matches...

Anal penetration with objects. Oral penetration...
Waking up at night, lack of appetite, infections, inability to play, involved in a fantasy world, distrustful of adults...

Daddy pinches me right here [vaginal area]...
Urinary tract infection, throwing up, rubbing herself violently. Very quiet. Screamed if you touched her. Wears layers of clothes on a hot summer day. Lies in bed and shakes, says she never sleeps, covers up tightly to stop shivering...

Really rough touching of my breasts, being pushed, held down, hands on my shoulders, sore in the breast and mouth area. His lips coming down on me. Tears. Sensation of the pressure. Crying. Lying down in the bed. Things put in my mouth. Being French kissed. His penis in my mouth. Memory of white sticky stuff falling out, real gooey texture, colouration. Smothered, scared of choking...
These sensations enter my daily life... I remember a repeated nightmare of trying to fly down the stairs and I don't move. I'm stuck. Feeling of flight. From grade one on... Repetitive rape dreams... I remember not feeling a part of any group. I never ever felt I was a child, carefree. I felt a weight on me. A sense of being cut off, of not doing anything well enough. Multiple personalities. Depressed.

Digital penetration, fondling, anal penetration...
Vaginal bleeding, bled anally. Unable to sleep, throwing chairs, angry temper tantrums. Refused to get undressed, went to bed with clothes on, wet the bed, afraid, never liked bed. Headaches, stomach cramps, leg cramps, eczema from stress. Thumbsucking, biting, punching, screaming, hiding at night. Can't get excited about anything...

He sat on my stomach with all his weight and then he would put his penis in my mouth—he always hit me, punched me in the stomach first because I didn't want to do it...
Stomach-aches, sleep-walking, threw up in the morning after visiting father... "I felt very, very bad. I need help because I have to get it out of my mind. I can't carry it around all over me. It feels bad..."

I have memories of when I was in the crib. I think I was two or under. My main memory is... his penis in my mouth. I remember his hands and being touched genitally—never penetrated with his penis but touched... One time when I was twelve, thirteen, I remember him coming in my mouth after genital touching, stimulation... me feeling choked and thinking I was going to die...

Somehow I was responsible if it was happening, my being a bad person, there being something wrong with me. I spaced right out of my body, made a split to deal with things in my head. It forced me into excelling at school. Not trusting my own feelings, not trusting of other people. Difficulties being intimate. Screaming rages. Chronic back and neck problems, voice and throat constriction. Dissociating from what I'm feeling. A residue of rage...

Mostly he started touching my vagina with his fingers. He kissed me—not how you're supposed to kiss a kid. He'd kind of roll very close to me with no clothes on. I remember he made me grab with my hand and squeeze his prick... Sometimes he was driving the car and I was sitting on his knee and he would—I don't know—get off on it.

Physical reactions—my stomach started shaking, a kind of uncontrollable shaking... I was terrified he'd made me pregnant. I remember always hoping I'd never be alone with him. I felt very much inside myself, isolated, kind of in my own world. I felt scared a lot and constantly afraid that it would happen again and never knowing whether it would or not. I felt "other" or different. I had a sense that something was wrong with me that couldn't be corrected.

When I was young, he did a lot of things in front of the family; French kissing, fondling. Later, it was regular intercourse. At age ten, the sex got more and more violent and that's when I started to get hurt. It got perverse. I don't know what he used—he had dental instruments—I was different from something he was wanting—he put them inside me.

Constant bleeding inside, rectally, scar tissue... scared of the instruments... I definitely feared him. Concerned I'd get pregnant. I have bad dreams about his office and the paraphernalia... I was ostracized from everybody. I just didn't want to exist. I started to emotionally abuse people. I wanted people to hurt... I did a lot of drinking, a lot of drugs... I haven't cried since I was nine years old, my feelings were apart from me.

The acts were not isolated incidents, though even an isolated, one-time assault has significant consequences—not the least of which is living with the fear that if it happened once it can happen again.

The majority of children were abused by more than one offender: grandfather and father; father and mother; cousin and teacher; babysitter, brother, neighbourhood boys, and father; stepfather and uncle; father and day care operator; father, great-grandfather, boys, neighbour, school teachers, psychiatrist, foster father, stepbrother.

It happened in the child's own bed; in her crib; in her father's bed; in front of her father's friends; in the car; in the woods; at the dinner table; in a classroom; in the basement; in her uncle's office; in front of her sisters; in the TV room; on the kitchen counter; in the bathroom.

The abuse happened repeatedly: every weekend when a child visited her father; whenever her brother felt like it; at night; in the morning; whenever a child's stepfather got her alone; when she sat on his lap; when she was being carried upstairs; every summer when she stayed at her uncle's; as part of or instead of discipline or spankings; disguised as a game; as sex education. For many children, the abuse began in infancy and continued for three years or eight years or twenty years. For some it began in adolescence and ended when they were able to leave home.

Sexual abuse was a regular occurrence for some children, sporadic for others, and random for all. It was unpredictable. They had no control. It was a lesson in sexual terrorism: they could never be sure of who, when, how, why. They could never be safe.

It was also a lesson in male sexuality and male authority: whether the offender was male or female, men's definitions of what was good or bad ruled. They told the children they should like it; they ignored the children's tears, pain, and protests; they were gentle or violent according to whim and what got them what they wanted. They used authority and pornography and coercion, and justified it all by mother-blaming or victim-blaming or male prerogative. Abusers took no responsibility for their actions and ignored the damage and destruction.

Women's accounts of the sexual abuse they and their children experienced challenge many theories and assumptions about childhood sexual abuse and how and why it happens. Some theories suggest that children go along with the abuse willingly or unsuspectingly or innocently, unable to set or maintain boundaries. Some contend that, since children are sexual beings, sex with an adult is not, or not necessarily, terrifying or exploitive or damaging for a child but good for her. Nothing in survivors' and mothers' descriptions of the abuse and its effects supports these views. On the contrary, women's accounts indicate clearly that such generalizations are dangerous myths.

Child sexual abuse is inherently violent. Whether or not the abuser uses outright physical force to get his way, the abuse involves, at the very least, interference with and violation of a child's physical integrity. And it all has consequences.

As Elizabeth Stanko has noted, "The forms of sexual intrusion vary—it is not always genital nor always physical; none the less, the female child is likely to be affected by various forms of sexual intimidation." She points out that, although actual forced intercourse is most likely to be viewed by others as violent, even less obviously violent acts are damaging.

> The father who fondles his genitals while he stares at his daughter as she undresses invades his child's feelings of security or safety. The father who progresses from fondling to intercourse uses a pattern of intimidation and control. (Stanko 1985:23)

Perhaps from the abuser's perspective it is a matter of degree: if, for example, he doesn't actually rape the child or if he doesn't hit her, he may contend that he hasn't really hurt her. But from the child's perspective, it all hurts emotionally as well as physically.

Women we interviewed recalled the pain they felt as children when the abuser "would stick his fingers inside me"; when he "fingered me for a long time... so hard and so painfully"; "the gagging and choking" sensation when he made her take his penis in her mouth; the fear of being smothered by him. One woman said she remembers anal penetration, "but I don't know who or what—just pain." Children told their mothers of the pain when the abuser "puts pencils inside me"; "puts his penis in my bum"; "rubs my pee-pee—it hurts a lot."

Some children did not, at the time, express the pain they felt. In fact, several women remembered that they had tried very hard not to feel the pain of what the offender was doing to them or to feel or express anything at all. They tried to separate or dissociate themselves from what was being done to them. For example, one survivor said, "I would just lie there ramrod still." Another recalled that she would go "outside" her body trying to escape what was happening to her.

Trying not to feel the pain of the abuse can't undo the experience or its consequences. One mother told us her three-year-old girl said the abuse left her feeling "yucky inside" and she described herself as "a wrapped up dead person who can still move." While dissociation made it possible for some children to endure the abuse at the time, it too has serious effects—among them the deadening this little girl described—as well as memory loss, confusion, and self-estrangement. Splitting off from their experience, distancing themselves from the pain of what the abuser was doing to their bodies was the only recourse some children had to escape or resist the abuser.

Children who were abused as infants had no way of knowing what was happening to them, let alone resisting. One adult survivor described the earliest experiences of abuse she can recall: "Me, as an infant. A hand. I'm naked. A hand and a vagina. A hand touching my vagina. Manipulation. Fondling. Age two. Very dark. Me looking down on it. Dissociated."

Another woman who was first abused when she was an infant said, "My father had the power to come and go in the night, to be touching me," and she was left with "vagueness around not knowing if it was real." What is real to her now is her memory of "lots of fear... like a nightmare—pressure on my chest, funny feelings in my cunt, powerless feelings."

The powerless feelings, the fear and confusion, and the pain of what the abuser was doing to them made some babies and

young children cry. It was one of the only ways they had of saying "no," of communicating that they didn't like what was being
done to them. Others simply endured it, unable to know or to
communicate in any way that what the offender was doing was
wrong. The abuse was simply a fact of life; it had begun so early
in their lives that they had no other reality to draw on to resist or
counter the abuse or even to recognize it as abuse.

One adult survivor's account of her earliest memory of the
abuse illustrates how vulnerable and easily manipulated a child
is in an abuser's hands. She sees herself as an infant, "very small
and just about the same size as my father's penis"; her memory is
of her father holding her close to his penis and, she says, "I'd
grab for it and put it in my mouth and suck on it, just like any
baby would with any object that's put in front of them."

Others recalled the confusion of being awakened at night
and taken, in a disoriented state, to be abused before being put
back to bed again. It would be understandably difficult for these
children to know whether the abuse was real or a terrible dream.
For some it has been a long struggle to cut through the confusion, to remember and to realize what really happened.

Obviously an abuser who puts his fingers in his infant daughter's vagina as she is lying in her crib is using force, though he
does not have to hit her or invent games or use threats or say
anything to get his way. He can simply act, he can just do it. Unless he's caught in the act, at most, he may have to answer for her
tears or deny any responsibility for them. And who can challenge
his word? The child is unable to speak and powerless to resist. It
may be years before she can realize that what the abuser has
been doing to her is wrong, and so begin to find ways to resist
him or the next abuser who comes along.

But what resistance will work? Whether the abuse began
when she was an infant or four years old or twelve, what can she
do? The descriptions women provided in our interviews reveal a
continuum of coercion, a multiplicity of effective strategies, tactics, and manoeuvres available to abusers to enable them to get
their way, to use children as objects for sexual gratification.
These children did not comply willingly. They did not initiate the

sexual abuse. They did not choose it. They were coerced and manoeuvered into positions where they could not refuse.

The Continuum of Coercion

Force, constraint, compulsion, control, bullying, overpowering, bondage and violence are all synonyms for coercion. Women's accounts show that the coercion abusers used was not always physical force, though many were clearly violent at one time or another. Some did hit and punch; others threatened to. Some used constraint, forcibly confining the child by holding her tightly by the arms or holding her down or even tying her up with ropes. Others—particularly, as we've seen, when the children they abused were very young—simply overpowered their victims, exercising control over them, compelling them to comply with the abuse either by virtue of the abuser's physical presence or by parental or adult authority.

Most children experienced more than one form of coercion. For example, if using force didn't secure the child's compliance or if violence wasn't a "turn on" for abusers, they could and did use disguises or trickery to get their way. In fact, many children were compelled and controlled—and confused—by the abuser's power to name or disguise what he was doing to them as something other than abuse, by making his abuse of the child into a game, by disguising the abuse as affection or sex education or part of punishment or discipline.

Abusers' Use of Outright Violence

Women's descriptions of the childhood sexual abuse they or their children experienced contain many examples of the abuser's exercise of physical force and violence. Several women specifically referred to being raped. One woman recalled her father took her out to the barn and raped her. Another woman remembers several childhood incidents of rape; one involved "a bunch of boys attacking me and raping me—I had to be treated with cold cloths on my vagina so the swelling would go down and I would heal." She was also raped by a teacher and by a high school counsellor and his friend, among others.

Some women referred to incidents of "attempted rape." One, who recalled having been sexually abused by her uncle when she was three, said that when she was thirteen

> [He]... tried to rape me... I was getting ready to go to a dance and my uncle came into the house... He followed me into the bedroom and tried to put his arms around me, tried to kiss me and I got really frightened. He said, "I know you want it too"... I can remember him throwing me on the bed and trying to get on top of me. But then he got off as if something made him change his mind... He told me he'd kill me if I told. I wasn't supposed to tell anybody. And he put his hand around my throat as if to choke me.

Another woman said that she was sodomized. She remembers her father choking her, his hands on her throat, and added that she didn't know "what word to call it—rape? Molest?"

While some women actually used the term "rape" in describing the abuse they'd experienced, those who did not use the term certainly could have. Surely the little boy who was held down and forced to perform oral sex on his father was raped. Surely the children who endured anal and vaginal penetration by their fathers' penises or fingers or by pencils or other objects, were raped. Surely the little girl who, in her mother's words, "was made to orally stimulate" her grandparents was raped.

Women recalled as children being held down or having the abusers lying on top of them. One woman remembers being held down on the couch and abused by her brother who was twelve years her senior. Another child was held on her father's lap while he molested her. A young girl and boy were forced by their older brother's threats, "usually with knives," to fondle and masturbate each other and him. A fourteen-month-old little girl had, in her mother's words, "suffered some sort of vaginal assault, anal and oral assault" as well as being tied up and, her mother suspects, drugged.

When this child and her sister, who was also abused from a very early age, were given dolls to help them communicate to a counsellor what had happened to them, their demonstrations indicated the force their father had used on them. Their mother recalled:

> My youngest daughter had the little girl doll lying on her back with the little boy doll trying to put his penis in her mouth, only it wouldn't fit. [Her older sister] said "Oh no, it works like this." She flipped the dolls over so the boy doll was on the bottom and the little girl doll was on top of the penis but [the younger daughter] flipped them back over and jammed the penis in so it would fit.

This woman remembers also that one of her daughters had "finger print bruises" on her thighs when she came home from visiting her father and that there was blood in her daughter's bowel movements. Another woman said she had her four-year-old daughter "seen by a doctor because she had been bleeding vaginally" as a result of what the mother realized must have been sexual abuse, though the little girl initially denied it because she had blocked the incidents out of her memory.

All of these examples make it clear that the abusers used varying degrees of violence to compel their victims to perform and endure sexual acts beyond the children's choice or physical capacity. The examples also defy anyone to suggest that the abuse was "innocuous" or in any way "good" for the child.

Even when an abuser chose *not* to use the additional force required to make a child go beyond certain limits—limits which, of course, are defined by the abuser rather than the child—there are still consequences. For instance, the woman whose uncle attempted to rape her talked about the long-term effects of what was "only" an attempted rape.

> But, you know, like, for *not* being raped, I was so frightened of any men around his age. I was frightened of black cars because he drove a black car. I was treated for depression. I was on tranquillizers. I was very nervous. At school I couldn't read out loud anymore because my voice would shake. And I still have that problem and it's from the experience.

While many abusers clearly used physical force, it's important to be mindful also of the consequences of abusers' less obvious violence. One woman's childhood experience illustrates how an abuser's authority and a child's innocence work in concert. She said her stepfather "fondled" her from the time she was four and a half years old, "but it seems that intercourse was always there too." She recalled being in her stepfather's bed and "There was blood on the sheets and he said, 'Don't show your mom these sheets.' That confused me, it didn't make sense to me." On another occasion, she said, "I remember him coming inside me and him saying to wash it out but I didn't know how to or why." When she drew the line at oral sex—"I said 'no' to doing oral sex on him"—he persisted with his demand but, she said, "I just refused" and he apparently accepted her refusal. Accordingly, this woman feels justified in saying "He didn't make me do anything I didn't want to." Groomed from an early age by her stepfather to comply with his demands for intercourse, by her pre-teen years she could not recognize his abuse of her as abuse or see how he had forced her into intercourse. His acceptance of her refusal to perform oral sex compounded the problem, making her feel she was acting as an equal participant in a sexual relationship rather than succumbing to his force and the lessons of compliance he had taught her.

This taking on of responsibility is a particularly damaging and insidious by-product of abusers' skillful coercion and grooming of their victims. By twisting the definition of what he's doing, the abuser can manipulate the child's sense of what's going on and trap her into doing and believing what he wants. As a result, the child not only doesn't recognize the abuser's responsibility, she also can't see the abuse he's perpetrated.

A few abusers were open about what they were doing to the children. One woman said she was sexually abused not only by her father but also at his urging by his friends. Another woman recalled that, at age seven, "the very first time" her father molested her, "It happened when we were watching TV and my brother was there. So it was mostly when we were alone but it was in front of other people too." In addition to abusing her in her brother's presence, this man would "do stuff to me in front of his friends. They knew it was happening but it didn't bother them. I recall one of his friends making a comment that implied they knew what was happening. It was kinda 'ha ha ha, you bugger you.' There was a lot of sexual jokes and that sort of stuff." One woman said she was shocked when she remembered as a child going up to her father one day when there were guests at their house and "He put me on his lap and he had his hand down my pants right at the table. It was in a room full of other people!"

Not only did these men encounter no reproach from their friends—indeed, some received encouragement—openly abusing their daughters in front of other people seemed to be an added "kick"; flaunting the abuse seemed to give them an extra "charge." Of course, the children who were abused in this way suffered particular humiliation. They also learned that even if others knew about the abuse, they would not stop it and so the children's silence was effectively reinforced. Why would they tell when their father's friends obviously saw nothing wrong with abuse?

One survivor pointed out that because she wasn't obviously physically hurt by the abuser it was more difficult for her—and perhaps for others—to identify that what the offender was doing was, in fact, abusive. In her words, it was "really hard to see it as abuse. Black eyes, or whatever, would make it easier."

Violence and Authority

The many abusers who did use outright physical violence did so for apparently diverse reasons. In some cases, an abuser used violence to override a child's resistance and to force her to comply with his desires. Violence was a supplementary instrument in the abuser's exercise of his authority—authority derived from his status as the child's father, stepfather, teacher.

In other cases, however, abusers used violence because they didn't have sufficient authority without it. For example, most of the women who recalled being abused by brothers or other boys close to them in age described the abuse as clearly violent. Since these abusers lacked sufficient authority over their victims, they overpowered them.

Women's accounts of child sexual abuse by women also suggest a connection between the abuser's degree of authority and the use of outright violence. One woman described the abuse by her mother as more obviously violent than abuse by her father. This adult survivor recalled first being sexually abused by her father, from the time she was a baby. Her father acted out what he wanted. As she grew up he also played on her sympathy for him when he was ill to manoeuvre her into being abused by him. She recalled at least one occasion, when she was seven, "Both of them [father and mother] together... them using me sexually, using me to get them off sexually with each other—a real sicko scene!"

Her recollections of her mother abusing her began with an incident when she was two or three years old: "I remember being between her legs and her stimulating herself on my body." Later, her mother's abuse was clearly violent. Looking back, the survivor sees this abuse as a reaction to and punishment for what her mother apparently considered to be her daughter's complicity in the sexual abuse by the father. However, there is no denying the severity and pain of the abuse by her mother. She described physical assaults by her mother as "life threatening abuse" and cited examples of her mother chasing her, holding a knife to her neck and "trying to hang me once," as well as violent sexual abuse.

> I have memories of my mother being sexually abusive. The reality of this is really different to me. It feels like a reactive thing to what was going on with my father. I remember being tied up, tied to a chair and being touched genitally. It was more punishing and humiliating. It feels like a reaction to my father having been incestuous.

Another account of sexual abuse by a woman—a grandmother who abused not only her own daughter but also her granddaughter and grandson—reveals that the woman acted together with her husband. She is described by her daughter as "emotionally very insecure; she can't do anything without my father."

One of the adult survivors we interviewed told us that she

has begun to remember sexually abusing her younger brother when she was a child. Unlike her father who had abused her from the time she was two, she insists on taking full responsibility, and she stopped the abuse as soon as her brother resisted.

> It must have been difficult for [my brother]... I still have difficulty sorting it out in my own mind. It stopped of its own accord—it ended and never would happen again. Somewhere in there I must have figured it out—or [my brother] did. He must have said "no" and I said okay. That was that. And that's when it clicked in my head that this was wrong.

She has talked to her brother about the abuse and is surprised that he doesn't blame her. Instead, he is angry at their father, contending that his sister was acting out the abuse she had suffered herself. She, however, is filled with regret that she "didn't make the connection, that you just don't do that to someone" and is struggling to understand how her abusive behaviour is an offshoot of her own abuse.

Another incident of abuse by a woman reported in our interviews involved a babysitter who molested a four-year-old girl once, but did not pursue her when the child resisted by running away.

> She was helping me to get my bathing suit off. It was a red one-piece suit. When she dried me off, she dropped the towel and she was running both hands over my body. She was kind of talking, but crooning; I don't know if she was even using words. And she put her hands between my legs and she started rubbing me. She wasn't holding me tightly or anything but I had the feeling of breaking away and I ran, I think to the bedroom or something.

It seems significant that this abuser—a woman in a role of lesser authority than a father, for example—allowed the child to escape. Without suggesting that a male babysitter in this situation would have pursued the child or used force to get her to give in to his demands, the accounts provided in our interviews indicate that male offenders did use force to overcome such resistance when their authority alone was insufficient.

In trying to understand how and why women sexually abuse

children we must consider the authority factor that figures in survivors' accounts. For example, women's relative lack of authority (in society generally and in the family) helps to explain how a woman could be coerced into abusing a child together with her husband. But did the woman who used overt violence in abusing her daughter do so because she wanted to punish her daughter for having been abused by the woman's husband? Did she do it because it was a safer outlet for her anger than challenging her husband for abusing? Why did she use sexual abuse as punishment? Did her husband's abuse of the child give her a kind of permission to abuse which she didn't have otherwise? Did she see her daughter as damaged goods, easy prey, or simply available?

Does the woman babysitter's apparent willingness to allow the child to run away reflect her own lack of authority or her recognition of the child's right to refuse unwanted touching? Are women who lack even the limited authority of a mother less likely generally to overpower a child than boys in a similar situation? And, if an adult survivor could as a child respect her brother's right to say no, what possible excuse can an adult offender offer for overriding a child's resistance?

Violence as a "Turn On" for the Abuser

It seems that some abusers were physically violent simply because it gave them pleasure. An abuser who forces a child to endure anal, oral, or vaginal penetration is clearly putting his own pleasure and desires above the child's pain. For some abusers, it was perhaps a matter of just not bothering to think about the consequences of their actions, of just doing what they wanted regardless of the effects; for others their sexual pleasure apparently depended on the child's pain.

One abuser not only sexually assaulted his four-year-old daughter but also, as part of the abuse, tortured her by tying her up with a rope and setting fire to the ends of the rope. He took pictures of her tied up, and framed them. His ex-wife, the child's mother, recalled her horror in receiving the pictures as a Christmas gift from him.

Several women described childhood experiences of sexual abuse that reflect an escalating connection between their pain and the abuser's pleasure. One adult survivor, for instance, has memories of "fondling" and digital penetration from infancy to age two; memories when she was age five to seven of him coming into her room, sitting on her bed, touching her breasts—"he's being gentle." But by the time she was eleven, the abuser was "rough," holding her down, hurting her, ignoring her tears, putting his penis in her mouth.

Another woman, who was abused from the age of four by her uncle, described him as "very nice" at the beginning. When she was eight, "he started to change gradually, he stopped being nice" and began to have intercourse with her.

> We had regular intercourse from age eight or nine. When I was older it happened at his office and it got a little more perverse.

Her uncle, a dentist, used dental instruments in abusing the child. She also remembered that he "used to string me up and tickle my feet. My wrists get numb still... I can't stand things being stuck in me; any penetration hurts, of any orifice."

She described him as a man who began by being an affectionate uncle, a man who, to outsiders, was "intelligent, patriarchal, a politician, a driven professional, an evangelical Christian, a friend of a prominent preacher," a man with "the ideal family life." To his niece, "He was a first class little wimp with a penis he couldn't do anything about." He blamed his sexual abuse of the child on an out-of-control sexual organ, apparently— certainly conveniently for him—disconnected from his conscience.

Not only did this man disregard the consequences of inflicting pain for his sexual pleasure, he managed to make the child he abused feel that *her* inadequacy prompted his violence. He vilified her, essentially for growing up.

> He didn't like fucking me because I had pubic hair. He would slap me. I was developing breasts; he hated that... I was surprised. I thought men enjoyed breasts. He used to hit me on my breasts. He started cutting me a little, hurting me. He shaved my pubic hair, he slapped me.

And, while hurting her he conveyed the message to her that "somehow *he* was hurt"—as though she had hurt him by the very fact of her physical development.

Other abusers also shifted responsibility, blamed their victims, and berated the children's physical or sexual inadequacy. One woman recalled the abuser's anger because she wasn't developing fast enough: "He'd jump on me in the morning and stick his fingers in me... and say, 'when are you going to get tits on you?' " Other abusers were reportedly "excited" when their daughters began menstruation. Rather than communicating a positive message to these young women about their bodies' development, these men saw the onset of menstruation as an excuse for having intercourse with them—as though the abusers felt justified in treating them as adult women once menstruation began.

It is not uncommon for victims of childhood sexual abuse to grow up hating their own bodies. Not only do offenders hurt and damage and often berate the children's bodies, the children themselves often feel their bodies are bad. When an abuser makes the child believe the abuse is her fault, not his, she is left with only her body to blame.

Several women we interviewed spoke of how their bodies betrayed them by responding to what one called the abuser's "priming" of her body. Some children were left with the sense that it was because their bodies responded, because their bodies showed they were "turned on," that the abuser escalated his demands. Other children experienced pain because they "went rigid," lay very still, and tried to prevent their bodies from responding to the abuser's manipulations. One woman said she realized as a child that she had to "fake it," to fake orgasm because if she didn't the abuser refused to stop stroking her or penetrating her until she had "come."

Abusers chose to see children's sexuality as tailored to their own wishes. One survivor expressed her astonishment and indignation at the abuser's arrogance and presumption. She recalled being about six years old and her stepfather sitting her on a counter top, taking off her pants, spreading her legs and "He did cunnilingus on me and stroked me and went 'goo-goo' all over me." She said, "What was I supposed to do, get all excited at that age?"

Generally, their victims' feelings or responses were irrelevant—resistance, pain, any expression of feelings the abuser construed as negative were simply overridden in his pursuit of what he wanted. In some cases, a child's suffering was actually part of the abuser's pleasure. It is clear that abusers have many effective weapons in their arsenals, all of which have serious consequences for those who fall prey to them.

Abusers' Use of Disguises

The continuum of child sexual abuse includes various forms of sexual intimidation and intrusion, from what is often called "fondling" to rape. Certainly most of the women we interviewed described a range of abuses: an uncle "grabbing at me" or "making comments about my breasts"; a grandfather "drying me after a bath and touching my body and fondling my genitals"; a father "touching me sexually as he carried me in his arms"; as well as incidents of brutal sexual assaults which we've already discussed.

Similarly, the continuum of abusers' coercion ranges from abusers simply acting on an infant lying in her crib to sophisticated tricks and manoeuvres to outright violence. And in many cases, children's experiences ran the gamut, as the following account illustrates.

> Dad used to bathe me and my brother when we were young. There was some fiddling going on in the tub. I remember him fondling me. He was setting us up to be sexual with each other. Setting us up!... I also remember porn, oral sex—with everything involved—in my bedroom.

What we see in women's accounts is that when outright violence was *not* used by abusers it was either because they simply chose not to use it—and, of course, the choice is theirs— or because other tactics worked better for them. The other tactics women described involve disguises: disguising the abuse as something else—as a game, as punishment, as sex education, or as affection.

The term "disguises" reflects abusers' attempts to avoid discovery by outsiders as well as to mask it for their victims. Disguises make it difficult for the children to recognize the abuse and, thus, difficult for them to talk about it as abuse or to be believed if they tell.

One of the most damaging effects of disguises as a form of coercion is the child's confusion about whether the abuse was really wrong, whether it was really abuse at all. For the children it was a no win situation. The abusers always won because they had the authority to define what they were doing. Their strategies robbed the children of language, of memory, of recourse, and, often, of a sense of reality itself.

Abuse Disguised as a Game

Disguising sexual abuse as a game was a particularly effective strategy used by several abusers. It drew children to them and made recognition of or resistance to the abuse all but impossible. One woman's description illustrates the abuser's skill.

> When I was really young, he made it into a game. He made a kid want to be with him. He's fun. He's into puppeteering. He has a child-like sense of humour. He's enjoyable when he's not abusing. He's excellent with kids. It's hard to see it as abuse.

Giving the impression of being "good with kids" provided an extra layer of protection for the abuser, protection against intervention that he might risk if he was obviously hurtful in his dealings with children.

Another effective strategy was employed by a father who told his daughter that what he was doing to her was a game: "He asked me to play a not nice game—'snakes and ladders,' a pretend game." This "game" consisted of "Daddy saying mean things to me and rubbing my pee-pee. It hurts a lot. Daddy feels sad and I was mad." As much as it hurt her and as angry as it made her, how would this three-year-old be able to communicate what her father was actually doing? The only language she had to describe it was the abuser's language—it was a "game." And because he defined it as a game, and a "pretend game" at that, how could she recognize it as abuse or even as real? It was only her mother's concern about the child's "acting out" behaviour that eventually made verbal disclosure possible.

Several mothers recalled that their children's "acting out" made them realize the children had been abused. One woman described her daughter's behaviour.

> She was lying on the bed, lifting her legs in the air, putting her fingers in her vaginal area and pulling it open. She asked if I wanted to play with her.

When her mother asked what she meant, "She said her daddy played with her down there like that, that with his 'snake,' he goes up and down between her legs."

This child inadvertently disclosed through her behaviour that she'd been abused; her father had told her he would kill her mother if she told anyone about their "playing."

Another mother described her daughter's physical problems, her nightmares, her talking in her sleep, and other behaviour more obviously indicative of abuse.

> I was giving my daughter a bath and she put her hands on either side of her thighs and said "see my fur." Once in the bath she had her finger in her vagina and I asked her what she was doing. She said "getting the food out."

The abuser—who'd played "games" with his daughter, including games involving the family pet—when confronted by the child's mother, dismissed the child's account and "put it down to her imagination." The little girl herself could not articulate what her father had done to her and would not talk about it when asked, insisting it was "secret." His authority to invoke secrecy and to define and mask what he did to her silenced the child. It was only through her mother's insight, persistence and determination that the abuser was eventually stopped.

Several adult survivors who'd experienced abuse disguised as a game were silenced because of the abusers' tactics and because of family and societal attitudes that a generation or more ago meant less awareness of child sexual abuse as a problem. One woman recalled abuse by several adult males in her family including her father, uncle and grandfather. Her father's abuse of her began when she was a year and a half old and progressed over the years from fondling to oral sex. Of abuse by her grandfather she said:

> I have a sense of being five or six. He kept licorice candy in his pants pockets and he used to get us to get it out of his pockets and he'd play games around that. He wore those pants that were loose and had big pockets. Sometimes we'd look in one pocket and there wouldn't be anything in it and we'd have to check the other pocket and then we'd find he had a hard-on.

Her uncle made crass sexual jokes, grabbed his nieces' breasts and "made lecherous looks" at the children. He was "humoured" by the family, and his nieces were "made to give him a hug good-night and sit on his lap." This survivor grew up in a sexualized atmosphere with messages that this kind of sexual "play" was not really abusive, that it was something to be tolerated rather than resisted.

In some cases the abusers, by virtue of their being close in age to their victims, were seen more as the victims' peers than as authority figures. This meant that, as one woman suggested, what they did didn't really "count" to her as abuse. Another woman described her brother as "playing around" with the pins from a bowling game they had as children: "The bowling pins were small enough to go inside me... " Still another described a game of marbles—her older cousin "would play marbles and he would aim for my vagina and that started the whole thing." It led to more clearly sexually abusive behaviour. "Then when we were up in his room, he would tell me to touch his penis and he would touch his penis in front of me when we were alone."

The "games" abusers used sometimes served as a mask for the abuse and sometimes as a precursor of direct sexual aggression. They were clearly effective tricks which produced confused, silenced victims.

Abuse Disguised as Punishment

Some abusers disguised their sexual abuse of children as punishment for wrong-doing. While this disguise usually involved more force or violence than was evident when abusers used games as a cover, the effects on their victims were similar. The children were understandably confused about whether what was done to them was actually abuse and they were also silenced.

When an abuser uses punishment such as spankings to mask his sexual abuse of a child, the child is hard-pressed to articulate what's wrong. A father is considered to have the right to discipline his child. For the child to complain or protest means that she must challenge his authority. She must overcome her own sense of having done something wrong in order to realize, and then to say, that she didn't deserve this punishment. But the abuser's ability to name and define what he's doing robs the child of the words she'd need to explain effectively.

For example, one child had been physically assaulted by her stepfather for years—"he would kick me and punch me a lot in the stomach, he used to throw me against the wall." She says, "I didn't know why these things were happening to me, the only reason given was that I was bad." Even when her younger brother disclosed that their stepfather had sexually abused him and that he'd witnessed the stepfather's abuse of his sister, this little girl could not separate the sexual assaults from the hitting and punishment. She had great difficulty believing that what he'd done to her sexually was abuse because he'd taught her that she was "bad" and deserved whatever treatment he meted out.

In other cases, abusers did not actually hit or even spank the child but rather molested her *instead* of spanking her. One adult survivor said, "I remember I got my new shoes dirty and my father warned me that I would 'get it' at home. He put his hands up my nightie and felt my vagina and bum instead of my getting spanked." Another abuser evidently took precautions in order to give a false impression to anyone who might be listening when he was supposedly spanking his child. This woman remembers being spanked as a child "in secret, with the bedroom doors closed, being forced to take my clothes or pants off and I usually got hit once but then he'd put his hand on me and hit his own hand so it sounded harder than it was. And then he'd fondle me." She recalls on other occasions "being spanked and fondled genitally at the same time." Even when these children were not hit or spanked, the threat and very real possibility of such treatment was clearly present and served as a sort of "back up" for the abuser in enforcing his will.

The messages transmitted to children who were sexually abused under the guise of punishment were devastating. One survivor noted, "I felt humiliation, sexual arousal, and pain all at once." Such experiences had a lasting impact on this child's understanding of her sexuality. A child who is sexually abused instead of being spanked feels complicit and "caught." The message she carries with her afterwards is that she has been a "bad girl"; bad girls deserve punishment; sexual abuse is the punishment you get if you are bad.

One woman described how her father punished her when he discovered she'd been sexually abused. "He caught me with [the coach of the baseball team], he got angry, tied me to a pillar in the church basement and left me there." On another occasion when her father got angry with her, he apparently considered that because she had already been abused she was a suitable outlet for his own sexual aggression. He took her out to the barn and raped her, explaining it to her by saying she was a whore and "this [rape] is what I wanted." The message was: "It didn't really matter what he did because you can't hurt a whore."

She described the fears resulting from being tied up in the church basement.

> It was like he left me in hell—it was so dark, damp, and cold. My fear of the devil came out of that experience. I was always afraid of being abandoned and murdered. I can't stand the thought of being buried in the ground.

Her father's abuse of her conveyed to her, too, that she was "damaged goods," that the abuse was her fault, that sexual "use" is all she was good for, and that abuse is appropriate punishment for abuse.

This child never told anyone and repressed as best she could the memory of what he'd done to her. She felt marked for life as a suitable target for abuse. In fact, she remembers fourteen different offenders throughout her childhood and adolescence. For this woman and many others we interviewed, the abuser's ability to deceive, and his ability to convince children of their complicity and responsibility in a sexual abuse situation fostered the confusion, inability to tell and self-blame that are prerequisites for a cycle of continuing abuse.

Abuse Disguised as Sex Education

Several abusers took different advantage of their authority, derived either from being the child's father or uncle or simply someone "older and wiser." Rather than using the guise of punishment to cover their sexually abusive behaviour, these abusers pretended to be teaching the child about sex.

One adult survivor recalled an evening from her childhood when her mother was out visiting a relative, and her father told her he was going to give her sex education.

> He was sitting behind me. I was at the table and his chair was beside the fireplace. The next thing I know he's saying to me "have a look at it [his penis]." It was ugly. I didn't like it. I turned away... When he showed me his penis he was going to explain to me how you made babies. That was the preamble to it.

Later, "He took me up to bed... I got in bed and he got in bed... I remember not liking it. Then Mom came home and he suddenly was getting out of bed." Although her memory of what her father actually did to her is sketchy, this woman does remember that, as a child, she felt it wasn't right. She felt helpless, with no control over the situation, and no way to get her father out of her bed. Her sense is that he told her not to tell anyone, that it was "their secret" which, of course, only added to her powerlessness.

Another woman had a similar experience which combined the disguise of sex education with orders to keep it all a secret—

though in this case the abuser was not her father but a brother more than twenty years her senior. He told her, "He was teaching me about sex because Mommy hadn't taught him." To supplement the authority his age provided he said, "Don't tell Mom or she'll have a heart attack and die."

Abusers, as we've noted, often used a combination of tactics to coerce the child into complying, however unwillingly, with the abuse. In the examples cited above, the abuser used his authority and demands for secrecy combined with the disguise of abuse as sex education. Children look to adults to teach them things and they're encouraged to obey adults even when it doesn't feel quite right or they don't understand what they're being asked to do.

One adult survivor remembers her father taking her "downstairs to a study where there was a bed and he had me take my clothes off and get into a sleeping bag with him." She described him "encouraging me to get close to him and kind of giving me a sex lesson." She didn't want to go with him or do what he wanted her to do. "My stomach started shaking, it's something I still experience to this day, a kind of uncontrollable shaking"; but it was clear to her that she had to obey her father's authority.

Some abusers used pornography as part of their "education" of their victims. They showed children pornographic photographs or films and required them to do what the women and children in the pictures did as a "turn on" for themselves. Some used pornography to set the stage for the abuse and encouraged the children to accept and replicate the male dominance and female submission in the pornography. One woman recalled that her uncle used to read pornography; he never abused her without reading it first.

Another woman recalled her father using pornography to initiate and normalize the sexual contact he wanted.

> I remember him using porn on me when I was twelve, thirteen. I remember him saying "isn't this nice"—pictures of penises, vaginas, intercourse—no taste, style, real ugly—no nothing. It was disgusting.

> I'd stand there and look at them and he'd start playing with me [sexually].

The experience of these children certainly challenges the notions that pornography is harmless, that men use it only to fantasize, and that there is no link between pornography and men's sexual violence against women and children.

But whatever additional means they employed, the two keys to all the disguises abusers used, including the disguise of sex education, are the abuser's authority and his exploitation of a child's innocence and deference to adults' authority.

This exploitation is clear in most accounts of child sexual abuse and certainly in the following account of a child abused by her uncle as well as by her father. Using sex education as one of his preambles to abuse, her father proceeded to actual intercourse. When his daughter became pregnant at thirteen, she was sent to live with her aunt and uncle. Her uncle took over: he said to her, "Do you want to have a healthy baby?" When the child said she did he told her, "For a healthy baby you have to have sex." She had received no information from her parents about reproduction or sex—other than her father's so-called sex education. As she explained, she was vulnerable and confused and ripe for her uncle's ploys.

> I thought maybe there was some truth to it, maybe you have to keep doing it. He started touching me, hugging me. Being touched was a big thing, something not horrible. But it progressed from there.

One woman remembers an occasion as a child when she was "terrified that the abuser had made me pregnant so I stayed up for a few hours and worried and finally went and asked him. He just laughed and said 'of course not, dear.' He thought it was cute!"

Of course, these men did not teach their victims about sex. They taught them lessons of submission, passivity and powerlessness. When their "education" is also to be kept secret, they are being taught that sex is something to be hidden, not talked about or acknowledged openly. They are taught the abuser's definitions and standards of sexuality which are reinforced by pornography or by the next abuser who comes along. They are taught that abuse is sex. They are taught that male-defined sex is what women are for. And the coercion, tricks and disguises the abusers use confuse child victims, trap them, and deny them the right or opportunity to define their sexuality for themselves.

Abuse Disguised as Affection

Lack of affection was common in the family life of many of the survivors we interviewed. Some said that they were, in fact, "starved" for affection and, in several cases, they outlined how the abuser played on their hunger and their desire to please, how they pretended the abuse was an offering of affection. The children had no reference point from which to understand that they were being manipulated and that it was wrong.

As one woman explained, "I had a lot of good feelings around it [the abuse]." In the absence of other physically affectionate people in her life, she was vulnerable to the abuser who was the kind of person who hugged her and patted her on the head. Of course, the abuser did more than that; but, given the abuser's apparently innocent overtures, the responsibility for what followed seemed to the child to be hers, not the abuser's: "It started with fondling and I guess I was the right age to be sexually aroused. It gave me a lot of guilt."

Another woman remembers what she called "a confusion of things: I felt special. I felt loved. I felt I was getting attention I didn't feel in other ways. I remember getting touched and I felt a craving for affection and touch." Then, when the abuse escalated she felt frightened, terrified, confused and tried to get it to stop but, of course, to no avail. She did have a sense of betrayal but saw it all as her fault. "I thought, my father loves me and I want to be with him but something is going to happen and he isn't going to take care of me." Even though she rightly recognized his betrayal she was trapped, powerless to act.

Several women described similar uneasiness as the abuser turned the affection they longed for into abuse. For others, however, it was years before any such feelings emerged. One woman said: "I was his favourite child, the youngest, the baby of the family." Another woman recalled that by about the age of twelve she was disgusted by it, but she assumed her experience simply reflected how things are in the world. "I thought every man was that way."

Often the children who were caught in these abusive situations had been deluded by the abusers into believing they were equal partners in a love relationship. One abuser bought a ring for the little girl he abused and told her that people wouldn't understand their relationship so not to tell. He said he didn't want *her* to get in trouble.

Children's sense of responsibility and complicity in what the abuser does to them and the secrecy that surrounds the "relationship" traps them, leaving them with little recourse. Some women described how they tried to negotiate for changes in the "relationship" when they realized that somehow, something about it was wrong. Their accounts make it clear just how powerless and unequal they really were in the situation.

One child tried speaking directly to her stepfather who was abusing her, telling him how she felt, and asking him to stop "loving" her like this.

> This one time he was lying naked next to me and it was really evident that he had a hard-on and I was sexually aroused. I was confused by what I was feeling inside. I thought that something wasn't normal about my sexual response. Up until then it had never been so intense... I said, "I don't want you to love me like this, I want you to love me like a father." His reply was: "I do love you like a father does, but stiff pricks have no conscience." So that really confused me.

His response confused her and left her feeling that she had no choice and no way to stop the abuse: she had taken responsibility for trying to understand and to articulate what she wanted and needed, only to be met with the abuser's total abdication of his responsibility. What else could she do but give in to him? And if the abuser was not responsible for what he was doing to her then the child could only conclude that the responsibility was hers, that she wasn't "normal," that it was her fault for being "aroused."

By disguising sexual abuse as affection, abusers may be able to rationalize to themselves that what they are doing is not harmful or coercive. They may try to hold to the notion that a "sexual relationship" between an adult and a child can be a positive thing. However, not one woman's account showed the so-called "relationship" to be positive. All of them indicate that the idea of abuse as a sexual relationship—with the equality and mutuality that term implies—is ludicrous when applied to an adult's sexual exploitation of a child. Survivors' experiences of such relationships show the coercion abusers used and the harm to the child.

✳ It is coercion when the abuser uses his authority, his superior physical size, his greater life experience, his decision-making capabilities, and his power to name what he does as something other than abuse, and then blames the victim. Sometimes an abuser used a combination of all these things to violate the child's physical integrity, and to use the child as an outlet for his sexual desires without any regard for the harm to her.

A child—particularly a child who is deprived of affection except as it is disguised as sexual abuse—learns that her primary value is sexual. Through the abuse—often by more than one abuser in her life—she learns that sex is all she's "good for." These lessons affect her in childhood and for years after. Survivors spoke of still struggling as adults to define their own sexuality, trying to undo how it had been distorted by the abuse. They tried to make sense of their memories of their bodies' responses to the abusers' manipulations.

And, of course, even when survivors succeed in seeing through the abusers' attempts to disguise abuse as affection, there are myriad effects to cope with. One woman described the abuser's tactics.

> He would always read, always [be] smiling at me when we were alone, always [be] nice, showing affection. He'd never ever speak loud to me. He'd say, "come here, I want to see you," coaxing. He'd always make me hold his penis and lie down beside him and he would finger me.

At the time, the abuse was physically hurtful; years later, she remembers this hurt as well as the abuser's insistence that she not tell anyone about what he did. She realizes now that he was abusing her, not being affectionate. It was confusing for her because as a child it was the first sign of affection in her life. The confusion persists in her adult sexual relationships.

Childhood sexual abuse has a profound negative impact on a child's life. But abuse disguised as affection has particularly insidious effects. Primary among them is confusion about who is responsible. It is a confusion deliberately or at least uncaringly fostered by abusers. It distorts children's own sense of their sexuality and retards their process of recognizing the abusers' acts as abuse. For the abuser it is an effective ploy, one that lets him have his way with a child while abdicating responsibility. Furthermore, the effects of abuse disguised as affection repeatedly thwart survivors in their attainment of the genuine love and caring that are the most basic of human needs.

Facing the Reality

Realizing just what abusers do and how they do it means we must not ever excuse their actions or put their needs above those of the children they abused. We cannot blame the victim. We cannot deny the reality of the abusers' authority and weapons. We must recognize the powerlessness of children.

Children do try to tell. Even those children who are beaten and tricked and manipulated into silence and robbed of the language with which to speak and be believed. Even those children who are too young to put it into words. Even children for whom the only viable recourse becomes trying to repress the very memory of what the abuser has done to them. They all try in a variety of non-verbal or indirect ways to communicate their pain and confusion. The problem is that too many children are not heard or understood or believed.

It's clear that the abuse hurts and distorts and damages. It's clear that children do not initiate it or provoke it but are coerced by the abuser into taking responsibility for it.

Seeing what abusers do to children also means confronting the reality and the consequences of men's authority in our society to make the rules, to name their actions to suit themselves, and to define sex, violence and sexuality. It means confronting male sexuality, the connection between a man's pleasure and another's pain that is so apparent in the accounts of abuse. It means recognizing men's objectification of children's and women's bodies. It means confronting the fact that, to the abuser when he's abusing, no matter how he may treat her at other times, the child is invisible except as an outlet for his sexual aggression.

Not every man is a sexual abuser. But it is hard, given women and children's repeated experiences of abuse and other men's tacit or open support for the abuser's actions, to challenge the adult survivor who assumed all men would be abusive. Indeed, Dr. Roland Summit has said that "all males are susceptible" to committing child sexual abuse and that "mothers and daughters should be prepared to defend themselves against the trusted and loved man in their lives." (Grescoe 1981:36)

It is also hard to answer the woman who asked, "Is this a natural thing of males? Like cats, Tom cats, wild cats, they jump on their mates and beat them and have sex with them." Of course, unlike cats, these men have the capacity to make choices, to justify them, and to construct a world that reflects those choices.

Seeing how these men betrayed children's trust and innocence and the authority of parenthood, how they took what they wanted with wanton disregard of the consequences for those they abused, it is easy to conclude, as Alice Miller suggests, that children "merely provide fathers with the cheapest possible way of getting their pleasure." (Miller 1984:123)

Realizing how children were repeatedly abused by a father, a father's friend, an uncle, a brother, a grandfather, a cousin, a school counsellor—and later on how, as women, they were assaulted by a stranger or a husband or a friend—also means recognizing the sexual terrorism that pervades our lives and leaves us with no safe place, no way of knowing which of us will be next, or when. As one adult survivor put it in talking about her nightmares in which both she and her mother were raped: "It was as though there's nothing I can do about it, my time has come, I just have to take it."

Of course, we *can* do something about it, as the efforts of the women we interviewed demonstrate. But first we must face the reality of child sexual abuse and avoid averting our eyes from the horror. We can learn from the adult survivors, and from the mothers of children who were abused, what they did to survive, how they coped, how they are overcoming the damage and how they are finding exits from the cycle of abuse.

References

Grescoe, A. 1981. Nowhere to Run. *Homemaker's Magazine.* April:26-44.

Miller, A. 1984. *Thou Shalt Not Be Aware: Society's Betrayal of the Child.* New York: New American Library.

Stanko, E. 1985. *Intimate Intrusions: Women's Experience of Male Violence.* London: Routledge & Kegan Paul.

III

The Consequences of Childhood Sexual Abuse

The Survivor's Cycle: A Conceptual Framework

CHILDHOOD sexual abuse sets in motion a cycle of distortion, confusion, conflict, and accommodation. Children who have been sexually abused feel different from their peers. They have a secret and feelings of shame. They feel they are bad and wrong. They believe people dislike them, or would if they knew them well. Even the means children develop to cope with the abuse make them feel counterfeit and deceitful. They feel guilty when they receive praise and too deserving of criticism. They don't trust their own feelings or perceptions of reality. They feel estranged from themselves, and are often unable to articulate or even to identify what their feelings are. Many find ways to block the emotions that are too confusing and painful to acknowledge. Those who manage to establish some positive sense of themselves must struggle to maintain it.

None of the women we interviewed had understood as children that what the abusers did to them was actually abuse. With that primary fact concealed and obscured, so too was the reality that they had been manipulated, terrorized, and violated. Without the empowerment of this understanding, they were trapped in the cycle.

While respecting the fact that each survivor's experience is unique, it is possible to chart the cycle of experience common to women and children who've been abused. Diagram I, the Survivor's Cycle, reflects the very similar yet distinct sequence of experience and set of beliefs about themselves which survivors share as a result of the abuse. The Survivor's Cycle is an attempt to provide a conceptual framework for understanding the various ways women and children survive. In this chapter we use the Cycle as a framework for presenting what women told us about the consequences of childhood sexual abuse and how they've lived with them.

The Cycle begins where we all begin: as innocent, dependent, needy children. Remembering our vulnerability as children makes it possible to understand the effects of the violation and exploitation that is child sexual abuse. We can see how the abuser's invasion of childhood and his manipulation of a child's vulnerability wreaks havoc that takes years to undo.

According to women's accounts of how the abuse affected them, the consequences of sexual abuse are interconnected and cumulative. The consequences women have described fit the following categories: confusion, self-estrangement, the development of survival skills, entrapment, and negative sense of self.

When a child is sexually abused she experiences *confusion* about her rights and abilities, her physical and emotional boundaries, and even about what is real. She is confused about what is happening to her, about why she doesn't like it when the abuser tells her she should; about what she can do to stop it, about how to say "no," and about who's responsible for the abuse.

The confusion is profound and causes serious internal conflict. Confusion is central to the cycle of consequences a survivor experiences. It pervades all aspects of her development from

DIAGRAM 1

The Survivor's Cycle

Childhood: Every child is vulnerable, dependent, innocent, needy.

Child is Sexually Abused:
(physical, emotional, mental
violation and abuse)

The Cycle Continues

Negative Sense of Self:
I'm a bad person, everyone is
better than me.
I don't deserve better.
I'm a phoney.
If they really knew me they'd
dislike and be disgusted by
me.
I deserve whatever I get.
I don't know who I am.

Abuse Causes Confusion:
What's he doing?
I don't understand what's
happening to me.
I don't like this but how can I stop
it? What is normal?
Where can I be safe?
I can't do anything right.
I don't know what's real, what's
right.

I'm Trapped:
It's my fault.
I must keep the secret to survive.
I am responsible: I didn't stop it or
tell anyone.
I am responsible for who I have
become.
I can't change anything.
I can't change my life or myself.

Self-Estrangement:
I'm always wrong, I can't be like
everyone else.
I'm not normal.
I'm not important.
No one cares how I feel.
My feelings don't count.
What I want doesn't matter.
I don't want to be me.

Survival Skills:
I have to hide inside myself.
I have to protect myself.
I can't let people see who/how I
really am.
How can I keep from exposing the
real me?

childhood on. Confusion is a key for abusers too: the child's confusion is part of the abuser's empowerment.

For the child, confusion leads to *self-estrangement*: the child's reality doesn't match the abuser's reality or the reality she perceives in the rest of her world. She feels different, wrong, stupid and confuses feeling bad with being bad. She gets the message that her feelings don't count, and nobody cares. She resolves the conflict by convincing herself that her feelings are the problem. She tries to adjust to other people's reality by repressing or overriding her own thoughts and feelings.

Separated from her feelings and still in conflict, a child tries to accommodate herself to her situation by developing *survival skills*. She may become what some survivors called "a people pleaser" or a "helper," trying to meet other people's needs. She may aim for perfection—becoming an *A* student or a superior athlete or the stereotype of a good little girl and eventually the perfect wife and mother. Or she may "act out" by being the class clown or by being daring—stealing or talking back to adults. She may try to escape—as a child, by running away from home; by overeating or conversely by starving herself in order to "hide" in her body; by fantasizing or lying or blocking her memories of what was done to her. As an adult, she may "run" from one job or city or relationship to another; she may try to escape through drugs and alcohol. She may attempt suicide as a way to break free. Particularly as she grows older, she may use her sexuality—giving people what she perceives they want from her, by "sleeping around," or selling them what they want, by becoming involved in prostitution.

The survival skills women and children use are positive choices. They are both strategies for coping and strategies of resistance. Some of them work, at least for a time. As old skills wear out, new ones take their place. But because they stem from the abuse and the alienation it causes, even the most effective survival skills seal the trap the abuser set and perpetuate the cycle.

A sexually abused child is *trapped* by the abuser's lies and disguises. She grows up keeping the abuser's secret in order to protect her mother or sisters or brothers, to protect the abuser, or to protect herself from the uncertainty of disclosure. A child's feeling of shame and the abuser's denial of responsibility work together to convince her the abuse is her fault. She feels responsible, if not for the abuse itself, then for not stopping it. She is trapped also by the skills she develops which allow her to survive but which leave her feeling counterfeit, a fake, a hypocrite. If she succeeds in blocking memories of the abuse, she will feel flawed without knowing why. She comes to believe everyone would hate her if they learned her secret.

Alienated from herself and entrapped in guilt, secrecy and complicity, she loses a sense of the innocent child she was, and develops a *negative sense of self*. She can't see how the reasonable, justifiable needs she had as a child were exploited and distorted by the abuser.

The cycle continues. In her adult relationships the survivor grapples with her confusion about who she really is, what her needs are, what her rights are, what she is responsible for, what she deserves. The cycle produces its own energy, continually reinforcing itself unless and until it is broken.

The consequences a survivor experiences are influenced by her age at onset of the abuse and by the kinds of coercion and manipulation the abuser employs. Obviously, a child abused from infancy has no frame of reference other than the abuse. It is the dominating fact of her life. She has had no chance to develop any resources for dealing with the abuse, no way to think about it, no direct way to communicate her distress and no knowledge of life without it. For such a child, the abuse permeates her childhood development.

The older a child is when the abuse begins the more potential resources she has to draw on. However, even a child of six or eight or twelve experiences profound confusion and disorientation in the face of abuse disguised, for example, as affection or sex education or punishment. Whatever ability she has to realize the abuse is wrong or to protest against it is undermined by the abuser's authority to define what he's doing as something other than abuse and his power to override any attempts the child makes to stop the abuse. And though a child may be less confused when the abuser uses outright violence to enforce his will, nevertheless she has little recourse but to internalize her pain and powerlessness.

Children and adult survivors are also impeded in their attempts to make sense of their experience of abuse and its consequences by lessons they learn from abusers. Abusers avoid taking responsibility by denying, minimizing, or rationalizing the abuse and by blaming the victim. It's not surprising, then, that many survivors tried to deny their experience by blocking their memory of it or by accepting the abusers' definitions. Some survivors referred to the sexual abuse as a sexual "relationship" and said they'd grown up thinking of the abuser as their lover or boyfriend. They tended to minimize what the abuser had done to them. Several women told us the abuser hadn't hurt them physically or "forced" them to do anything. They were unable for years to see the abuser's coercion and manipulation for what it was or to see that the abuse was a violation no matter how gently it was done.

It is very difficult for a child to extricate herself from the abuser's justification for the abuse. The abuser's rationalizations seem plausible at the time. Several women recalled believing the abuser's explanations such as, "I was the only one who understood his needs," or "Mom won't be sexual with him or do what he likes."

Similarly, many women said they'd accepted responsibility for the abuse, believing it happened because they wanted affection, or liked feeling special to the abuser. Some blamed themselves because they kept the secret. The abuser, by rationalizing the abuse and transferring the responsibility for it to the child, absolves himself of responsibility and makes it very difficult for the child to realize it's not her fault. These strategies serve an abuser well but they don't work well for a survivor—indeed they lock her into a cycle of self-doubt, self-blame, and confusion.

Not every survivor experiences the consequences of sexual abuse in the same way, and the differences must be respected, but the Survivor's Cycle shows the connections that do exist. All of us who've had training in femininity—whether or not we've been sexually abused—can see our experience reflected in elements of the Cycle. Most importantly, the Cycle makes it clear that how a survivor feels, and what she does about it, is a consequence of what was done *to* her, not a result of her personal flaws, inadequacies, or imperfections.

What the Survivor's Cycle exposes is cause for justified anger as well as understanding, but most of all hope. By gaining a perspective on the consequences of the abuse, it becomes possible to see a way out. The women we interviewed affirmed that. Their accounts of the damage they and their children have experienced must be seen in the context of their survival. They are surviving and that in itself is a major accomplishment. How they have survived, how they are undoing the damage and reversing the Cycle—which we discuss in the chapter *Exits: Reclaiming Self*—provides encouragement for us all.

The Confusion Resulting from Abuse

Women who were sexually abused as children said the abuse left them feeling bewildered, ashamed, guilty, embarrassed, terrorized, and fearful. When we asked how they had felt about themselves they used words such as "bad," " wrong," " weird," and "different." It was not clear to them as children that the abuse was not their fault but the abuser's. Neither was it clear to many of them that the abuse was wrong or something they had the right to resist. The abuse and the abuser's disguising of it confused them. They experienced a profound gap between their own experience of the abuse and what the abuser wanted, expected, and demanded of them. They struggled in vain to make sense of what was happening to them. Unable to resolve the conflict, children internalized it and blamed themselves, concluding either that the abuse was their fault or that they were "bad" for not liking it or for not stopping it.

The confusion they experienced took several forms:
- confusion about authority—a child's sense of the validity of her own judgement, perception and rights;
- confusion about what's real and what's not;
- confusion related to autonomy—a child's sense of boundaries and limits, her sense of where she leaves off and the rest of the world begins;
- confusion about her own abilities or competence.

Confusion About Authority

One of the tasks of childhood is to learn to recognize and trust your own authority. Children must learn how to perceive the difference between right and wrong and between what feels right and what does not. They learn by observation, imitation, questioning or by instruction from someone who is considered to be older and wiser. They also learn by using their own thoughts and feelings.

Adults have authority over children: the power to tell children what to do, to force children to obey, to punish them if they disobey, and to disregard children's feelings. Any adult is a powerful force for a child to contend with. An abuser misuses his authority and confounds his victim's perceptions and judgement. If a child is frightened of a single adult then she will likely be on guard, suspicious, and fearful of adults generally whether they are known to her or are strangers. Or she may be too trusting of any adult's authority and completely relinquish her own good sense in that way. Inasmuch as her reality and personal authority are distorted by the abuser and represented to her as inaccurate or wrong, she will either be overwhelmed or have to struggle intensely to trust and believe in her own perceptions and good judgement.

Many women who spoke with us said the abusers had used covert or overt force. Many abusers also maintained control in their homes by means of emotional and physical violence directed towards the members of their family. For the children these men sexually abused, violence was a normalized practice. It was part of the abuse as well as the discipline or punishment children expected if they misbehaved.

One woman we interviewed said she lived in fear of her father. She had been abused by him from infancy and was thoroughly intimidated by his general violence within their home. She believed him when he said, "I'd like to kill you." The only way she could cope with the situation was to acquiesce to his wishes and try to stay out of his way. Her experience was that she did not have the right either to complain or to expect better treatment. She had no authority.

The theme of children's powerlessness is repeated again and again by the women who spoke with us. One child, who became pregnant as a result of sexual abuse, said she tried to tell her mother that her father had done sexual things to her. Her mother, in turn, confronted her father who denied responsibility. He used the word "penetration" in his denial and the child was unable to counter his denial because she did not know the meaning or significance of that word. Her mother believed the father.

This child did not feel knowledgeable or strong enough to assert herself. Her attitude towards adults' authority had been firmly established from a very young age.

> I respected adults. I listened to them and besides, I knew not to tell Mother anything. "The less I know the better I like it," she would say.

This child had perceived correctly that her father was completely in charge. Her mother deferred to her father's decisions and judgement. His word was respected. He could do as he wished.

One woman said she didn't know why the abuse was happening—she could only understand that her father "wanted it." This child obeyed. She accepted her father on his terms. As a consequence she did not learn to develop her own authority as a child. She was trained to accept his wishes and follow his lead despite the consequences. She described how her father/abuser used not only his authority as father or elder, but also the authority of the printed word to leave an impression that what he was doing was acceptable. He gave his pre-teenage daughter an article from a magazine that suggested sexual abuse of children is "normal" and induced her to doubt herself and to believe that what he was doing to her was "not as bad as it was" and "very common."

For several children, confusion about their own authority was compounded by the responses they received when they tried to stop or avoid the abuser. One woman remembered trying to avoid contact with her sexually abusive uncle, "but there was pressure to be nice to him. When I refused to go near him, my feelings were never backed up by the adults around me." Other survivors who told adults about the abuse were met with disbelief or denial; one was advised "not to rock the boat." These responses left children feeling they had no right to protest and no alternative but to go along with what the abuser wanted.

Those children who directly or indirectly confronted the abuser fared no better. One survivor recalled that at about age twelve she told her brother about their father's sexual abuse of her and together they talked to their father. Her father admitted the abuse "was a wrong thing to do and he was sorry... and it would never happen again." In spite of the abuser's promise, however, the abuse continued. In addition to feeling trapped and betrayed, this child also learned that her rights could be overridden no matter what assurances to the contrary she received.

Personal authority is developed through experiences which teach a child that she can trust her own thoughts and feelings. A child who is sexually abused loses confidence in her ability to develop an accurate understanding and appropriate responses to situations and conditions in her life. When the abuser lies to her or ignores or dismisses her feelings, he instills self-doubt in the child. Instead of learning to trust themselves, sexually abused children come to distrust their own thoughts, feelings, and their own developing sense of authority and rights.

Confusion About What's Real

Like sleight-of-hand magicians, abusers used their authority and skill to misdirect, surprise and confuse their victims about what was really going on. Whatever devices they used to disguise the sexual abuse—sex education, a game, love, a bed-wetting check—the effect was the same: the children were unable to establish or maintain an accurate sense about what was being done to them.

When we asked women what they thought as children about the abuse, one replied, "It didn't feel right [but] I had no conception of what was happening." Another said it made her feel "weird" and "embarrassed"; she recalled knowing "something was wrong, it was a secret," though she couldn't really say what she thought of it.

Some women we interviewed recalled that when they were children the abuse seemed unreal to them because the abuser came in the night. They literally couldn't see him or what he was doing clearly. The abuser didn't say anything when he was abusing or after the fact.

A child looks to adults to tell her what's going on and how she's doing. In the absence of any acknowledgement of the abuse or their feelings about it, children were confused about whether it was real or a bad dream and confused about why they had the feelings they had. What they experienced during the night didn't seem real during the day. The abuser's reality—his implicit or explicit denial that anything was wrong or even that anything happened—overpowered the child's sense of reality.

Several survivors said they'd needed validation of their childhood experience of abuse. One woman said she had wanted someone to tell her what was going on. Another said that as a child she needed to know people sympathized or would listen to her. Noting that the abuse meant she couldn't think her own thoughts, one survivor said that anything to reinforce knowing herself and her feelings would have helped in dealing with the abuse. Other survivors suggested that acknowledgement of the abuse would have offset their confusion and powerlessness and given them a fighting chance to find and use their own internal resources to make sense of their experience. It would have conveyed also—as one woman explained—"that I was okay, that what he was doing to me was wrong and that I deserved the affection I wanted." Looking back, another woman thinks that even if adults around her couldn't take away the pain, it would have helped if they'd at least acknowledged what she was going through: "Beyond someone applying a band-aid, what I needed was a whole lot of tender loving care and somebody to re-affirm that I was a good person."

Without such acknowledgement, sexually abused children conclude the abuse is their fault. They struggle to create a reality that deals with their confusion. For example, one little girl described her daddy as "really nice" but she had nightmares in which he turned into a tiger. When he was abusing her, his eyes reminded her of a tiger's eyes. Too young to be able to conceptualize good and bad in one person, she split her father into two—the nice daddy and the tiger. An adult survivor recalled how her repeated nightmares of being immobilized, unable to move, curtailed the abuse she'd endured from the age of two and enabled her to block the memory of what her father did to her.

Children who were sexually abused under the abuser's guise of a special, close relationship often suppressed their confusion and accepted the abuser's version of reality. As one woman explained, even though she was "mixed up and confused" because her father sexually abused her from infancy, "I grew up feeling that he cared about me and cared about what happened to me." Other women said they began to think of themselves as the abuser's girlfriend or lover. One survivor told us she believed she would marry her stepfather when she finished high school: "We'd move to Wisconsin. We even had the place picked out, and I'd have more of his children." Another woman said "as a child all I knew was this great love for him," adding that it's only recently she's been able to feel anger towards the abuser.

Some children tried to reason with the abusers. They tried to negotiate for the attention and love they wanted and to convince the abuser to stop abusing. But children's openness and honesty were no match for abusers' deception and denial.

It's not just the offender, however, who confuses things for the child. Society's expectations and assumptions also misdirect her. One woman said that she encouraged people to think that she liked her father because "the assumption [was] that you loved your parents and I didn't know that you were allowed to dislike them." Instead of allowing herself her real feelings, this child tried for years to convince herself that she liked him. She believes that if he had been charged for abusing her she would have lied and said it didn't happen. The truth was that she hated going to visit him and was always afraid that something would happen. She wanted to be good. She didn't know that it would be acceptable to tell the truth and so she tried to make the lie become the truth.

Another woman lived the same kind of contradiction. She said, "Maybe it was that he kept telling me that he was a great guy, so I believed him. And I didn't know anybody who hated him except my mother." As a child, she believed that "if all these people liked him, he must be okay." It would be many years before she sorted through the distortions to find the truth.

One survivor said, "I thought I was being loved and that my mother was trying to keep my father and I apart and that this was his way of relating to me." She didn't understand what her father was doing to her. As a child she had wet her bed until she was eight or nine years old. At one point she reasoned, "I was being touched because my father was checking to see if I had wet the bed." She, like other children, did her best to sort it out by herself. She trusted the abuser and tried to use his explanations, implied and expressed, as the basis for her understanding.

One woman's description of an incident when she was nine underlines how children try to do what's expected of them and to adjust to adults' reality. When this child's grandfather died her father indicated he wanted "some kind of physical comfort." She responded "by basically doing the same thing I did when I was three," and her father rubbed his erect penis against her body. But, unlike when she was younger, this time he ejaculated and told her to take care of cleaning up the bed. The woman recalled her mother discovering the still-soiled sheets the next day.

> . . . She got angry and accused me of, I guess, initiating something sexually with my father. I don't really remember, but I do remember that she was angry. So I tried to convince her that I'd wet the bed.

To be convincing, the child made herself actually wet her bed. She told us that she has had urinary tract and kidney problems over the years, and she believes that these problems originated with that incident. She did her best, as a nine-year-old, both to protect herself from her mother's wrath and to accommodate her father's sexual abuse, at no small cost to herself.

Many of the survivors we interviewed, despite their best efforts, failed to sort out what was happening to them. They had no choice but to adjust their own sense of reality and to accommodate themselves to what the abusers wanted.

Confusion about Physical, Emotional and Intellectual Limits

A child's primary task in childhood is to learn everything. One of the most basic things a child must learn about is autonomy: the understanding that there are legitimate boundaries between herself and others. Children who aren't sexually abused learn that they can say "no," that they can object when someone touches them in a way they don't like. They get support from the adults in their lives for establishing their boundaries. They learn that if someone bullies them or hurts them they can talk about it and learn how to handle the situation. But, depending on their age when the abuse begins, children who are sexually abused either never develop autonomy or their sense of it is unclear. Their right to autonomy is undermined by the abuser. They learn that any boundaries they have can be violated and that there's little, if anything, they can do about it.

Many women we interviewed described incidents of sexual abuse that were surprise attacks, with no warning, and in situations where children should expect to be safe. For example, more than one child experienced the abuser putting his finger in her vagina as he carried her upstairs or held her on his lap while he read her a story. Other survivors have very early memories of being woken up, as they slept in their cribs, by the abusers' manipulations of their bodies.

Women's comments on how the abuse made them feel as children consisted of words and phrases denoting powerlessness.

They spoke of trying to get away, of not knowing how to stop it, of having no choice, of not understanding and of feeling unsure, fearful, and helpless. The abuser's disregard of their feelings and of their right to physical integrity taught them that their feelings didn't count and that there was no safe place. Their efforts to stop the abuser failed.

One woman talked about realizing that she had no control to enforce her desire for physical distance from her father. She said:

> I did not like my dad being in bed with me. He was big and he was fat and I didn't like him and I didn't like [his penis] and I didn't like seeing it.

She knew that she wanted him to get out of her bed and that she felt very relieved when he went, but she didn't know how to make him leave. Another woman said she didn't have an analysis about why the abuse was happening: "All I wanted was for it to stop." She was first abused by an older cousin whose family she was staying with while her mother was in hospital. She was in a vulnerable position from the start—scared about what was happening to her mother, lonely, and confused. At the time, she was unable to challenge her cousin's authority or stop his sexualized "play" and abuse of her.

Several of the women who spoke with us described various strategies they'd used to try to set limits, enlist support, or regain some measure of personal control. One woman recalled trying to express her will physically: when the abuser came after her "the second time, I was pushing him away—I guess I felt it was wrong. I didn't like it. I was trying to get away." Similarly, another woman recalled trying to avoid her father, even going so far as locking the door of the room she was in to keep him out. However, "He would push the lock off the door. It was an ongoing scene and I could never get out of it... " She tried to get her mother to stay home from her night job, in the hope her mother could protect her, but she knew her mother needed money and an independent life. This ten-year-old child was too intimidated and confused to say exactly why she wanted her mother to stay home. When her mother told her she was "not being grateful for her working to make money to feed us," the child couldn't argue. Her own needs and feelings seemed inconsequential.

One woman's experience illustrates how a child's sense of boundaries is influenced not only by the abuser but also by the responses of other adults. She recalled climbing into bed with her parents once when she was unable to sleep. "My father pulled me close to him and he was rubbing his penis between my legs." She was facing her mother and had her back to her father. Although her mother had awoken, "She didn't help me or stop my father. She just rolled over." While her mother may not have realized what was happening, to the child her mother's lack of response suggested that the child had to accept what her father was doing to her whether she liked it or not.

Children did try in a variety of ways to set and enforce personal boundaries. One survivor who'd been sexually abused from an early age by several adult males remembered being invited to a girlfriend's to play with some young boys who were visiting. She recalled being nervous about going to play with the boys and "putting on ten pairs of underpants that day," as a kind of armour, in preparation for their visit. She'd suspected that the boys would want "more than to play in the hay barn. And they did. And I ran out. They were playing hot dogs and buns."

Some children found that dissociation established a boundary the offender could not break. One survivor said, "I would just be silent during the abuse. In order to do that I'd drift out of myself." She both escaped and cushioned her awareness of the abuse by allowing her consciousness to drift out of her body. She would eventually create other personalities within herself to avoid conscious knowledge of the abuse as well as her own feelings.

Another woman described a similar strategy.

I would go into the fog—sounds would become muffled, my equilibrium was off—I would pinch me to feel myself. I was in a void, not here with you. I had to concentrate like hell to feel partially there.

As she grew up she "used booze and drugs so I didn't notice the fog." A third woman explained, "I think I just repressed it [the abuse] so quickly when I was a kid... I was like out of my body really." Leaving their own bodies in the hands of the abuser was the only way these children could survive the experience. It was the only way they could create a boundary between themselves and the abuse.

One survivor described attempting to take control of her situation by establishing an intellectual boundary. Abused from the age of four and unable to stop it, she tried to re-define her experience by taking an "aggressive stance." She said, "I never pleaded with him" to stop; instead over time she convinced herself that "I was fucking him."

Some children fought back more directly. One woman described the "terrorist activity" she and her older sister had carried out against their father who sexually abused her.

> We would tease him, conspire to embarrass him. We'd give him a big hug and kiss him when he was uncomfortable, or catch him with his pants down when he was changing in the morning from his pyjamas into his clothes.

They tried to take advantage of "his fear of being exposed, his shyness about his body... to catch him out sexually, catch him with his pants down—literally." Their strategy, in spite of their relative lack of power over their father, had some effect: "I think he got scared and withdrew a bit. I'm not sure why because he certainly had the power." But the effect was limited; her father's abuse of her, which began when she was one and a half, continued until she was old enough to leave home.

Other children confronted the abuser or told an adult they thought could help. Confronting the abuser had little effect. The children's pleas were no match for the abuser's ability to rationalize what he was doing, to confuse, or to override the child's objections. One woman recalled her father's repeated promises that "he would never do it again... but, of course, he would."

One thirteen-year-old overcame her uncle's threats to kill her if she told anyone that he'd tried to rape her. A month after the event, she did tell her mother. In turn, her mother and father had her uncle committed to a psychiatric hospital. While her parents acted promptly to protect their daughter, they didn't explain to her what they'd done. To the child it seemed her uncle had just disappeared and might reappear at any moment. Her fears and feelings were not dealt with in the way she needed. As a result of not knowing what had happened to her uncle, she continued to be haunted by his threats. Further, the psychiatrist her parents arranged for her to see reminded her of her uncle which made it impossible for her to open up to him and talk about the abuse.

Similarly, another child who eventually decided to speak directly to an adult about the abuse she'd experienced was also apparently left in the dark about what response she'd elicited. She recalled that the abuse by her cousin stopped after she told her aunt. "She must have talked to my cousin's mother. I was smart for telling her because I knew she would do something about it, because I knew she hated my cousin." However, this child's abuse by other men, including one of her teachers, continued for several years. Although she obviously had a sense of her right to boundaries, she did not know how to enforce it effectively on her own.

For many survivors, it took years to learn how to assert their autonomy. One young woman had tried a variety of ways to stop the abuse she'd endured from age one until finally, at eighteen, one day the abuser hit her "for no reason. I went hysterical. He tried to come into my room. I grabbed scissors. I told him to get away and never come near me again." Another woman described how her brothers enlisted her help to deal with their father once when he was acting really dangerously, driving around with guns in the car, scaring people. Her brothers thought she had power over him because one time they'd had a fight and she'd beaten him up. "I'd used my weight to hold him down. He never bothered me sexually after that." She noted how wrong her brothers' assumption was; the only hold she'd ever felt she had over her father was sex—and that, of course, was not really a matter of her power over him but *his* desire and power to sexually abuse her.

In most cases the abuse had already gone on for years before survivors were able to challenge the abuser's authority or devise effective strategies to protect themselves. One woman recalled her father's insults, accusations, and proprietary advances continued into her teens and early twenties.

> Later on as I grew older, without his saying anything, I had the feeling that he considered me "his woman." . . . When I started dating he would accuse me of being a whore, a slut and once when I was about twenty-two I was dressing in the bedroom and he came in and put both hands on my breasts and started telling me about this gorgeous body that I had and, the way he said it, it was like a man talking to any woman—there was no father-daughter relationship there at all.

This daughter's feelings and choices were secondary to her father's. Her only option was to expose him. But she believed that to expose the sexual abuse would destroy her family, humiliate her further, and leave her in the position of having her word measured against her father's denials. She also knew that her mother was "petrified" and brow beaten by her father. Under these circumstances, she couldn't convince herself that her situation would improve with disclosure of his sexual exploitation of her. As a result, she had to forfeit her own autonomy and for years endured the abuse.

Sexually abused children learn from their experience to distrust and disregard their own judgement. The abuse, the abuser and others' responses distort and blur a child's sense of her own legitimate physical, emotional and intellectual boundaries.

Confusion About Personal Competency

To develop a sense of competency, a child must acquire confidence in her abilities. It involves simple things like learning to kick a ball or play a game. It includes developing independence from her parents and learning social skills. To develop the confidence she needs, a child requires support and affirmation from the adults in her life. For example, when she learns to catch a ball or figure out a puzzle, she needs an adult to encourage her, to say, "That's really good; let's see if you can do it again." She also needs the opportunity to be independent, to function on her own with her peers.

Sexually abused children have a hard time feeling competent. The women we interviewed told us that as children, instead of learning they were important and valuable people, they felt incompetent and full of self-doubt. Some were confused because the abuser was at times a loving father who taught them to read or play sports but at other times was sexually abusive. A child in this situation is unable to accept freely the affirmation her father provides for fear of being abused by him.

Affection, attention and abuse were bound together by several abusers. One woman told us she had desperately wanted the affection and attention she received from her grandfather but they were tied to his sexual abuse of her. Another survivor remembered that, "With my uncle, I wanted the affection so I'm not sure I would have wanted it [the abuse] to stop. But I tried to show him I didn't like the sexual abuse... "

Sexual abuse also undermines a child's ability to be independent. The abuser's violation of a child's bodily integrity and privacy makes her vulnerable and fearful. She can't feel safe. She lacks the confidence she needs to become independent. In addition, a child's experience of being unable to stop the abuse, combined with her doubts about the validity of her own perceptions of reality, makes her feel incompetent. Sexually abused children live with stress and with the suppression of their own reality. Children abused from infancy do not know life without this tension and duality. Their ability to act on their own behalf is eroded by the abuser.

Having a secret, trying to hide the truth of their experience— perhaps even from themselves—forces children to withdraw further. It makes them mistrustful of affirmation or recognition of their positive traits. One woman explained, "for sure it made me feel uncertain of taking in recognition or attention. It had some element of something bad about it." She grew up feeling unworthy, uncertain and undeserving.

... Not trusting my own feelings. Not trusting my own intuition about things. I didn't feel trusting of other people around me much at all... I think it contributed to having difficulty in taking in positive things from people. Whether touch or other kinds of caring. It contributed to having difficulties being intimate. Not just sexually, but intimate with feelings.

With her friends, in social settings, she could not talk about what was happening at home. Eventually, like so many other abused children, she blocked off conscious awareness of the abuse.

These children could not be open or honest with others for fear of revealing their secret. They lived in hiding. In their confusion their sense of themselves became inseparable from a sense of shame and fear of discovery.

One woman described an "uncontrollable kind of fear" that kept her constantly on her guard as a child.

Because the abuse was not named as such, my whole life revolved around him... the more I had to keep the secret, the more isolated I started to feel with other people. I was okay in large groups, but not on one to one.

Intimacy with other people frightened her because she believed that if anyone had looked at her a certain way or even asked a certain question she would "blurt the whole thing out." As an adolescent, she believed that exposing the "secret" would expose her own dishonesty and "badness." In constant turmoil, she had to minimize her contact and intimacy with her mother, brother, and peers in order to feel any measure of safety and control.

Many survivors told us they hadn't made friends as children. One woman explained this by saying "I felt odd with kids in school." Another said, "I think I felt other or different." One woman now sees how the abuse affected not only her feelings about herself, but also her ability to engage and interact freely with others.

I felt punished and robbed of the freedom to relate to my peers... it took that away. At the same time, when people were talking, I appeared ignorant when I wasn't because I couldn't say what was happening.

Like other survivors, she feared rejection if she was honest so she hid within herself and pretended to be like everyone else. Some children made the camouflage their "identity."

With no authority or control, no support and validation for their thoughts and feelings, and devoting much of their energy to hiding the truth of their lives from themselves and from others, these children could not establish or develop their own competence.

The Crisis of Confusion

Living under these conditions creates a conflict within a child between her own sense of reality and the abuser's construction of reality. When her inner reality is not supported or reflected more generally in the world, this conflict will eventually become a crisis. It's a double bind: if the child tells she faces the possibility of further humiliation and probable retaliation; if she doesn't tell she must accept the abuser's ability to define reality and continue the abuse.

Despite the potential horrors, children did try to tell what was happening to them. When they were misunderstood, ignored and disbelieved, some kept trying, but many gave up. Powerless to change their situation, they had to find a way to live with it.

One woman talked about feeling like she "lived in two worlds."

> ... On the one hand I was really depressed and unhappy and what I called "felt sorry for myself." I used to lie in bed at night sometimes and list all the bad things that had happened to me and wish that I could tell somebody.

She felt "bad for thinking those things" and dismissed her feelings as self-pity. She said her night-time world was "home." In her daily life, she felt she carried something around with her, but couldn't identify what "it" was. She couldn't justify her depression so she didn't show it. Like other children, she had no choice but to adopt the abuser's reality in place of her own.

To live with childhood sexual abuse is to live with trauma.

The dual reality of abused children's lives causes emotional and intellectual crisis. To continue to function these children had to resolve the crisis. They had to choose which reality they would live with in the world. In the end they all had to accept their powerlessness to change their situation.

Self-Estrangement

Locked in a struggle with the abuser, the most viable option for most sexually abused children was to remove the one combatant they could control—themselves. "Blocking out" or "letting go" of their own reality was a necessary and common resolution to an otherwise unendurable situation of perpetual inner turmoil, pain and conflict.

When the women we interviewed talked about how they felt about themselves their comments reflected self-rejecting and negative attitudes. One woman said that she felt "guilty." She believed it was wrong to enjoy herself in her own body. She shouldn't like herself. When she was asked how the abuse made her feel about her family, she responded by talking about how her *family* felt about *her*:

> That I was an inconvenience. I was a hindrance. I wasn't good for anything for them. I never pleased them, ever.

Like so many other children, she believed she was to blame for the abuse because she wasn't good and she was at fault. Isolated in a tension-filled home and discouraged by both parents from making friends when she was a child, she could only accept the often repeated judgement that she was a faulty, inadequate and burdensome child who deserved what she got.

Other women expressed similar feelings. One woman who was abused sexually by both parents said that, although it is still hard for her to separate which feelings originated from her mother's abuse and which from her father's, "Somehow it still focuses back on me being a bad person—there being something wrong with me." By the time she graduated from high school, she had blocked all conscious memory of the abuse by either parent. She was estranged from herself and it was a small step to disengage from the specific fact of the sexual abuse itself. She carried a sense of being bad and wrong as a person for years to come.

One woman who was abused from infancy by her father said she believed him when "the messages that he gave me were along the lines of his lack of control and my control." She explained how he cemented this idea in her consciousness.

> I think there's a possibility of my sister [having been abused as well], but I think if anything happened with her that it stopped and he just concentrated on me. I think that solidified his argument of me having some kind of special ability.

This child survived by creating "splits" in her personality to avoid having full conscious memory of her experiences.

Although it was a self-protective strategy, she found that her "splits" were also used against her by some of the men she later encountered. She said, for instance, that one boyfriend would "corner me and we'd have sex. He knew that I wouldn't remember it and that I was powerless."

To describe their ability to disengage from their direct experiences of continual exploitation and abuse as children, other women we interviewed used phrases like "blocked it out of my mind," "blanked it out," or "forgot really fast." In fact, the majority of the women mentioned memory loss or mind blocking as a primary obstacle to their recognition and recollection of the abuse as adults.

One woman spoke of her ability to control her general awareness as well as specific memory of her experiences. She said, "I choose not to remember." She told us that to this day she can blank out whenever and whatever she chooses.

> I have a good automatic shut-off valve and I do that easily still. I can just walk through and forget what I just saw or did a half hour ago. I have to force myself to concentrate. If I want to, I have the best memory. I can read a script and learn it in one night.

Abused by her stepfather from age one through eighteen, she developed a facility to control her mind and memory which she can now employ in a positive way. And, as it did for many other women, this ability enabled her to remain functional despite her confusion, powerlessness, fear and guilt. It enabled her to behave "normally" when she was with friends or other family members.

Several women commented on an inability they now have in remembering parts of their childhood. One woman in particular described "selective" memory:

> Age three to ten is blank and my dad is snow; like TV snow. Seven to ten I remember school, not at home.

Another woman recalled, when she was eight years old, trying to tell her mother about being abused by four boys. The next day, however,

> I couldn't remember what happened. I tried to think about it and couldn't remember it. I felt completely traumatized, like a part of my memory had slipped and gone away... it was almost like a shock.

There is no doubt that she was in shock: mentally, emotionally and physically. Her mind "slipped" the experience away overnight.

One woman we interviewed talked about how she lost her memory of her father's abuse, regained it, and lost it again.

> As an adolescent I blocked it out until age seventeen. There was a TV program on sexual abuse—her face in the shadows—it triggered my memory. It was too much at the time and I suppressed it again.

The most constructive thing this teenager could do was block what she couldn't deal with.

What these women described is the establishment of an intellectual barrier to their experience: an absence of conscious knowing. Like those children who "left their bodies" during the abuse, this form of self-estrangement is a result of powerlessness. It is a crisis solution. For some, it developed into what psychiatrists call "multiple personality disorder" and what survivors call "multiplexity." One woman told us she created other personalities within herself to avoid conscious knowledge of the abuse. But as another survivor pointed out, blanking out the experience can heighten the confusion: "You're just left with the repercussions," without any reasonable explanation for them.

For the survivor, the result is loss of partial or full use of her emotional and intellectual ability to distinguish or recognize her own feelings and thoughts. She loses the ability to know herself and to feel good about herself until she can recollect the lost pieces of her life.

Survival Skills

Survival skills are abused children's attempts to deal with a situation they are powerless to change. Survivors develop many skills to help them cope with the abuse and take some control of their lives. Their survival skills can be attempts to call attention to the fact that something is radically wrong or to escape their experience or to mask it from themselves and from others. Many survivors develop skills which do all that at the same time.

By becoming an *A* student, or the class clown, or the most helpful child imaginable, a young survivor gets a measure of affirmation. Her behaviour is acceptable to at least some of the people around her. By fitting in, by gaining approval—if only from her peers—she can counteract to some extent her feelings of being different or bad. But this same behaviour can also hide what's really going on and thus prevent detection of the abuse. Who would believe, for example, that a child who cares for others, who jokes all the time or does well in school, is really unhappy and hurting?

Survivors who "act out," who try to run away or who lie or fantasize or abuse drugs and alcohol or try to kill themselves are more obviously troubled or angry. They may repress their feelings less than survivors who seek the acceptance of others but they too are hiding the real problem. And they get little or no positive attention. Their behaviour alienates the people around them. They are often punished or dismissed as incorrigible. If someone tries to find out why they are behaving in such un-

acceptable ways, the very expression of interest, with its attendant questioning, poses the threat of exposure. The survivor may
also reject offers of caring as inadequate or as censure—further
evidence that she's undeserving or that no one really understands. The fact that survivors use a variety of skills together at
different times complicates matters further, both for the survivor
herself and for those who would try to help.

As a sexually abused child grows into adolescence and adulthood, she must confront more directly that part of herself which
was most directly assaulted—her sexuality. She must refine or
adjust her survival skills to cope with relationships and sex. For
many women, the options they faced as children are reflected in
the ways they dealt with adult sexuality: some tried to avoid sexual relationships; some sought acceptance through sex; some
sought sexual power. In personal relationships, sexual and
otherwise, most survivors felt safe only if they could maintain
detachment and control.

While all survival skills are positive, creative responses to an
impossible situation, survivors are also trapped by them. In the
pages that follow, women's accounts show how survival skills
work. They also show how the very skills that enabled survivors
to function, disguised the real pain of their lives and
camouflaged their feelings even from themselves.

Intellectualizing

Some women told us they'd found the safest way to fit in and
be acceptable was to respond to situations as much as possible
from an intellectual or analytical posture. Their feelings were
confusing. Allowing their feelings to surface at all was often
painful or frightening. They could more effectively control their
thoughts than their emotions. It was safer to stay in their heads,
and block out their feelings. Doing so also enabled them to keep
their distance from other people or to control them. Some
women referred to being "analytical" or "intellectualizing"
while others talked about being "defended" or adopting a
"defensive stance."

One woman was especially clear about the development of

these survival skills in her repertoire. Feeling estranged from herself, she retreated to a reliance on her analytical capabilities, and a detachment from people around her. The sexual abuse she experienced at home by both her mother and father made her split to deal with things in her head. She said she totally intellectualized everything, and, "It forced me into excelling at school." She saw her body as the source of her humiliation and pain so it made sense to separate herself from it. She had a fine mind, and came from a middle class family that valued intellectual achievement and presumed she would go on to post-secondary education. However, she also found some problems with her strategy: "It propelled me into a defended or defensive stance generally," and it resulted in an "intellectual acting out... confronting teachers and feeling restricted" in late high school. Nevertheless, she recognizes that it served as an important anchor in her life: "I had to do well. School was the only place I was going to get any strokes."

Another adult survivor talked about feeling she had thought through things before her friends did. When she was seven her father and mother separated and her father began sexually abusing her. She described feeling confusion and conflict about her parents' divorce, about her father, and about the abuse. Her confusion, her sense of having "grown up faster" than her friends, and her ambivalence about her relationships with the boys at school led her to become analytical early on in high school as a way of trying to deal with her confusion. She used her intellect to grapple with what she sensed was more than just biological differences between men and women, or what she would now call the "sex-role conditioning."

She also used her analytical abilities to try to build a sense of identity in her uneasy relationships with schoolmates. Although she wanted to be accepted and liked, she would only "compromise" to a certain point. She felt she maintained "... a sense of integrity. Dignity is sort of [a] corny [way to say it, but] I wouldn't just do whatever they wanted." Because she was developing her abilities to analyze, she could disagree with her contemporaries, articulate her reasons, and in this way gain a positive sense of independence.

She said she used her budding understanding of feminism to begin to frame a sense of herself as having identifiable values. School became a place she could assert herself. She said, "I was known in school as a 'women's libber'.... " She was developing limits she could enforce at least with her peers. Because she was sexually abused as a child, her sense of safety was directly related to her ability to build and defend a sense of identity and respect and control in her relationships with others.

Another woman also talked about having developed her "intellectual side, putting a lot of energy into valuing thinking," while at the same time not knowing her feelings. Although this strategy kept her feelings at bay, it provided only limited protection. Being cut off from her feelings meant she didn't recognize when she was being harmed or taken advantage of, and so, in her words, she "didn't have the capacity to say 'no.' "

One woman told us she got caught in the double bind of developing both her intellect and a sense of perfectionism. She said she felt like nothing she ever did was good enough or high enough for her. "I was upset because I got ninety-one and someone else got ninety-seven. That has done me in. I felt shitty, not worthwhile, my marks were not high enough. I was never good enough." Her academic success was all the more remarkable considering that initially the abuse had made it difficult for her to concentrate and pay attention at school. She remembered in grade one she urinated on the classroom floor and was caught masturbating in public. But she later found in her school life the outlet she needed to cope with the sexual abuse by her alcoholic father. School provided her with a sense of control over her own life and distracted her from the problems at home.

For one young woman, excelling at school provided a bond between herself and her one good friend in childhood. She said they were both angry and didn't know why, and both were distant from their stepfathers. They were the same age and "We were both manipulative. We also liked to be leaders of a group and we were both intelligent, at the top of our class."

For another young woman, however, intellectual and

analytical abilities became a barrier to friendship and a source of resentment.

> I was isolated, lonely. I am most angry about using my intellect to keep my life together rather than using it to build a life for me. I did it, but I'm still so encumbered with it.

Nevertheless, she was able to keep her life together. For her, as for other survivors, developing these abilities enabled her to have a measure of control over her life and gave some survivors a useful veneer of success that lasted well into adulthood.

Hiding

Feeling different from everybody else, many sexually abused children attempt to hide. Several survivors told us they learned how to withdraw, disappear, or fade into the group in order to avoid feeling too exposed. They tried to avoid or disengage from most social interactions as a way of navigating through life without letting others see their confusion, self-loathing, and insecurity.

For some it seems to have been a way to guarantee privacy and space. One child who'd been abused by family members, friends, and strangers suffered major depression in her teens and tried to will herself to die. She also attempted suicide once. She recalled that in childhood, "... I liked my physical and emotional space. I wanted to be left alone to think and read and be..." The youngest of five girls, she was described by her parents as hard working but emotionally distant. Withdrawing was one way of coping.

One woman described herself as an average student, which she said allowed her to "fade into the group" and get by without being noticed: "I was very passive. My teachers just ignored me." Another survivor who was abused from age one through eighteen by her stepfather, characterized herself as a loner. Whenever she went out to parties, she was always "off to the side." Her way of coping with being in public places was to stay in the shadows and not draw attention to herself. She didn't feel good enough about herself to make friends throughout elementary school. In high school she had one friend whom she described as "an outcast too: homely, thick glasses, a likable personality." A decade later, they are still best friends.

Being invisible can become a way of life. One of the women we interviewed said she has only recently discovered that she still spends a great deal of time in hiding: "I realized recently how easily I can hide. I disappear. I withdraw. I'm there but not there." Withdrawal, which in childhood provided a needed cushion between herself and the world, has carried over into her adult life and become a barrier.

Another woman, when asked how the sexual abuse affected her, said, "For a long time I hid in my religion. I used religion. I became a spiritual person." It was an obvious refuge for her. She grew up in rural farming communities and her family's social life was church-oriented. The church must have seemed like a peaceful sanctuary from abuse by her grandfather, father, brothers, uncle, and others.

Several of the mothers we interviewed said hiding is one of the behaviours their children have exhibited since the abuse took place. One woman described how her four-and-a-half-year-old daughter often runs and hides when someone comes to their front door. On occasion she's fled from the room when a guest enters. According to her mother, this child is raucous in their home when guests are not present, but extraordinarily shy publicly.

Another mother described behaviour which is reminiscent of many adult survivors' fear and uncertainty; specifically, fear of men or boys. She said her four-year-old daughter became quite withdrawn towards the mother's current male partner when he was present in the home. Her daughter was afraid to be with him unless she was there. Since, as far as the mother knows, this man has not harmed the child in any way, the mother believes the behaviour is directly related to the sexual abuse her daughter suffered at the hands of her father and a friend of his.

Many women described changes in their children's behaviour that were inexplicable to them until after the disclosure of abuse. One woman said when her husband came home from work, her daughter would go to her room and hide until supper time. Although puzzling at the time, the mother now understands that her daughter could not speak of what her father had been doing to her. All she could do was try to hide from him.

The many ways survivors hide or try to be invisible are acts of protection born of powerlessness and insecurity. They are a result of the fear and loss of trust sexual abuse promotes in a child. The children whose mothers we interviewed will have more opportunity, time, and assistance to sort out and come to terms with their feelings about themselves and those around them. The abuse is known, they have been believed, and their mothers are determined to support them in their healing. The adult survivors we interviewed, on the other hand, were left to struggle alone, trying to adjust and adapt to these feelings as a condition of their lives.

Being Passive

Sexual abuse teaches children that no defences they have will stave off a determined offender. They have no choice but to comply with the offender's implicit or explicit demands. They are trapped in a situation they cannot change and are confused or frightened into silent compliance.

Passivity in response to sexual abuse is an understandable response which many survivors described. As one woman said, "If somebody forced me I would have done anything, I would have lain there in a comatose state and done what I thought was supposed to be done." Like someone lost in the forest, a child who is unable to determine a safe way out of her situation will often simply stay put and hope for rescue.

One adult survivor said she felt she had to submit to her father's abuse to "appease" him, although she felt "detached," "awkward" and "dirty." He would begin by showing her pornography (which he had already told her she would enjoy), then he would touch her in sexual ways.

I'd stand there and look at them [pornographic pictures], and he'd start playing with me. The hardest part is that I was so passive. He'd get horny, laugh and smile. I would laugh too, to appease him. Pat his head, take care of him. I felt awful."

He ignored her silent, passive resistance, and performed oral sex on her and put his fingers in her vagina. She remained passive because she could not think of anything else to do. She felt she had to acquiesce to his wishes.

Another woman described a consequence of having told someone about being sexually abused. Although she didn't remember who she told, she recalled what happened next.

... He [the abuser] came after me on it. I just grovelled and felt terror. A feeling of being threatened and like I wouldn't survive.

This experience of humiliation and fear was a powerful lesson in the wisdom of passivity, a clear warning not to speak or protest again. She did not repeat her "mistake."

For a significant number of adult survivors, compliance and passivity became a general life pattern. Passivity is a survival skill survivors learned directly in the experience of being sexually abused and developed into a strategy for coping with new situations in both public and private interactions.

The confusion and distortion created by the abuse affects the child's ability to trust her own perceptions. Since the abuser is an adult and by definition "right," the child must construe her own perceptions as "wrong." She learns, as one survivor put it, to rely on "cues" from those around her. These cues inform her conduct and replace her own decision-making and thought processes.

One survivor, whose abuse by her father began at age four and continued for five years, recounted an extreme form of passivity development. She described consciously conforming to people around her, as completely as she was able to do. Like other children, she wanted to be "normal." Since she didn't feel she was normal, she tried to learn how to behave normally by meeting the expectations of others.

I was behaving like a victim, period. Totally. It was an aspect of my being. I dealt with the world as a victim. I was passive, conforming. I

didn't know what I wanted. I put others' concerns first. All my attitudes cued off other people. I had no sense of self, autonomy, or
sense of worth.

Several survivors gave examples of their passivity in sexual
relationships, indicating that their attempts to take cues from
other people extended into their adult lives. One woman said she
was unable to trust her own intuition or feelings, nor did she feel
able to trust those around her. Although she has developed a
general indifference to what men think of her, in the past she
found it difficult when a man was sexually interested in her and
interested in her in other ways.

Most of the men I was involved with I felt they were interested in
me, but sexually I felt I couldn't assert myself with them. And I distanced myself about caring whether they thought I was attractive.

Another woman we interviewed used words like "victim"
and "passive" interchangeably when commenting on her relationships with the men in her life. She described the pattern as
one which persists to the present day.

I carried on the passive pattern with my first boyfriend. With my
husband now I'm doing it out of duty—it's what I should do. I've
carried on in the same victim pattern.

Passivity for this woman has resulted in a complete absence
of sexual desire. She calls herself an "ice victim," implying that
she is frigid as a result of being acted upon without asserting her
needs.

That's what it is when you are an ice victim. You let it rule you or
you decide you are going to rule it and if you do it's an uphill path
and that's what it's like for the rest of your life.

Another woman talked about expecting her lovers to be responsible for her sexual and emotional well-being. She did not
expect herself to have to reciprocate. She talked about a depen-
dency or, as she put it, "a victim place" from which she defended
the one-sided nature of the relationships.

I expected my lovers to give me an orgasm and be responsible for
me. In all ways. Being responsible for me emotionally too. Because I

was so invested in this together, sexual image of myself. Always expecting my lovers to be right there for me, but I didn't have to be there for them.

Until she came to understand that this pattern was rooted in childhood sexual abuse, this woman accepted the passive role.

One woman who spoke of feeling like a victim was not optimistic about her ability to change.

It's like a part of you has been taken away and you never get it back. There is irreparable damage done to your soul. I try desperately hard to be whole. I'm missing pieces. It's very hard to do—to attain that goal [of wholeness].

At this point in her life she has recalled a great deal about what was done to her as a child, and is realizing its continuing effect on her entire life. In spite of her lack of optimism, she and the other women we interviewed are no longer accepting their situations passively; they are struggling to undo the damage.

Using Humour

A principal aim of sexually abused children is to survive the abuse without making it worse. Several of the women we interviewed used humour as a mask for their feelings and as a way to feel more powerful and in control. It also provided a way to get the attention they desperately wanted but could not ask for directly for fear of exposing themselves or the abuser. They found that being the clown, trickster, jester, or buffoon worked fairly well, at least for short periods of time.

One woman recalled that when she was six years old, her uncle told her what "they" were doing was all right and a special "secret." Though she sensed it was "bad," and feared it could get worse, she didn't know what to do. As she grew older, humour became her refuge.

I was the Court Jester, slap stick, black humour. I would kick myself and fall down, literally. "Aren't I clumsy?"

Nonsense was safe; playing the fool was safe. Talking about what was really on her mind was not safe. She developed a bravado and wit which came in handy on more than one occasion. Once, she used her humour as a weapon to intimidate and confuse boys who tried to rape her.

> I was almost gang raped and I used it [humour] to talk my way out of it. The new me said, "Okay, I may get raped or killed, but one of you is going with me. Which one of you big boys is brave enough to go first?" It worked. I laughed at them and [got] out of the rape.

Laughter usually suggests personal ease and a lack of fear. Being able to mask her fear with laughter worked well for her that day.

Another survivor talked about how she believed that being "funny" gave people the impression that she was fine. She was not fine; she was abused by her father for the first time at age seven and for years after that. She also had to endure the indignities of her father's attempted abuse of her best friend and exposing himself to a babysitter. However, "because I was very bubbly, funny, everyone thought I was this well-adjusted, happy kid." She also described herself as being a "loud, funny jock," and said that being able to use humour, particularly sarcasm, made her feel more powerful.

> So definitely the humour and sarcasm was a way of fighting—protecting myself. And I would certainly risk humiliating guys. That felt good.

One woman recalled being the class clown. She didn't use humour to intimidate others but, she said, "I'd make jokes in class and get the attention I didn't get at home." Emotionally neglected in an angry home where her father was a working professional with a drug addiction, she found humour helped her mask a troubled home life. Unfortunately, her use of humour didn't protect her from the English teacher who abused her when she was fourteen years old.

Being funny, sarcastic, or a wit had clear advantages for these women. It got them some attention, provided some protection, gave them a way to fit in, and made people think they were happy when they weren't. In addition, it gave them a sense that they had some control over the reactions of other people.

Being A Helper

Being helpful is a trait which our culture encourages in female children, valuing it as a useful skill for women in adult relationships. Women are often expected to take care of the emotional well-being of others. Survivors of childhood abuse learn this role particularly well: their emotional safety depends on everything and everyone around them being all right. Their thoughts, of necessity, often center upon taking care of others. Sometimes that is the source of their only sense of personal value. One way to escape from the "bad" feeling inside is to "be good" on the outside. The child picks up clues from those around her to determine what is and is not acceptable behaviour.

Some adult survivors we interviewed talked about either being responsible for, or assuming responsibility for, the care and protection of others as their primary way of establishing and maintaining relationships. One woman said she felt she was more mother than sister to her siblings. She followed the lead of her mother whom she describes as "bossy, always controlling." Unfortunately, she believes her behaviour created an emotional distance from her siblings which still exists today.

Sexually abused by her stepfather from age one until she left home at age eighteen, she was secretive, unhappy and lonely. Fearing her mother's disapproval, and her stepfather's abuse and threats, she learned that her only hope to stay safe was to obey orders and to see that her siblings did so as well. In addition, she tried to avoid competing with her mother and to take care of her mother's feelings at the expense of her own confidence and recognition of her own abilities:

> I was a C+ student and I never lifted a book. Mom was doing her high school at the same time, and she was very competitive with me. I protected her and let her have the As.

As a result, though she would have liked to attend university, "I never felt I could do it academically." She was first and foremost a slave to members of her family and only secondarily, if at all, a person in her own right.

Being a helper, however, is not necessarily without benefits.

One woman, whose mother was often ill and took tranquillizers daily, found that she could safely receive and express non-sexual love as she cared for her younger sister with whom she formed a loving bond.

Another woman talked about how she became the "take no shit" counsellor for her friends when they were troubled by problems in their relationships with their boyfriends. She described her attitude as "quite obnoxious" towards her male peers. She believes this kept them at a distance. She "pretty much thought they were jerks." Since she felt comfortable being critical of the boys, and she gave out good advice, she became an important support to her girlfriends when they were struggling and confused. For example:

> My close friend was constantly being messed around. I would say it was his fault and not hers which she told me recently was not what other people would say to her.

Helping others functioned for many women as a survival skill which gave them an identity and a legitimate role. It also enabled them to establish parameters in their relationships and, sometimes, control. Helping others was also a way to forestall the impossible question of how to help themselves.

Acting Out

While many children who are sexually abused develop survival skills which will help them fit in and conform to adults' expectations, some "act out." Several women we interviewed talked about their children's aggressive, destructive behaviour. They couldn't account for it until they discovered that these children were being sexually abused. Then, as one mother put it, "It all made so much sense." Women described their children as "unbearable," "tough," and repeatedly involved in power struggles with adults as well as other children.

One woman said her daughters, who were both sexually abused by their father, constantly fought with each other. The elder, who was five years old, also threw dishes on the floor and wrecked furniture. When questioned, the child cited her father's proprietary rights and authority as an explanation: "Daddy said all of this is his and I can do what I want." Her parents had separated. Her father had told her she was "magic" and tried to persuade her to live with him by promising her a ranch, a horse, her own bedroom. He tried to discredit her mother as "crazy" and to encourage the child's defiance of her mother. When this child disclosed the abuse, it was clear she hated and feared her father and was terribly confused by him.

Other women described their children's biting and pinching, their troubles relinquishing power, their temper tantrums, the destruction of their possessions, and changes in play behaviours. One mother talked about how her three-year-old went from drawing "happy pictures... to black scribbles with very angry lines." Another woman talked about how her seven-year-old child does art work where she "annihilates offenders... with balloon stomachs and she pops the balloon." These children couldn't find words to express their rage and despair. They communicated through drawings and through aggression.

Several adult survivors described similar feelings and behaviours. They talked about misbehaving in school or at home. Some performed sexually explicit acts, others peed on the floor in the classroom or regularly challenged adults' authority. One woman explained that she "acted out" a lot in school because "I had a secret, you know." She was incredibly fearful as a child, "watching and listening all the time for some calamity to fall." She also felt acutely different from other children—right down to her shoes.

> I was quite bright, but really shy—tormented is my memory. I remember how we used to leave our shoes outside the classroom door. I thought my shoes were noticeably different than all the others. It made me think of witches being burned and stuff.

Her "acting out" was bravado to mask her fears and perhaps distract attention from her sense of being different. Other survivors said they too felt as if their experience of sexual abuse was a visible mark on their bodies, there for all to see. If they couldn't conceal it, they could pretend they didn't care what other people thought of them.

Another woman said she used to steal because she felt that people and the world owed her something. Although she felt guilty and responsible for her stepfather's sexual demands of her, she lived with an indefinable sense that she was being exploited and deserved something in return.

Another adult survivor told the story of how she got caught stealing money from her father who abused her. She recalled her parents suspected her of stealing and they set her up. When her mother confronted her she denied it. But her mother had kept track of how much money was in her father's pockets. Still, the survivor believed her father would defend her. "I thought he would cover up for me—or come to me. I was insulted that he betrayed me. He's getting all this. I felt used."

Some adult survivors, in retrospect, see their behaviour as a cry for help from a troubled child which unfortunately elicited punishment and disapproval that only added to their bad feelings about themselves. For others, "acting out" was a mask to conceal their secret. And for some, it was as direct an expression as they could manage of their rage and confusion.

Escaping: Running, Fantasizing, Lying

Survivors described several ways they attempted to escape the reality of the abuse. Some women recalled literally running away from home in an effort to stop the abuse. Others tried to endure the abuse by escaping into a fantasy world or by telling lies about their lives. Since they couldn't actually leave the situation, they tried to run away from themselves and their feelings.

One woman said she made an escape attempt at age seven. She ran away from home only to return out of fear that her father would take out his anger towards her on her mother. She recalled that her father regularly beat her brothers and sister as well as her mother. As a child, she worried about adding to her mother's problems. While she decided she couldn't run away from home altogether, she escaped for a day at a time by playing hooky from school and going off by herself for long walks. She remembered feeling humiliated when her grade two teacher read out the attendance records in class, noting that she had been absent a total of sixty days during the year. Finally, at fifteen, she left home for good. At eighteen she married a man who she hoped would fix everything that was wrong, but he sexually abused her and their children. For her there was no escape.

Another woman told us she left home at age seventeen. Then she corrected herself saying that in fact, it was more like running away from home which she had also tried to do when she was a young child. On that first attempt she realized she was unprepared to fend for herself but, "I was scared to go back. So I went to the police so that they would come back with me. I'd be protected." The police, however, took her home to her parents. As soon as the police left, her parents dragged her in the house and proceeded to beat her for having tried to run away. She realized that if she were to leave again, she would have to be better prepared to make her own way in the world. When she finally left for good at seventeen, it was a struggle.

> I didn't know how to survive at first. I think of it as at seventeen I started living, being born. So I had to learn everything from day one starting at seventeen years of age.

Although she was alone, lacked social skills, and was deeply distrustful, she began to live her own life, confident it would be better than the life she'd left behind.

Some women continued to run as adults: one told us she had moved between Ottawa, Montreal, Victoria, and Vancouver several times, struggling to make a living and unable to settle down.

For many survivors, running meant finding escapes, when they were children, through books and fantasies. One woman recalled being too intimidated by her abusive father to run away from home, so she ran away in her mind. She remembered, in particular, one family vacation when she discovered a cache of fairy tales in her grandparents' basement.

> I read them and sat by the pool. It was a treasured time: positive, idyllic, relaxed, little periods of time, really good. I was away from people and full of books.

Some women described fantasizing about being taken away from the abuser. Others imagined having sexual power over boys where they were dominant and completely in control. One woman said she fantasized about excelling in sports because she was very insecure about her academic abilities and intelligence.

A mother we interviewed said she was afraid that her daughter would be unable to believe that the "super powers" in her fantasy life weren't real. She described her five-year-old daughter and her two-and-a-half-year-old son (both sexually abused) as "overly imaginative... being so involved in a fantasy world to the extent that they forgot where they were." Another woman expressed concern that her children were confusing "ghosts and goblins" with abusers.

For other children their imaginary worlds were terrifying. One woman remembered having violent fantasies, full of "blood, gore, and power-tripping... " She now recognizes that she was trying to deal with her fear and powerlessness. These children used their imaginations to cope with a reality they couldn't otherwise control.

In some cases, adult survivors remembered using a combination of lies and fantasy as a survival skill to hide their reality from others and from themselves. One woman described herself as a child who was aloof, very serious, mature beyond her years, and quite hardened. She said her fantasies and lies created a web of distortion that even she had trouble keeping in order.

> Like the outside is not matching the inside at all. I have friends. They don't have me. I begin to believe in my pretend world, and when my reality would surface I would pretend that wasn't real. That's a real nuts place to be.

Nevertheless she maintained some measure of control of her own consciousness and stayed safely hidden most of the time.

She told us, however, about one incident when she was almost found out. She was pregnant with her stepfather's baby and living in an unwed mothers' home. She was lonely, had never dated and needed to feel important to somebody. All the other residents were writing and receiving letters from their boyfriends. She said she "discovered a want" inside herself and she "used that want to create the lie." She wanted to have a boyfriend; her lie was to create an imaginary boyfriend to whom she wrote sexually explicit letters. She actually sent them to the abuser "because I believed that's what he wanted to hear from me." As well, she had become "thoroughly entrenched in the fantasy of being his girlfriend."

To her horror, one of her letters was returned and opened by the staff of the home. When confronted she sustained the lie by portraying herself to the staff and other residents as a drug-taking sleaze bucket, though, in fact, she was neither. In retrospect she realizes that she wanted someone to see through the lie and question how she got pregnant. She wanted the abuse to be discovered.

Another woman recalled consciously lying on a regular basis to hide the abuse. She told us that "by age eight I was conscious of lying and, tracking it from age twelve up,... I had more and more to lie about."

For one survivor lying to people was a way to hurt people "even just for a second." With her stories, she would "suck people in for a day or two and then blow their minds and walk away." Her mother believed she was mentally ill. The woman herself said, "I may have been. I don't remember." In retrospect, she believes she was "probably seeking attention." She was sexually abused by her uncle with whom she spent the summer and recalled that she dreaded going back to school each September "to nothing, no attention."

Whether they used lying or fantasizing as survival skills to endure the abuse or tried running away from home as a way to stop it, the damage they'd sustained at the abusers' hands followed them. Though there was no escape for them as children, eventually survivors struggled to understand their survival skills and to reverse the consequences of the abuse.

Drugging and Drinking
Several of the women told us they turned to drugs and/or alcohol to cope with the abuse. It was one way to change or mask

how they felt inside and to create an artificial emotional reality for themselves. One woman talked about "falling into the bottle for twenty years." She said, "No one put a bottle in my hand. The person who poured it down my throat was me. The basic reason for my becoming an alcoholic was that was my choice of coping with life." Her father's alcoholism made drinking a familiar means of numbing and distancing herself from the trapped and helpless position she was in.

Another woman, who was first abused by her stepfather when she was twelve years old, began using drugs when she was eighteen and began drinking when she was twenty. Today she is recovering. She stopped taking hard drugs when she started drinking, though she said, "I'd still take the odd valium... " She stopped drinking when she was twenty-six years old. As she explained it:

> The drugs and alcohol were a form of denial, but even after they were no longer in my system I denied, I minimized, I rationalized and justified, the whole bit.

She continued to feel deeply ashamed and personally responsible for the abuse until she spoke with other survivors several years later.

The women we interviewed now link their abuse of drugs and alcohol specifically to the sexual abuse. When asked how the abuse affected her one woman said, "I did a lot of drinking. A lot of drugs." Another woman replied, "During high school and college I used alcohol." At the time, however, many of these women simply believed they were innately and inexplicably bad or wrong. Only when they stopped using alcohol could they see the connection between their drinking and their childhood experiences.

One woman, who became a stripper at one point as a means of supporting herself, used wine and beer at first, then LSD, mescaline, and marijuana in order to do it. "I had to be drunk to do it. It was weird. I always wanted to be a dancer, and I was a good one, but not a stripper." Although she was both alcoholic and drug-addicted at an early age, she no longer is.

Women used these substances to control and mask their own internal pain. As one woman explained, it was often a calculated and deliberate act performed in despair and resignation.

> I used to take pills. Never enough. I would lay them out and look at them and think about it a lot. Valium, anti-depressants. Eight at a time.

The pills didn't kill her or kill the pain, but at least they dulled it. Although alcoholism and drug abuse are dangerous, destructive responses to the experience of sexual abuse, they were the most effective recourse some survivors could find.

Considering and Attempting Suicide

All survival skills are an attempt to protect or care for oneself. The primary experience of some survivors was that to live was to be in pain. The survival skills they'd developed were inadequate. They had no sense of the future beyond a continuation of the pain. In such circumstances it seemed the most caring thing they could do for themselves was to choose *not* to continue to live.

While attempting suicide is not a survival skill like all the others, asserting the right to choose to die and acting on that choice can be seen as a proclamation of self, of will.

We will never know how many victims of childhood sexual abuse have made that choice as an escape from sexual abuse. We can assume that, before they acted, few had told of the abuse, or were heard if they did tell. Doubtless many suicide attempts stem from experiences of sexual abuse, whether or not the survivor recognizes that as the cause at the time. Sometimes these are indeed attempts at a permanent escape; in other cases they are the actions of a self-destructive rage.

While suicide attempts are often assumed to be cries for help, several adult survivors we interviewed spoke of suicide plans and attempts as a decision based on the fact that they found no joy, no good reason to continue to exist given the conditions of their lives. As a consequence of the abuse, they felt estranged from themselves and from everyone around them. They had no sense of being able to influence or improve their own lives. They found nothing to hold on to and no one to hold on for.

One woman who made an attempt at suicide when she was a teenager explained that she was not really living anyway: "I wasn't present when I was with somebody." She said she had long since "separated" herself from her own experience and was living a disconnected and superficial existence. She didn't feel real to herself and wasn't connected in any meaningful way with anyone else. She felt she had nothing to lose except perhaps the continuing experience of chronic depression, hopelessness, and powerlessness.

Similarly, another woman said she felt unreal and essentially non-existent as a result of being abused as a child. Her sense of isolation peaked in her first year of graduate school. She was depressed and exhausted from the effort it took to continue covering how she really felt about herself and her life. Unable to articulate her needs made her situation intolerable.

> All my energy was used in covering... I just couldn't find words to ask for help. Words were lost. I made a suicide plan.

Though suicide seemed easier than the facade, she eventually decided she couldn't do it. She continued to consider suicide but she found reasons to choose survival. She said her suicidal intentions had not come from a wish to be dead or to hurt someone else; they were the result of an inner sense of defeat, a sense which has only recently abated.

> It was an internal struggle. I was so withdrawn that I was gone. I had lost the struggle and the inner didn't match the outer. It was only this summer that suicide disappeared as the alternative.

While many children survived by separating themselves from their own experience, this separation can also obliterate reasons for enduring the trouble of living. It can blur the distinction between the end of the painful experience and the end of one's self.

Two women told us they had felt certain they would not endure beyond young adulthood. One of them recalled that as a child she had no aspirations, no plans for the future. "I didn't want to live. I thought I would kill myself by age eighteen. I didn't like life enough. I never planned past age twenty." Hospitalized for two suicide attempts when she was a teenager, she said people had asked her what was wrong, but never asked if she was being abused. Now in her thirties, she says she can imagine things to live for, whereas for many years previous she'd seen no escape from the abuser.

The other woman said she hadn't wanted to live to be thirty. She recalled that for years, "I had been trying so hard to kill me—carving myself, slashing, taking pills." She was first sexually abused as a young child by her uncle and repeatedly sexually and physically abused by her foster father and foster brothers. By the time she was placed in a foster home which was free from abuse, she could no longer tolerate any expression of caring or concern directed towards her. She only wanted to die. She says the turning point for her was being in a mental institution following a nervous breakdown in her mid-twenties: she faced the fact nobody was going to help her. She remembered coming to the realization that the decision to live or die was hers alone: "I wanted to live. I don't know why. But I didn't want to die."

For the women we interviewed, considering suicide was an attempt to take control of the only choice they felt they had left: whether or not to continue to endure. Thus, while dying precludes the possibility of survival in the literal sense, the decision to commit suicide can be self-affirming in that it is a refusal to continue to live with unceasing pain. Acting on that decision is exercising personal choice.

As an adjunct to this general case, some survivors told us that the experience of considering and/or attempting suicide quite unexpectedly led them to discover in themselves a will to survive that was stronger than their despair. Though they couldn't fully understand it, somehow they found ways to live.

Struggling with Intimacy and Sexuality

Given the source of their trauma, it is not surprising that most women have survival skills which are bound up with their sexuality. Survivors are not able to come to an understanding of sexuality based on their own wishes, but on the sexual definitions and demands of those who abused them. As a result, many survivors described their own sexuality as distorted, conflicted, and confused. For them, sexuality was not a source of pleasure, but of fear and pain.

We asked women how the abuse made them feel about their sexuality and about their expectations of relationships. Most said they are still sorting out how to have positive feelings about their own sexuality and sexual relationships. The survivors who are lesbian stated very clearly that being abused as children in no way caused their lesbianism, though for some being sexually involved with women added to the confusion the abuse had created in them. Most importantly, though, issues of sexuality were similar for all survivors, lesbian and heterosexual.

Survivors' efforts to establish their sexual integrity take place in a society where women's sexuality has traditionally been defined in terms of what meets men's desires. Men's projections of their own cravings onto the female body obscure women's sexuality. Men objectify the female body, relating to it in pieces, severed from women's identity. In consequence, women's sense of self is fragmented into pieces which reflect male sexual demands. Women struggle to collect the pieces and to define themselves as integrated intellectual, emotional, physical, and sexual beings.

This struggle is infinitely more difficult for child sexual abuse survivors. Survivors have lived through destructive experiences, very often at the hands of more than one offender. As a result, their sense of themselves is in small sharp splinters. Many women fear that once collected, these fragments would not reflect an image of themselves but instead another shadow of their abuser.

Survivors have received intensive lessons in the distorting power of male sexuality. By their actions and words abusers superimposed their own definitions of sexuality on their innocent, vulnerable victims. They distorted and often nearly obliterated these children's emerging sense of themselves as human beings. Abusers overwhelmed the children's emotional and physical feelings with their own definitions of what they were doing. Many of these children grew up unable to distinguish their own sexual feelings from what the abusers had done to them. Their sexual feelings are associated with the abuse, the abuse with the abuser's sexual demands, and sexual demands with sexual feelings.

This circle precludes the possibility of these children developing a sense of their sexual selves. Instead it surrounds survivors with the image of what the abusers want them to be. As if in a hall of mirrors, survivors react to these images in many ways. Some try to hide, some remain immobile, some try to run; some turn in upon themselves, some turn against all others, some smile, some laugh; some try to destroy themselves or the reflections, some embrace them.

These images become particularly immediate during adolescence, when young people are faced with trying to come to terms with their own and others' sexual expectations. Nowhere is there acknowledgement that many young women who were sexually abused as children live with the consequences of that abuse. Survivors feel tainted, conflicted, and vulnerable as they search for a way to negotiate this difficult and often agonizing aspect of their lives.

Most survivors we interviewed faced this test before they'd been able to sort out their experience of sexual abuse. Few had any idea that their confusion or fear about sexuality in their adolescence was linked to the abuse. Most just did their best to find ways to cope without making things worse, without prolonging their own pain or causing pain to others. To the extent that they were unsuccessful they blamed themselves, attributing their failure to their own inadequacies or unworthiness.

Adult survivors told us they'd adopted a variety of roles in relation to the sexual expectations of others. These roles divide into three main categories: rejecting sex, seeking acceptance, and seeking control. These roles were not rigid; some women used two or even three at the same time. Others alternated among them according to their abilities and needs, as well as the situations with which they were faced. Examining these roles makes it possible to understand the confusion which characterized most of these women's efforts to learn to exist as adult women with a positive sense of their sexuality.

—Rejecting Sex

Most of the adult survivors we talked with said there were periods in their lives when they did not want to be sexual. Many simply did not feel any sexual impulse or arousal. For those who felt arousal, it was accompanied by other less desirable feelings, such as shame, powerlessness, humiliation and fear. Several women said they've never found a sexual encounter physically pleasurable and do not feel motivated to explore further possibilities.

Many survivors told us they had what some called "body memory" of the abuse during their adult sexual experiences. The physical sensations prompted them to recall the abuse; those memories invaded their attempts at intimacy. As one woman explained:

> I have felt really dirty, bad about feeling sexual and have sometimes mixed up my lover, who is very trusting, with the abusers. In other words, I have had memories.

One survivor described how remembering the abuse she'd experienced has affected her:

> It threw my sexuality up in the air. I was very angry. Up until I remembered I enjoyed my sexuality. I liked myself. I liked my body. I liked making love with women. And then, I felt really vulnerable in terms of my sexuality. I kept getting flashbacks when I was being sexual and I'd shut down. I'd go numb and leave my body. When I was with men I was numb all the time. Nobody ever noticed.

This woman's response to the flashbacks was to use the same survival skills she'd used as a child: she cut off sensation and dissociated from her physical self. It is a creative solution for a child who has no other way to protect herself, but a very troubling one for an adult who had previously enjoyed sex. Her reactions have prompted her to try to come to terms with the problems in her relationships.

> I have had an overwhelming urge to withdraw from relationships as soon as I felt they were loving relationships. I didn't know how to say "no" in sexual relationships so my safety came from finding other ways not to be there. My sexuality is changing [but] I'm not

comfortable or willing to be sexual yet.

Some adult survivors found they can't tolerate having certain parts of their bodies touched. One woman described the associations which still plague her:

> Those sensations [of the abuse] enter my daily life. I am repulsed at the thought of French kissing. Anything in my mouth. I don't want anything in my mouth, and I tell my boyfriend I don't. Strange sensations of being touched on my face, touched on my breasts— and it's a turn off—it just happens. If I was aroused, it ended there. He [the offender] touched my right breast more than the other one.

Experiences like these left survivors feeling their bodies are alien, dangerous, or not their own. The problem was compounded for some women when their sexual responses also triggered specific emotions connected to the abuse. One woman outlined her experience.

> I feel like there's a connection between shame, humiliation and sexual arousal for me. When I feel aroused I start to feel humiliated. I am just beginning to learn how to move through that. I have fear about being passive. I have fear about loss of control. My sexual protection was to be active in responding, but sort of faking it. I used to feel fear and almost repulsion at sexual arousal. Not at the beginning, but at the wrong time—right at the height of arousal.

For her, sexual relationships are very difficult: "It's real hard to trust a sexual partner. I feel safe on the street and most unsafe in my own bed or the bed of a lover."

The way sexual abuse trains survivors to become accustomed to specific arousal patterns was also described by another woman. One of the abusers physically immobilized her, taunted and humiliated her during the sexual abuse. These experiences taught her that it wasn't okay to feel sexual. She is struggling to undo the link between arousal and shame.

> I have had long periods of time of not being sexual. I think [the abuse] has contributed to sado-masochistic fantasies. It's difficult to experience someone else's sexual energy coming towards me without feeling powerless. Memories come up for me when I'm sexual.

> It's difficult to enjoy being sexual. I enjoy it to some point and then I have S/M fantasies—then have to break through the fantasies to feel pleasure. It's hard to be seen to enjoy sexuality, to let go and enjoy [it] in front of someone else.

One woman we interviewed talked about her reluctance to accept or enjoy her physical self.

> I was in my twenties before I looked at my body naked. I can't have sex without the lights off. If I masturbate, I masturbate under the covers so no one can see it—a constant conflict of I'd like to enjoy it, but you're not supposed to enjoy it.

Survivors learned to hide or cover sexual feelings in a number of ways. One woman started to describe how her father's abuse made her feel about living with him, but ended up talking about how being around him made her feel fearful of her own sexuality.

> As an adolescent it made me feel wary of my father. Really hesitant about feeling sexual or exploring my sexuality because of what he might do with it. Like it wasn't okay, safe to be sexual or to take pleasure in my body, experience it.

Since sexuality is integral to who we are and since adolescence is an important time to explore, develop and express our individuality, the kind of self-protection this woman required exacted a price in terms of her personal development. Fear of attracting her father's attention limited her choices and curtailed her expression of her emerging sense of herself. This repression continues even though her father no longer constitutes a threat.

> Generally the abuse made me afraid to experience myself as sexual. Opening feels scary to me; it's scary to feel vulnerability and openness at the same time. Integration of sexuality into a sense of myself is still hard. . . I haven't sustained a relationship where it's been sexual over a long time. I'm never fully present as part of the relationship.

Other women also talked about avoiding relationships and the attentions of those they see as threatening. One woman said that she spent four years avoiding sex or men. Another survivor described a continuing impulse to guard against feelings she associates with being vulnerable.

> It still affects me sexually. It's hard for me to let go, or let myself feel . . . for when I do start feeling, another part wants to put the lid on fast.

Though avoiding their sexual feelings does not eliminate the confusion and distortion that stem from the childhood assaults, survivors who abstained from sex made a self-affirming choice for themselves. In order to experience sexual feeling fully, it is necessary to be physically and emotionally open and vulnerable. Sexuality requires an ability to risk expressing both sexual initiative and responsiveness. Many survivors were unable or unwilling to take this risk.

For many survivors, the abuse they'd experienced made any involvement in sexual relationships impossible. One woman recalled believing in adolescence that she could never have a relationship with a man. She saw people around her enjoying sex and wondered how they could. She said, "I had this feeling that I'd never know what great sex was."

Several women said they continue to avoid sexual entanglements because they feel threatened by other people's sexual need or desire, even where that desire grows out of a close, intimate relationship. One woman told us that she had never experienced sexual desire. She and her husband have decided not to have sex because she does not want to. She expressed a sense of loss.

> You know you're missing something really neat and you can't have it. You feel deprived of something you should have through no action of your own, no fault of your own, no conscious choice.

Though she said that she felt some guilt about the lack of a sexual relationship with her husband, and saw sex as "a normal part of marriage," she is managing to be true to her own feelings. When we asked her how the abuse made her feel about her sexuality, she summed it up by saying, "Basically it has taken it away from me." She feels it's gone and she has no choice about it. For her, to feel sexual was to feel bad; to choose to be sexual with someone else meant choosing to open up to negative feelings within herself and towards her partner. Though her regret and frustration are clear, she has been able to build a relationship with her husband which provides her with a valuable resource in what she called "a constant battle" with the consequences of sexual abuse.

For this survivor and others, rejecting sexual involvement has been one way to protect themselves. It's a form of resistance to the expectations of others. It is re-affirming in that it asserts a power denied them when they were abused as children. It is a choice which has given them as adults the necessary freedom to learn to love themselves while continuing to search for ways to express their love for others and to accept others' expressions of love for them.

—Seeking Acceptance

Survivors' descriptions of their lives showed that the confusion and self-hatred engendered by sexual abuse caused them to become detached from understanding or trusting their own thoughts and feelings. To survive childhood sexual abuse many of these women had become very "other oriented." Their struggle to find a sanctuary in the acceptance and approval of others extended to their sexual relations.

This search for acceptance takes place in the context of a gender-divided society which prescribes a subordinate position for women. Survivors of child sexual abuse have direct and debilitating experience of women's sexual subordination. They were trained as children to submit to abusers' demands and their gratification. Survivors learned to comply in order to protect themselves from what they feared would be more violent abuse if they resisted. They'd had to concede the greater power or authority of the abuser, and resign themselves to his demands. What they'd learned dominated their growing up and their attempts to negotiate their role as adolescents and then as adult women. For some survivors accommodating others' demands became a strategy; for others, it was the outcome of their inability to say "no" to anyone.

Though many of the women we interviewed said they didn't enjoy sex, they submitted to the expectations of sexual partners. One woman suggested the abuse has made her shut off sexually: "I don't feel anything. I don't want to feel." For her, having sexual relations is a chore, a duty she must accept. She commends her husband for his patience and understanding of her efforts to overcome the effects of the abuse and to discover her own sexual pleasure.

Other women talked about trying to have sexual relations as a way to meet unspoken social expectations. One survivor explained that the abuse had taught her that a relationship wasn't real unless sex was involved. Although sex wasn't important to her, she believed having a relationship would show her parents she was well-adjusted. To accomplish her goal she developed what she laughingly called "a great system: I never slept with anyone I didn't love but I fell in love in ten minutes!" Falling in love justified having sex and, in turn, sex was a means to an end, the relationship that would demonstrate that she was normal.

One woman recounted trying to relate sexually to men in a variety of ways. She recalled, "I went through a period where I had a series of one-night stands and affairs," rather than having intimate relationships. But the repeated abuse she'd suffered as a child, coupled with what she felt were sub-human sexual experiences as an adult, confirmed her belief that men are conditioned to be predatory and women to be receptive. She has struggled to reconcile the conflicts she feels.

> There have been periods of having a lot of contact and there have been long times without having any male contact whatsoever. And I'm sorry for that. It's because I think men are important. Their humanness is as important as ours is. But I didn't know how to deal with them, or trust that what I was hearing was genuine. And when I've tried to have a relationship it's been incredibly difficult. I pull away from that intimacy.

She was unable to integrate her belief in the importance of having heterosexual relationships with her actual experiences with men. She and many other women persisted despite their fears and discomfort.

One survivor said her sexuality was accompanied by a sense that being sexual was bad, and also by a fear of sex.

> I was afraid that something would happen to me—especially that I would get pregnant. It's like I wanted sex or I wanted something, but all that would happen was that I would get "done to."

A survivor of sexual abuse by her father, she, too, was aware of the predatory nature of much of men's sexual interest. She remembers definitely having a sense that men were getting their needs met. For her there wasn't a lot of difference between what happened with boys in high school and the abuse she'd experienced; she felt a lot of the same isolation and fear.

Survivors' understanding of male sexual demands was undeniably influenced by the abuse, and it was re-affirmed by even their non-abusive adolescent and adult experiences. As one woman told us:

> I think I saw relationships with boys as sexual—that you had to put out. And it was clear to me that your friends were the girls and the relationships with boys were—if you were lucky—a friend, but the sexual part was clear. It was an integral part of those relationships.

Many young women, whether or not they have been abused, might share this perception of adolescent relationships. Similarly, the survivor who recalled believing that "having a date meant going out and going to bed" was perhaps only more direct and less romantic than other girls her age in her assessment of what boys generally want.

Some survivors apparently thought, however, that they'd be that much more acceptable if they took the initiative in acting on their understanding that what boys and men wanted from them was sex. One survivor began early. She recalled how she coped in elementary school.

> I would always be willing to play "Truth or Dare" and I'd do it with a number of boys—I might be the only girl there. And I would say stuff like "there's nothing wrong with sex and it's natural"—not that I felt natural about it though... I remember being after one boy and finally getting him into the bushes and being really sur-

prised that he didn't know how to kiss. When I was six, seven...
I'd do things like go and undress for boys in the woods.

She told us that it was a way of getting attention and having
them like her. She'd understood her real value to her father was
sexual; sex, therefore, seemed the logical way to win approval
from her male peers.

Another survivor remembers trying to play out what she
perceived to be her role of meeting men's sexual needs. The
reactions she received, however, indicated that she had
misunderstood how men want women to behave sexually. She
didn't realize that while women are expected to do what men
want, men insist on maintaining the authority to define that.

> I was completely confused. I always felt like I was supposed to be
> the one to satisfy the man and that I was supposed to be the active
> one. But I realize that most men prefer women to be passive sexual
> partners and when they'd be with me and I'd be very active, and ag-
> gressive even, they'd treat me abusively. It would make them feel
> frustrated, I suppose, because they didn't have control of me. They'd
> want me to stay still and they'd get angry because they thought I was
> just trying to tease them or that I wasn't letting them have control
> and some men thought I was a whore.

Although these experiences confused her, taking an aggressive stance with men was the strategy she'd learned from her father. Abused by him from infancy, she was made to believe that
she was responsible for giving him erections. She was also sexually abused by a series of men, including two of her teachers.
This woman tried to be acceptable and in control at the same
time. Taking the sexual initiative also became for her a way to
try to protect herself. At thirteen, faced with a gang of boys who
threatened to rape her, she recalls thinking

> ... the only way of getting control was for me to be the active one,
> sexually, so I took over and had sex with the brother because the
> friend had threatened that the brother was going to rape me too. I
> figured I'd beat them to the punch.

In trying to protect herself in this way, however, she inadvertently also gave protection to her assailants; they could claim that she consented to the rape.

Other survivors also told us they'd decided that the best sexual defence was a good offence. One woman talked about trying to be sexually assertive as a defence, not against assailants, but to deal with her discomfort with her own sexuality. She attributes being very cut off from her sexuality to the abuse.

> I was always expecting other people to take care of my sexuality, to take responsibility for my sexuality. Always looking for someone to "give" me an orgasm. Not wanting to admit that I'm a woman. Dressing in dark colors, big clothes and hiding my body.

Avoiding monogamous attachments, avoiding intimacy, she covered up her real feelings and submitted to the notion that a variety of relationships would make her happy.

> I also acted really sexual—as this real sexually hungry woman who's really open about sex and comfortable with it. That was a defence for my discomfort. And always having trouble with commitment. Always sleeping around. Really hurting my lovers. Thinking that to be sexually promiscuous is "the way." Thinking that that will bring me happiness.

But using this strategy only added to survivors' confusion and self-hatred. One woman explained how the strategy developed.

> What happened was after I was abused by my cousin I adopted a behaviour where I started picking men up. I call them "the men." So I was learning something here. I just have the feeling I was being trained to be promiscuous. It was a hard time.

She described how the abuse and her responses to it made her feel about herself:

> The abuse made me feel real dirty, and bad, and like trashy. Which are all feelings that come back now and again. And when I started picking up men and adopting promiscuous behaviour I felt completely out of control. Like I couldn't stop. And I didn't know what was wrong with me.

The insight which this survivor and others articulated was developed after a long struggle to sort out their feelings. As one woman pointed out, the guilt and shame still linger.

> I'm learning so much. It's hard to project back to then. I still think of myself as a slut... that had to do with the promiscuity.

In retrospect, these women can see how their sexual behaviour and their feelings about it are a consequence of the sexual domination they'd experienced as children. The abuse distorted survivors' sense of their sexuality. It taught them that they must try at all costs to accommodate men's sexual demands. For some, accommodating meant "putting out," even before they were asked. For others it meant submitting, having sexual relationships out of duty or a desire to be "normal." For all, the struggle to define their own sexuality involved overcoming their need to be acceptable to others.

—Seeking Control

Looking back, it's clear to some survivors that they had tried to use the lessons they'd learned from abusers as a way of exercising sexual control. One woman commented that in her adult relationships, "It seemed the only two avenues of emotional expression were either to get angry or to sexualize." She has a sense of herself as a young woman being "very demanding sexually" and "quite compulsive" about what she saw as her "sexual need." In retrospect she said, "I was very much like my offender." She tried to dominate and control the sexual and emotional climate of her relationships as the abuser had dominated her. In time, she began to find more respectful and responsible ways to relate.

Several women said the abuse affected their sense of power and powerlessness in sexual relationships. One woman talked about how she took the upper hand in her relationship, although she was not able to sustain it.

> I had a one year relationship with a woman in Vancouver and Victoria. I was a bitch—she was a puppy dog... I couldn't stand lovemaking. I made her feel weird for wanting me... [She] was my first woman lover. After two months I left. She stayed in Victoria and I'd come home every two weekends. We tried living together. I couldn't

stand it. We broke up. I didn't feel good about being lesbian, about sex. I had no deep desire, so why bother. She was childlike—I was mature. It was hard for me to take. I didn't know why.

Not knowing how to negotiate a sexually intimate relationship, this woman used against her lover the same forms of manipulation the offender had used against her as a child: distortion, confusion, and blame. The fact that these women remain close friends is a testament to their commitment to each other.

Another woman said she's determined not to be abused again. The abuser had made her "feel like nothing." To protect herself she has limited the boundaries of her sexual expression and taken charge in her relationships.

I've been in a relationship with the same man for quite a while. He is not a strong person. I'm very strong and he's weak. I'm the dominant person. I don't know how I would relate to someone if they were dominant, or even if I could [relate]. I'm scared of letting go, I guess, because if I let go I could end up getting abused again. I never put it together like that before. It wasn't just the sexual abuse, it was everything. I've learned to loosen up, but I've always been on guard...

For her, it's a compromise between not having a relationship at all or having one she controls. She explained why she's had such a struggle to relate to men.

I was never equipped. I was never taught how to have relationships or relate even. Everything relationships were, I didn't want. There was no room to discuss—men had this vision of what I would do. I didn't do anything that they wanted. I did everything wrong trying to get started. Well, it wasn't wrong, I just didn't know what I was doing. I had to tumble through things in complete isolation. I was never equipped going into relationships. I had to find out for myself. I'm now forty-two years old and I've come to it by twenty-five years of trying to figure it out on my own.

One survivor told us what she'd learned as a result of the abuse was that "the way to a man's heart is through his penis... And the way to get to a man's penis was to be promiscuous." She believed her ability to arouse men sexually would get her the attention she wanted. That, together with her ability to disengage, "to become a block of ice in seconds," would give her the control she'd lacked as a child. Her conclusions were derived not only from the abuse she'd experienced but also from observations of her mother's relations with many men. She noted her mother had also been sexually abused from the age of nine; abuse her mother kept secret for forty years.

Three women told us they turned to prostitution as a way to take control of their lives and to obtain economic benefit. One woman outlined how she concluded that prostitution was a reasonable and viable choice for her.

> Because I had been so wrapped up in my father and his abuse of me, when I had my freedom from the abuse I felt immediate relief, but more loss than ever. I missed my peers. I didn't know how to fit in with them and their sexualities. And it was almost as though I decided, if I'm not going to have any fun with this, I might as well make some money at it.

When asked how the abuse made her feel about her sexuality she replied: "very powerful, frigid—I don't like the word frigid but that's the only available word to describe it." She felt she'd "missed the boat" in terms of ever being able to enjoy her sexuality. She believed she had the power to sell men what they wanted without fear of being sexually aroused herself. For her, prostitution represented a means of achieving both economic and sexual power over men.

Similarly, another survivor who told us she'd been involved in prostitution said it's clear to her now that she didn't like sex, so she got money for it. She described herself as someone who avoided her feelings and avoided even personal conversations with people. Having been sexually abused from age two into her teenage years, the idea of having impersonal sex with men and getting paid for it seemed to her less exploitative than the abuse had been. Indeed, she's thought about "the money I would have if he [the abuser] had had to pay me!" As far as she could tell as a teenager, the only careers were as a pimp or a prostitute, and it seemed like everybody in the world was a prostitute. To her prostitution meant "doing it honest,... there was some power, respect, control and dignity as a prostitute." To have more control, she tried to be "more and more high class, and not have to put time into the work."

As a young woman she was not emotionally connected to the abuse and its effects on her. What she understood was that the money and sense of independence she got through prostitution gave her more choice and control than she'd had as an abused child. Another woman recalled having a similar view of prostitution as a way to have power.

> I used men. I got into prostitution. I didn't have a pimp. I felt powerful, in control. I called the shots. These guys were lucky to have my company. I was pleasing—not bitchy.

Although it's clearer now to these survivors that their feelings of control were relative to the powerlessness they'd experienced as children, one woman noted her continuing ambivalence about prostitution. The important thing for her is that she wasn't "a walking victim."

> It's me in control of my body and selling it. Sometimes it's me in control and the money. It pisses me off—except for a few times with one man—that I ever gave it away. I feel ripped off with men.

The sexual abuse all these women experienced as children defined their sexuality. The abuse trained them to satisfy men's sexual demands, even if it meant they had to disengage from their own sexual feelings to do it. It trained them to compartmentalize, to separate from their emotions and their bodies. It showed them men wanted to use their bodies for sexual gratification. How the abusers controlled them and their bodies taught survivors ways to relate to other people.

In response to this training, they tried to take whatever control they could and obtain some benefit. Their sense of sexuality became a tool for self-protection rather than an authentic expression of their feelings. Using sexuality in this way, however, created an obstacle between them and their own experience of pleasure and the sharing of sexual pleasure with others. It caused survivors to become more entrenched in the detachment of mind and body, thwarting the erotic power which originates in the unity of both. It also precluded their development of a sexuality that is self-directed and further exposed them to men's sexual violence, ostensibly as "willing" participants in prostitution.

Their choices were undeniably limited and not clearly understood by those around them. One woman said her family ostracized her. Some faced the condemnation society readily levels at women involved in prostitution. Others noted that men continued to exploit them. But these women survived—initially by finding some measure of empowerment in attempting to control men through sex and, eventually, by understanding the consequences of the abuse.

Contending with Changing Expectations

Survival skills are developed to function as a buffer either internally, externally, or both. In this sense they can be seen as damage-control techniques. Women told us that they honed and expanded their survival skills as they grew up and had to contend with changing social expectations and situations and as their needs changed. For instance, when a child starts school she may refine the people-pleasing skills she used at home. Or she may adopt entirely different skills, such as talking back to her teachers, either as a rebellion or perhaps as a cry for help. If she comes from a family where her mother is beaten or where there is drug and alcohol abuse, she must make decisions regarding how much of her life she is willing to let others know about. Moreover, if her family is economically disadvantaged or if she belongs to a racial minority in her community, her direct experience of isolation and oppression will be greatly increased. Will excelling at school work enable her to fit in and hide her many secrets—including the sexual abuse? Or will "going along with the gang" better ease her feelings of being different?

As a survivor reaches her teenage years she has to contend with boys and dating. If she is sexually attracted to women, she must reconcile that not only with the pressure to conform but also with her confused sexual feelings resulting from the abuse.

When the abuse is ongoing (as it was for most of the adult survivors we interviewed), she must simultaneously contend with fresh pain and confusion while scrambling to adapt to the social demands of relating to her peers. As she reaches adulthood, she must grapple with choices about employment as well as relationships, and with her ability to make choices given the powerlessness that has dominated her life and her perception of what her choices are.

The more secrets she has, the more she has to protect. The more she has to hide, the more dishonest she feels within herself and in her relationships with others. The more false she feels, the more her sense of personal integrity, worth and value diminishes. And on it goes, week after week, month after month, and year after year.

One survivor explained how she responded differently at different ages to expressions of sexual interest.

> When I was ten, there was this boy. He used to follow me around. I bloody near killed him... I couldn't stand that he liked me... I tried to get him to stop liking me. Punches, name calling... Finally... he left me alone... It was worse when I was fifteen. The boys started to talk to me and some of them were interested, showed signs of liking me. I panicked... I wouldn't leave the house...

In her adult relationships, however, she could not sustain the strategies of aggression or physical avoidance and instead tried emotional detachment and compliance, but found that these extreme reactions wouldn't agree with each other.

Another survivor recalled being lonely and unhappy as a child and trying various ways to fulfill her emotional needs. Her survival skills included hiding, escaping from her true feelings and seeking the approval of others.

> I'm overweight... I abuse my body with food. I'm still sucking my thumb as an adult. I used to steal... I used to take drugs... I would never tell anybody. No one knew what I was doing. I was really involved in theatre in high school. I was a cheer-leader, singer, I starred in plays. Whatever I did, I did the best...

Her masquerade was successful. She hid in plain view. She must have been a very good actress.

For another woman, survival skills were what she termed "yeses." They were her way to ask for help. Unfortunately, no one raised the question she was so desperately trying to elicit.

> There were never "noes," there was always "yeses." But the yes became more and more indirect. I became very sexual out in public with him [the abuser], and I know I wanted people to question that kind of behaviour. My changing from extrovert to aloof at school was a "yes, please question this."

She remembered that "the nature of my recurring dreams were also a cry for help... there was always hope that somebody would come and fix it. Always. That's why the cries for help continued." As a young adult she became addicted to drugs and alcohol and involved in prostitution. Her sense of herself as a person worth helping grew weaker and weaker.

For this survivor and others, some survival skills were attempts to provoke a caring response and a way to seek help. Others were simply all they knew to do with their rage and powerlessness. While survivors' versatility constituted survival, it also drove them further away from a sense of themselves and further into the maze of confusion and distortion.

Entrapment

A child who is sexually abused becomes, in effect, who the abuser wants her to be. His reality dominates her life. It is his reality she tries either to accommodate or reject in developing her survival skills as she grows up. She becomes increasingly cut off from her experience and her own feelings about it. The longer the abuse goes undiscovered the more responsible she feels.

In our interviews, adult survivors talked about the various ways they were trapped by the abuser and by their own attempts to deal with the abuse. These women said they were trapped by the secrecy surrounding the abuse, by the fear and guilt and sense of complicity that the abuser fostered in them. In many ways, at various times in their lives, they had tried to find a way out of the trap. When their attempts failed, they blamed themselves and shouldered the responsibility. And so the trap closed more tightly until they discovered how to break free.

Secrecy

Abusers enforced secrecy directly and indirectly. For example, some simply told the child the abuse was secret and threatened dire consequences for her or others if she told anyone. Those men who sexually abused an infant could simply rely on her inability to talk about it. Others benefited from the fact that a young child often doesn't realize that what is being done to her is wrong in the first place, or is too ashamed to discuss it. Some could be confident that the child would not be believed even if she did tell.

Survivors internalized the abusers' messages. Some were convinced that it was their fault from the beginning. Despite the fact that many of the women we interviewed had not one but many reasons to remain silent, most tried to tell, however indirectly. One woman we interviewed recounted her attempts, as a twelve-year-old, to find some opening to disclose the secret. She was attending confirmation classes and she "kept bugging the Bishop with questions about the commandment about honouring thy father and mother." She kept hinting, "Well, what if they did something really bad?... " The Bishop's irritation with her questions left the child with the clear impression that "he wanted me to shut up."

Another woman remembers not trusting anyone other than the uncle who abused her. As a result she was dependent on him to guide her.

> He set it up that way. He always said, "I'll talk to her." I felt like only he cared enough to talk to me.

This man used the child's neediness, loyalty and confidence to protect himself, cutting her off from others who might have truly had her best interests as their first priority.

Many survivors were unable to trust their own judgement of people enough to recognize occasions when they might receive support for their disclosure of the abuse. If a child, or an adult, does not perceive an opportunity, then that opportunity might as well not exist. For some survivors the opportunities for disclosure were restricted by the circumstances in which they lived. For example, one woman recalled the isolation of growing up in farming communities, physically isolated from other families. Not only did she have little chance to compare her situation to the way others lived, her access to people who might have helped her was limited. The physical isolation of her family was confining and, because of the abuse, she didn't feel free at home.

Fear of reprisals made one woman feel the abuse was "okay as a secret." She was confused and unclear about whether she or her father was responsible for the abuse. As a result it seemed safer to her to be abused than to be exposed. She spent her time wishing for an escape as the abuse continued into her late teens.

Another survivor was trapped by her belief that adults wouldn't take her word over her uncle's. Given the survival skills she'd developed, which included lying and other secretive behaviour, she had good reason to assume she wouldn't be believed if she dared to tell the truth about the abuse.

One little girl eventually told her mother about the sexual abuse, even though to do so she had to overcome the fear her father had instilled in her, fear that God would know if she told anyone and that her mother would die. Another survivor, who was sexually abused by several neighbours and a boarder, said that the violence in her own home made her too fearful to disclose the abuse. Since the offenders were known to the family, she was afraid of what might happen if she told. Her father had a violent temper. She recalled having nightmares as a young child and "crying a lot." She was spanked and told to "shut up." Her response to this treatment was to conclude she had best "be. quiet and not make a fuss."

Even sympathetic, gentle inquiries from a family friend couldn't override one survivor's fear. Once, when she was pregnant by her stepfather, a friend came into the bedroom where she was lying on her bed crying and asked her to talk with him about what she was going through. She told him, "No, I can't tell you." Even when he suggested that he and his wife take a walk with her to the park, where they could "just talk," she could not bring herself to accept his offer. She sensed that he felt very helpless. She said, "That was the closest I came to ever breaking down and telling somebody directly." She felt badly for him and because of that, not out of concern for herself, she almost disclosed the abuse.

Another child believed that if she told anyone her father abused her, "I'd get hit. It was so simple. If I said anything I'd get in trouble." The fear many survivors felt had solid foundations. One child had witnessed the abuser raping her sister. Both girls lived in fear. The unlikelihood of being believed was also an impediment to telling: "No one believes you as a kid. People still don't give credence to a child's statements." Even today, this woman is not sure she would expose the abuser.

> I don't know what the purpose would be now. It doesn't change it... I am confused... I don't know. And it bothers me that I don't know.

Guilt

Since the experience of being abused creates in children a feeling of being wrong and bad, the progression to deciding they *are* guilty is a small step. At the best of times, children often confuse feeling bad with the state of being bad. As well, many abusers deliberately encouraged the child to feel complicit in the abuse. And for some survivors, guilt was a consequence of not being able to tell anyone what was happening to them or of the responses they received when they did tell.

One survivor, abused from age one, talked about how guilt set in at age fifteen. She responded by retreating into her room and spending most of her time there. She explained, "I really couldn't tell Mom. It was my fault. I didn't tell the counsellor I was seeing." Guilt for not telling also haunted another woman we interviewed. She remembers a childhood friend whose mother fired a babysitter for molesting her daughter. When her friend told her what had happened, "I felt bad for never saying no, for not standing up for myself."

But for this survivor and many others, abuse was, in one woman's words, "Something you do not tell people." To deal with abuse by her father and brother one woman said she sought solace and comfort in religion. Her religious convictions compelled her to "forgive" the abusers. By the time she felt free enough to experience the anger she had been denied, she had already excused them, "forgiven" them. This left her with the guilt. She said she spent a lot of time trying to understand what made them do it.

One woman we interviewed talked about feeling responsible for hurting both the abuser and her mother when she disclosed the sexual abuse under pressure of her stepfather's requests for visitation following the dissolution of the parents' relationship. Her mother's belief that the abuser should be exposed compounded the problem.

> Now there are two parents hurting and I'm to blame. She wants me to go to court, but she doesn't understand that I'm convinced it's my crime and I have been invisible for so long that the thought... it was just too overwhelming that the public would hear this. I felt really ashamed...

The survivor felt bad, guilty, and unlovable. She was convinced that she was a co-conspirator in the abuse. She did not have the perspective to explain all of this to her mother. She turned to alcohol and drugs to separate herself from the pain of feeling guilty and wrong.

One man instilled guilt in the child he abused by insisting she go to church with him to confess talking back to her mother. Though she realized how hypocritical he was, the guilt she felt immobilized her.

Another woman recalled that what overwhelmed all other feelings was shame and the overpowering sense of "seductress." Seeing herself as a seductress was a powerful, if distorted, way to understand herself. It became a survival skill for her. It was an outgrowth of how the abuser had, in her word, "twisted" her into believing the abuse was her fault. She remembers, "I wanted someone to tell me that it wasn't my fault... that I didn't need to feel guilty, I wasn't a bad little girl, and that I was loved." When this failed to happen she became estranged from herself: "I anaesthetized my body, I stopped feeling and I felt very much like a freak." Feeling like a freak and a seductress, she could not free herself from the trap for many years. When she did finally tell some friends about the abuse, their responses made her regret the decision and added to her reluctance to talk about her experiences.

> The admission of it to people made me feel more dirty—how they looked down at the ground, their faces got red, their uncomfortableness made me wish I hadn't mentioned it.

The response of several counsellors reinforced one woman's sense of shame or what she called "the stigma" of being abused. When she sought professional help because she experienced no sexual desire, she said she was told "there was no such thing as no sexual desire—so I thought it was me." She went to another counsellor who referred her to yet another. This counsellor told her that there was nothing wrong with her but that she didn't deal with sexual abuse and she suggested the woman see a psychiatrist. The survivor thought she was so flawed no one could relate to her.

The shame and feelings of complicity the abuse prompted were enormous obstacles for survivors to overcome. For many, the feelings developed from a sense that they were not exploited by the abuser but derived some benefit from the abuse. One survivor felt special because her father "really only bought *me* a Christmas present. No one else got one." She in turn felt "wrong" for disliking the abuse.

Another woman described how she would get money "over my allowance" and how her father would "be on my side" when she got into disagreements with her mother. As a result she felt she "used the abuse to get what I wanted." She had the illusion that she was pulling the strings.

The benefits were often simple things like being granted permission to go to the movies. As one woman explained, she considered she owed her father something in exchange for what he allowed her to do. She said she still "feels a lot of anger about that both towards him and towards myself—which is probably why to this day I hate owing anyone anything."

Another survivor talked about how she and her teenage friends got "payoffs" from her sexually abusive teacher. "He would do things like drive us home from school and buy liquor for us" and "one of the 'payoffs' for being with him was he'd let us skip his classes and not write 'absent' in the book." On one occasion, this teacher let the girl and her friend use his apartment when the two girls wanted to have sex with each other. She explained, "We were scared and we knew somehow we could do it there." But the teacher insisted on joining in: "Just before we were leaving we touched his penis or licked it or something like that to get him away." Because this young woman perceived that she was operating on an exchange basis, she could not discern how her teacher was exploiting her and her friend.

Survivors' inability to understand their exploitation and how to end it, was a consequence of living with sexual abuse as a regular occurrence. It was for so long a fact of their lives that they could have no perspective on it. They were trapped by the abuser's ability to distort reality and make them feel responsible for the abuse. They were further entrapped by the very skills they developed to endure the abuse. Lying or acting the class clown, for example, made it possible for these women to survive what was done to them, but also left them feeling false, guilty, and complicit in covering up the abuse.

Survivors were caught in a kind of slip-knot—the harder they tried to wrestle free, the more the knot tightened. But not resisting still left them restrained and added to their confusion and feelings of responsibility. They were increasingly immobilized and their sense that they deserved anything better faded away.

Negative Sense of Self

As we grow up we acquire a set of experiences and knowledge which determine our sense of who we are. We all encounter obstacles in our efforts to fit our experience and knowledge together into an integrated sense of ourselves. We may have to struggle to understand certain experiences or to know in retrospect how we've come to hold the beliefs we do. But children who are sexually abused must contend with the almost insurmountable obstacles of the lies and distortion inherent in the abuse. Their sense of their experience and acquisition of knowledge or beliefs is profoundly influenced by the abuse. Abuse denies survivors a positive sense of who they really are.

Many survivors we interviewed had lost a sense of themselves as ever having been vulnerable, innocent, dependent children. They assumed they must have been seductive, sexually aggressive little girls because the abuser had convinced them they had initiated the abuse. One woman recalled being told by the abuser that it all began because she liked to sit on his lap. It wasn't until she was twenty-four, when she talked about her experience, that she finally understood how natural it is for a child to want to sit on her father's lap. She realized she'd had a right to act on that common childhood desire and that she should have been able to do it without risk of sexual abuse. For the first time, she caught a glimpse of herself as the innocent child she had been.

For many other survivors such realizations came even later. The abusers had confused them about their rights and responsibilities and set them up to have continuing negative feelings about themselves. They were confused about what their experiences were and how they felt about them. By disregarding them the abuser rendered their needs invisible. The children became invisible to themselves as a result. Their history was obscured.

Mothers we interviewed referred to their children's fears of men, their discomfort with their own bodies, their uneasiness with other people, their fear of ever making a mistake. Abused from an early age, these children couldn't know the origins of their own thoughts, feelings or fears. Compounding the problem are the barriers a child creates to survive the abuse. If she succeeds in seeing past them, what she confronts is a negative image of herself—the guilt and shame for having been abused or for deceiving people about who she really is. The barriers also prevent anyone getting close enough to her to affirm her positive traits. She's left with no positive sense of herself. In addition, if a survivor can't see that she was wronged, if she can't recognize the injustice of the abuse, she can't explain or account for her experience or her feelings. It becomes increasingly difficult for her to assert her rights or needs, and so the cycle continues.

Several women said they grew up wondering if they were crazy. One survivor, who spent two years in a mental institution enduring electric shock treatments and being forced to take medication, decried the fact that no one validated her reality as a child or as a young adult. She contended that breakdown occurred because she had no way to express her feelings about the abuse she had experienced as a child. She sees a parallel between being an inmate in a mental institution and being a child: neither has rights. By learning how to "act sane," she was eventually discharged from the institution but she worries about the other women she met there who will never escape.

Many adult survivors talked about feeling incomplete, invisible, empty and lost. Some maintained over the years a hope that they could find the fulfillment, affirmation, and love they needed. But until they dealt with the abuse and its effects on them, all they could do was hope; they didn't know how to go after what they wanted, or make it happen. The confusion, the damaged self-esteem, the sense of being flawed and undeserving of respectful, caring attention from others followed them into their adult relationships.

Several women talked about staying in abusive relationships as adults because they felt undeserving of anything better. Some survivors simply had no way of knowing what a loving relationship is. One woman described her marriage to a handsome man who at first seemed gentle and affectionate. When she became pregnant he offered to marry her. She recalled that he only once told her he loved her, on their wedding day, never before or after. During their marriage, his abuse escalated: he took axes to the doors at night; her children watched while he beat her. For years this woman believed, "If this is love, I'd better hold on tight, it's all I'm going to get in my life." Her marriage was not unlike her childhood experiences.

One woman told us she felt doomed to fail in relationships. She believed she would somehow lose something if she got close to a man. For many years she couldn't understand how her fear was rooted in all she had lost as an abused child who had been exploited every time she got close to someone. She believed herself to be unworthy of a loving and lasting adult relationship and thought she had to accept men's demands with no regard for her own needs. Several other women felt inadequate because they couldn't understand or trust men. Though they suspected their uneasiness was related to the abuse, they perceived it, nevertheless, as one more flaw in themselves.

Sorting out the effects of the abuse enabled some survivors to overcome their distrustfulness or be clearer about it. One woman learned to give trust, if she felt that trust was deserved. She is particularly mistrustful of men. Another woman told us she feared having children because, chances are, they would be abused as she had been. Another woman has concluded that men are to be avoided: "They think with their penises and are governed by their sexuality." This assessment is derived from her experience of the tyranny of random and arbitrary abuses by men throughout her life, which good relationships with one or two men could not offset.

While sexual relationships were a focal point in many women's comments about their negative or incomplete sense of themselves, the problems extended to other aspects of their lives. One survivor told us her "sense of spirituality was cut off by the abuse." It's an aspect of her life she has spent a great deal of energy recovering. She spoke of her continuing efforts to avoid separating her spirituality from her intelligence or from her ability to feel positive, open and emotionally connected with her friends. Other survivors struggled to recollect and make use of talents and creativity they'd long devalued.

Several women found intimate friendships frightening. They referred to pushing people away, holding themselves apart from friends, being unable to trust them for fear of letting anyone get close. Unable to trust themselves, they couldn't trust others. It was a problem one woman remembered from early childhood.

> I remember not feeling part of any group. For example, going to and from school with kids—I wasn't really with them. I never ever felt I was a child, carefree, I felt I had a weight on me.

Another woman said, "Basically, I don't open myself to anybody." Others said they struggled with how to maintain intimacy given deeply negative feelings about themselves. They feared the consequences if the external image they'd constructed crumbled, revealing the hidden, horrible truth.

The distrust and fear that kept many survivors isolated, yet longing for intimacy, was a direct consequence of the abuse. It is perhaps the cruelest consequence of all: the loss of a positive sense of themselves which, in turn, alienated them from sources of potential comfort, love and acceptance. Unable to know or accept themselves, they couldn't accept love from anyone else. They felt despair and had little hope for the future. The cycle continued.

For the children of the mothers we interviewed, effective intervention and support means their reclaiming of themselves will not be burdened by decades of hiding and hating who they are. Adult survivors' experience shows the cycle can be broken. But it requires peeling away layers of self-doubt and negation.

Each of these women wanted to be someone other than who she was for some period of her life. Each felt "wrong" and "not good enough" to merit any caring and affirmation that came her way. Still, they have all endured. They have continued to learn about themselves and are continually striving to improve their lives. They have had to struggle through the distortions, lies, and secrets to re-frame their sense of who they are and find strengths and qualities they could value. If they had settled for the beliefs, thoughts, and feelings which the childhood sexual abuse initiated, they would have been unable to speak with us at all.

IV

Exits: Reclaiming Self

C HILD sexual abuse takes a dreadful toll. It distorts and, in some cases, it obliterates parts of a child's life. It overwhelms a child's very sense of self.

Yet what women told us about their lives reveals ways to undo the damage abuse causes. Their experience demonstrates that it is possible to recollect and reclaim what one survivor referred to as "some things in you no one can touch, the things you need to feel alive." Finding those inner resources and building on them is a crucial part of the process of finding exits from the cycle of childhood sexual abuse. It is not a linear, or even a circular, step-by-step process. Each woman or child must find her own way through it, a way that works for her.

It is a difficult process. There are serious struggles facing an adult survivor who tries to make sense of her experience in order to build on those "untouched" parts of herself and to break free from the cycle of abuse. There are major obstacles standing in the way of a mother who tries to stop the abuser's access and protect her child. But understanding how women and children make the journey and what both survivors and mothers had to contend with along the way, can teach us all how to be realistic and respectful in our efforts to help ourselves and others.

In this chapter we focus on the many lessons that emerge from survivors' courageous efforts to heal and from women's determination to protect and support their children.

Mothers Trying to Protect Their Children

Adult survivors told us that as children they desperately wanted to be rescued and protected, to be taken out of the abusive situation. They also said they needed someone to recognize the abuse they were experiencing. Such acknowledgement would have helped to offset survivors' confusion and powerlessness. It would have given them a fighting chance, a way to find the thread of a sense of themselves. The caring and sympathy they longed for would have communicated the critically important message that the abuse was not their fault.

Survivors told us that the protection a child needs requires more than simply removing the child from the abusive situation or temporarily stopping the abuser, though these are undeniably important acts. The child also needs the security of knowing the abuser won't be able to get at her again. Protection is a matter of heeding the child's cries, however indirect, and finding a way to let her know she is cared for and believed.

Survivors told us a child's cries for help will likely be muffled because of the confusion and secrecy in which she is trapped by the abuser. The child may also lack the words to express her experience. As well, being believed and validated may be uncommon experiences for her. As one woman explained, the child has to feel safe enough to talk about her experience, and to feel safe she must be believed.

Being believed is a really hard one. As soon as someone questions you, you doubt yourself more. It's hard enough just to say it—it feels so unreal—and to have someone doubt you when you say it or if people over-react or pity you or just don't say anything, then that puts you in some other weird place.

Unfortunately, the disclosures of the adult survivors we interviewed were met with disbelief, denial, or minimization of what the abuser had done to them.

Some women said, in retrospect, they realize they'd lacked the means to disclose clearly. As one said, "At age four, I didn't have the words to describe it." As several others pointed out, the pictures they drew or the poems they wrote or their "acting out"—which seemed to the children a clear cry for help—were lost on the adults around them. However, one adult survivor stated very persuasively her belief that "in every moment of a survivor's life, be it waking or sleeping, he or she is crying out for help and it is up to the community to become educated and aware enough to hear the cries, however indirect." The onus is on all of us to hear and to respond.

Significantly, what adult survivors said they had wanted and needed as children is precisely what our interviews with the mothers of sexually abused children indicate they provided. The current generation of mothers and their children live in a world where there is increased public consciousness of childhood sexual abuse. They have resources and options unheard of by the vast majority of adult survivors' mothers. Nevertheless, to protect their children, the women we interviewed had to fight with sensitivity and extraordinary determination to hear their children's indirect cries and to respond.

The mothers we interviewed told us that to provide protection for their children they first had to recognize that their children were, in fact, being abused. They had to trust their own instincts about their children's behaviour even, in several cases, in the face of the children's initial denials that there was abuse. They had to investigate, pay attention, ask questions of the children, and help them to feel safe enough finally to disclose their experience.

Most mothers found out about the abuse by paying attention

to their children's behaviour and by investigating further when that behaviour made them suspicious. If it sounds simple, it wasn't. One woman recounted listening to her daughter's seemingly constant complaints of a sore finger, a sore foot, a sore knee and so on. She said, "One morning, I just looked at her and asked her, 'what is it that really hurts?' She [the child] pointed to her genitals and I said 'why are they sore?' and she said 'because a dog licked them.' " This woman recalled that it took her a day or two to recover enough from the shock of what her daughter had said, but then she did act. "I just took the bull by the horns, so to speak. I said to my daughter 'I know it's not a dog, I know it's a person. Can you tell me who it is?' " The little girl wouldn't speak; the abuser had frightened her with threats that her mother would leave her if she told. Her mother helped her: "I said, 'I'll name some names and you tell me if I'm right.' We got it the first time—it was Grandpa." This woman and her family hid from the abuser; they went underground to protect the little girl and her brother from continued abuse. The woman reported the abuse to the police and to social workers and got medical care for her children. She also wrote a letter to her father, the abuser, confronting him with her knowledge of what he had done, and refusing to have any further contact or communication with either of her parents.

Another woman spoke about her struggle to accept the validity of her suspicions that her four-year-old daughter was being sexually abused. Her little girl was rubbing her genitals violently. She said that at first she didn't ask her directly because she didn't want to put ideas in her head. But she paid attention and added up all the other disturbing aspects of her child's behaviour—the biting and pinching, how she'd scream if anyone touched her, how she'd run to the bathroom when she came home from visiting her father, how she'd wear layers of clothes on a hot summer day. Within two months her daughter told her more directly. "I wrote down what she said: 'I asked him not to—he wouldn't quit.' That was all she said." The woman confronted her estranged husband who accused their daughter of lying. Thus began months of court appearances and visits to counsellors, with accusations that this woman was being hysterical and vindictive in her efforts to restrict the abuser's access to their child.

The children of all but two of the mothers we interviewed were under the age of five when the abuse was discovered. Consequently, their lack of facility with speech and language impeded or complicated both the children's disclosure and their mothers' efforts to understand their experience. One woman realized that because her daughter had been abused from the age of nine months, the little girl had no words to express what had been done to her.

The children who were old enough to speak directly about the abuse eventually did so. One woman remembered watching a television programme on child sexual abuse with her oldest daughter, who said that she thought that maybe her stepfather had sexually abused her. This woman then talked with her daughter about the abuse and asked her younger son if he too had been abused. In spite of his denial, she pursued counselling, enlisted the help of the local child abuse team, and had her children examined by doctors. Another woman, whose children revealed they were being sexually abused by their stepbrothers, immediately went to the authorities. She protected the young children by keeping the older boys away from them until the authorities responded.

All of the mothers we interviewed believed their children's disclosures. This in itself is critically important. As adult survivors indicated, being believed conveys to the child the possibility of openness and support. It helps to counter the effects of the abuser's tricks and manipulation. It gives the child the beginning of a sense of respect for her right to refuse contact that she does not want. And an adult's validation provides something for the child to hold on to and build from in breaking out of the cycle of abuse.

For mothers to act on their belief and protect their children required incredible persistence. Persistence in finding the support and assistance they and their children needed; in overcoming the abusers' denials of wrong-doing; and in convincing often disbelieving or constrained social workers and police and court officials to take their children's abuse seriously.

Mothers' Initial Reactions

The very first thing women had to deal with when faced with growing realization that their children were being sexually abused, was their own reactions. Most mothers did not have clear, direct disclosures from their children; they began to think about abuse because of their children's behaviour. They told us they were essentially unprepared to deal with it. Even those women who'd been abused themselves as children had blocked that experience or not yet dealt with it consciously. Before they confronted their own abuse or their children's, all they'd known was what they'd read about the subject in the newspapers or seen on television. As one woman noted, "It's such a hard thing to believe that an adult could do that to a child. It's something you don't think about before it happens." Another woman said that upon learning about child sexual abuse through her children's disclosure she was shocked: "I got sick. I went into a tunnel."

Yet women's shock and lack of preparation did not prevent them from investigating their children's troubling behaviour or from believing their eventual disclosures. One woman said she'd known about sexual abuse mostly theoretically and through case studies of the children she worked with in a community agency. She admitted that she'd had a hard time believing it happened to real flesh and blood children. She was, however, the one who identified it as something her own children were experiencing before they articulated it. Although she was in complete shock for the first few weeks, she acted swiftly when she realized what was happening.

This woman maintained that the reaction mothers often have when they begin to suspect their children have been abused— "that this can't be true"—should be called doubt, not denial. It is a natural reaction. She stated, "It's never a denial that the abuse actually occurred but a mass of doubt that clicks in and out." Other women spoke candidly about the doubts that plagued them and which they tried, apparently with some success, to mask from their children. One woman remembered that she felt the abuse had happened and she listened to her children for anything they said which would confirm her suspicions. But she also tried to tell herself she was wrong.

Another mother recalled thinking that sexual abuse was very rare and that it was too bizarre to happen in her life. She did research to try to explain away her child's physical symptoms and now thinks that was a desperate attempt to believe it wasn't happening. She fears initial attempts to talk to her child about the abuse scared the child because she had no idea what to do or say and she felt that she was handling it badly. But she read everything she could get her hands on and, by the time her daughter actually said she'd been abused, she could react appropriately. One woman said, "I believed my daughter... but I didn't know what to do about it." She informed herself right away by reading books and articles and by talking to the social services ministry's child abuse team. She recalled following their method of talking with children—things like "don't look horrified when the kids tell you." Another woman said that she just seemed to know what to say to her children when they disclosed the abuse. She attributed this sensitivity to what she realizes now was an unconscious knowledge that she herself had been sexually abused as a child. About two nights after her children's disclosure she woke up "with a silent scream in my head and I knew then it had happened to me but specific incidents started coming up for me maybe two months after."

For several of these mothers, realization of their own childhood experience of sexual abuse was intertwined with learning of their children's experience. One woman guessed within a few hours of getting her own first memory that what her daughter's behaviour indicated was that she too had been sexually abused. She said, "Everything made sense in terms of my behaviours and my children's behaviours, my semi-suicidal adolescence, going into psychology as a field, working with kids, the ways I kind of acquiesced to men or patriarchy without wanting to, my passivity." While it all added up it was also, in her words, "a real double whammy."

Whether or not women had realized or dealt with their own experience of abuse, their reactions to their children's disclosures were shock, horror and the desire to convince themselves they must be mistaken. But they all overcame those feelings (sooner rather than later) and acted to get help for their children.

Others' Reactions

In the process of getting help for their children, mothers themselves need support. Most of the women we interviewed turned to family and friends first. They met with varied responses such as shock, disbelief, denial and mother-blaming.

One woman explained that to avoid contact with her parents who had abused her children, she and her husband told everyone they knew about the abuse, everyone whom they felt the abusers would try to contact to get hold of them. She recalled that people were shocked—"they believed it because we told it to them and they knew we wouldn't lie—but there was a lot of disbelief. They didn't think it could happen to someone they know." Another woman said that the abuser's mother believed her account of the abuse as did everyone else she told except the members of the abuser's church.

Fear of disbelief and people's reluctance to believe that a child has been sexually abused can inhibit women or children from talking about their experience. One of the mothers we interviewed said she cut off contact with mutual friends of hers and her husband's (the abuser), because she didn't want to be in the position of trying to convince them to believe her children over her husband. Later, when she did talk with some of those people, her suspicion that they would support her husband was confirmed.

Another woman, who told her husband's family that her daughter and son had been abused by their stepbrothers, found that they saw sexual abuse of children as acceptable or at least inevitable. They said, "It happens in the best of families." Her husband's parents, in particular, adopted a stance not uncharacteristic of their generation: they minimized the damage caused by sexual abuse and declared "they didn't believe in any 'psychological bullshit,' as they put it." But she recalled that her sister-in-law said, "I was abused too, I know all about it."

Surrounded by such attitudes, it's not surprising this woman didn't tell anything else to unsupportive family members. Although some of her friends would not acknowledge that the boys would do something like that and blamed it all on the woman's husband, fortunately she found two women friends who gave her positive reinforcement.

In the absence of support women are particularly vulnerable to guilt and self-blame. Several talked about feeling guilty in spite of the fact they were doing everything they could to stop the abuse and help their children. Some noted that even though no one they talked to blamed them outright, they felt guilty anyway.

Others were castigated by social workers, police officers, judges, family members and others. One woman remembered her mother denounced her, saying, "How could you not know? I told you to watch out for that guy." That question haunted many mothers: "You make yourself feel guilty. You wonder how it could have passed you by. That's one of the first feelings you get—guilt." This self-blame makes support for mothers even more crucial. They need support which takes into account that, in one woman's words, "If you're not educated about sexual abuse, you don't see it. You feel it, but you don't know it's real."

Another woman pointed out that blame comes at mothers from all angles. Often the child will think a mother already knows about the abuse because mothers are assumed to have eyes in the back of their heads. Children think that a mother knows everything, and if she doesn't do anything to stop the abuse, they think she doesn't care. Added to that is the tendency women have to blame themselves, and the propensity of social service and criminal justice officials to divert responsibility from the abuser onto the mother and the victim or the family as a whole.

One woman we interviewed counselled mothers to recognize that they are not the non-offending parent but the supportive parent. Another urged mothers to remind themselves that it's not their fault, it's the offenders' fault. But thinking positively about themselves or having a sense of the validity of their own needs was a real struggle for most. As one woman explained, "The biggest thing is getting across to myself that I'm human and I do have feelings and I'm important too."

Some women did find that their families were helpful. They provided emotional support and, in one case, money to fight court battles to prevent the abuser from regaining access to the children. Others found friends they could talk with. One expressed her appreciation for the woman friend who stood by her all the way, phoned her every day and was just terrific. Another noted that her friends were quite supportive although one in particular who was very close to her couldn't handle it. Two relationships deteriorated over the first few months after the disclosure of abuse. It was necessary for one woman to keep trying until she found a friend who could be supportive and she recommended that mothers should continue to reach out to friends until they find the support they need.

For other women the important process of talking about what they were going through worked best with the help of counsellors or in support groups. Support groups for mothers ranked high on the list of the mothers' resources for keeping strong in order to help their children. Groups were a way for them to realize that abuse is not something that happens only to them and their children, that they were not alone with it. One woman said she is still in touch with a couple of women from a support group she attended several years ago. Women said it's particularly helpful to find other mothers who've been through similar experiences. Talking with other mothers or sympathetic counsellors was a welcome relief and source of strength because they were believed and accepted and got practical advice.

Of course, nowhere was denial more pronounced than among abusers. Every one of the mothers we interviewed said the abuser explicitly denied sexually abusing the children. One young man, who'd abused his stepsister and stepbrother, confessed to all of it when his stepmother confronted him but, at his father's urging, he consistently denied it to the police. Several other abusers not only claimed they were innocent, they either insisted on or agreed to a polygraph or a lie detector test to prove it. And, in all but one case, they passed the test.

Passing the test cannot be regarded as confirmation of their innocence, since many offenders have either justified their actions to themselves or experience a kind of split which makes it possible for them to lie smoothly and without the kind of stressful reaction which is measured by the machine. Nevertheless, abusers' denials make it significantly more difficult for the mothers to convince justice system officials and others to believe their children.

What several women found particularly galling was how readily abusers blamed the victims. One man reportedly told the police officer questioning him that he hadn't done anything wrong and maintained his four-year-old daughter had "tried to fellate him and many times he'd had to remove her physically from that situation." Another suggested the problem was not anything he'd done but his child's "big imagination." When one mother confronted her ex-husband with her suspicions about his sexual abuse of their daughter, he dismissed the suggestions that he would even think of "having sex" with his child as ludicrous. This woman later learned that his abuse had begun well before his cavalier dismissal of her concerns.

Women were furious at the abusers' abdication of responsibility and unabashed betrayal of their children's trust. They were also appalled by the abusers' attempts to scapegoat the children and by their apparent lack of remorse. One woman said abusers' callousness and irresponsibility are particularly hard to take because, in their innocence, "Children are very forgiving: all they want to hear is, 'I'm sorry, what I did was wrong.' "

And, of course, it is the mothers who had to deal with the consequences for the children of the abusers' actions: the confusion, hurt, sadness, fears and anger. While some children were openly angry, most exhibited a mixture of emotions, especially when their father was the abuser. One little girl was happy not to go back to see her father and said, "My daddy tells lies, he does mean things." But she's "sad he is that way" and asked her mother to "fix my daddy." Her mother described how this child and her sister acted out their fears and confusion after disclosure, in pretend telephone conversations:

> The kids talk on the phone. They say, "I don't want to see my daddy." They use different voices and one says, "I don't want to go to jail"; the other says, "You have to go to jail."

Other women described their children's reactions: the temper tantrums, the anger seemingly directed inward; the nightmares based in fear that their disclosure would prompt the abuser to hurt them or their mother; the fear that their mother would be angry with them because they'd been abused; the feeling that they'd done something wrong for that to have happened to them. One little girl was, as far as her mother could tell, clearly angry: she said she hated the day care operator who abused her, that it was his fault and tried to explain to her mother that his wife didn't hurt her. Nevertheless, she couldn't sleep at night and her mother worried that the rage she expressed she also folded in on herself.

The abuse of course affected the relationship between the mothers and children. Some women talked about a distance in the relationship—they sensed they were growing apart from their children. One woman said she thinks her children had it in their minds that she wouldn't love them as much once she knew about the abuse.

Mothers said they felt inadequate to help and were confused by their children's behaviour. They struggled with feeling very sorry for them and very protective while at the same time trying to provide what one woman referred to as the guidance, firmness, and discipline children need. She asserted that if they could have gotten some justice from the systems they went to for help, they would have had some confidence. But in trying to get justice, protection, and support for their children, women had to contend with seemingly endless difficulties. They tried valiantly to do the right thing and they succeeded in spite of the obstacles.

Systems' Responses

Women's strategies for stopping the abuse of their children consisted primarily of trying to remove the abusers' opportunity to abuse. However, when they turned to the social service and criminal justice systems for help, these mothers entered an incomprehensible maze of frustrating inaction and apparent buckpassing, with only occasional help from individual professionals.

In one case the woman was seeking protection for all three of her children—her daughter who had told her directly about abuse by her stepfather, and her two younger sons who would not talk openly about it but exhibited signs of having been abused. This woman contacted the social welfare ministry and a social worker came within a couple of days to talk with the children. The youngest child was too afraid to say anything but the older children disclosed to the social worker. Based on what the children said, the social worker reported the case to the police.

The mother recalled: "The police contacted me shortly after. They kept setting up appointments to interview the kids and then they kept cancelling them. So the kids would be ready for these interviews and then they wouldn't happen." This delay left the children and their mother in a state of limbo and can only have undermined for the children the positive effects of being believed by their mother and social worker.

In the interim the abuser was continuing to have visits with his son. The boy was "talking about penises all the time." When he came home talking about his father's penis, the woman called her social worker, who put an end to the visits. The father responded with an application to Family Court for access to his son. Shortly before the hearing the boy disclosed that his father had sexually abused him. This mother told us that the social worker, testifying at the hearing, told the judge that while children are sometimes reluctant to speak about their abuse, what they do say should be believed. Encouraged by the groundwork laid by the social worker, the mother then testified about what the boy had disclosed. She reported that the judge seemed to believe the child's disclosure, but ordered a psychological assessment of the mother, the father and all three of the children.

The psychologist who conducted the assessment said the father denied abusing the children but acknowledged that the children clearly saw their father as the abuser. Accordingly, he recommended the father have no access to the children. The children's father did not attend the hearing at which the psychological assessment was to be presented and the judge was to make the final decision on access. Ultimately access was denied.

The police carried on the criminal investigation which included administering a polygraph test to the abuser. Soon after, to the mother's surprise, the Crown Counsel quashed the case. She asked him why. She said, "He gave me a real run-around and he wouldn't change his decision. In fact, he went to the point of defending him [the abuser]," saying he should be given credit for going to a programme for sex offenders. The mother also told us that criminal justice system personnel tried to convince her that her children would be further victimized by court. She concluded that they said that to try to get her off their back.

This woman has continued to pursue the case for more than three years. Her first priority was to restrict her ex-husband's access to the children, a task which she accomplished. However, even though she had contact with a number of professionals who deal with sexual abuse, she was unable to get the therapy her children needed. She told us that she couldn't get help for years, because nobody would pay. Eventually she got financial help after a woman in a support group she attended told her about the availability of criminal injury compensation.

The abuser was never prosecuted. A police officer re-interviewed the children and sent the file to a new Crown Counsel, but to no avail. The mother concluded: "It's a very frustrating system that you have to deal with out there."

Another woman's account of her experience illustrates similar difficulties. The social worker she contacted called in the police to tape record the disclosure of the woman's four-year-old daughter. They were unsuccessful because the child wouldn't talk. Her behaviour, however, convinced her mother and the social worker that she was being sexually abused. The police said

they were going to administer a polygraph test on the child's father. The woman recalled that she and her parents both warned
the officer of a split personality they'd seen in this man, and told
him that he was a professional con artist. The police officer assured them that "he wouldn't fall for anything." The next week,
however, the officer phoned the woman to come to the police
station to talk about the polygraph test.

> When I got there, the officer said he'd done his work and now his
> job was to convince me that my husband was innocent, that he'd
> passed the polygraph test with flying colours.

She reminded the officer of the report from the child's doctor
which noted evidence of sexual abuse and asked him if he felt her
daughter had been sexually abused. He said he wasn't going to
deny that it could have happened. But the officer then argued
that since the father said that he had "left the child with no other
man and never out of his eyesight and [since] you say the same
thing... unless you're willing to confess to me right now that
you did it yourself, this file will be closed because of lack of evidence." Apparently, the officer believed the polygraph test was
irrefutable evidence that the child's father was innocent. His
powers of deduction then led him to accuse the child's mother.

The woman was very frightened. "In trying to protect my
daughter from being abused, suddenly I felt I would have to protect myself from being accused. I never thought that would happen... It scared me because I had always felt the police were
there to protect you." With the option of pursuing charges
against her husband effectively removed, she continued her
battle in family court to prevent the abuser from having access to
her daughter. She noted that she could continue because luckily
the social workers didn't back down. With their support on her
side and with her father paying the legal bills (because she
couldn't get Legal Aid), she was able to go on.

She succeeded in spite of the frustrations she encountered in
the court system. She recalled: "The court dates would be about
once a month but they were just stupid legal games where you'd
spend hours in court to have your case only come up to set a

court date for another day."

This woman said that an accidental meeting with a woman who worked for a community-based sexual abuse service provided the crucial assistance. "If I hadn't met her I wouldn't have gone to the sexual abuse counsellor." The evidence of this counsellor was decisive in preventing her husband from having access to their daughter.

Luck again played a role. Support from sympathetic social workers, a community agency, and a skilled counsellor were also very significant in this woman's successful effort to deny the abuser access to the child. But her own determination to protect her child must not be underestimated. She not only stood up to her husband's threats and violence to herself and her parents, she withstood the police officer's frightening accusation and persisted through the court process.

This mother left no stone unturned in investigating her daughter's disturbing physical and emotional symptoms and getting her the help she needed. When her husband's lawyer suggested that the redness and soreness in the little girl's vaginal area may have been caused not by sexual abuse but by the child drinking apple juice, the woman contacted a major apple juice producer to find out whether this could be true. She told us the company provided her with a laboratory technician's report disputing the suggestion and contacted the lawyer to warn him against using the "apple juice theory" in court. The tragedy is that this woman and many of the others we interviewed had to deal with such a frustrating and intimidating process in order to get protection for their abused children, and that they received so little support along the way.

Some women did have positive experiences with individual police officers, social workers, lawyers, and doctors; occasionally with justice system officials; and more often with counsellors, therapists and community-based agencies. One woman spoke about the positive response she received from a community agency. She recalled that the workers had expertise in the issue of child sexual abuse from which they were able to give practical information about the role of systems' officials and the criminal justice process. This information had not been forthcoming from social workers and justice system personnel themselves. The agency workers provided assistance and support: "They never made me feel guilty or rotten" and once they "even let me sleep on the sofa" after a particularly exhausting day in court.

Unfortunately, most women's experiences indicated a serious lack of sensitivity and understanding regarding child sexual abuse. Women cited patronizing, condescending, and stupid behaviour by professionals; implicit and explicit accusations that they were "horrendous" parents; intimations that they were over-reacting, vengeful, and hysterical; charges that the abuse was "a ploy because we were separating, that I was trying to get back at him"; a therapist who "ended up shaking my daughter by the shoulders saying 'you have to talk to me, you have to talk to me' "; a "tough doctor" who assured the child there'd be no physical examination and then proceeded to do one. Women were denied information by social welfare and court system personnel as their cases proceeded, and were told repeatedly "there's nothing we can do" by the officials to whom they turned for help.

Women and Children Reclaiming Their Lives

Breaking the cycle of childhood sexual abuse involves a long process of healing. It is a process of renaming and understanding as well as reclaiming what was damaged and distorted by the abuser. All aspects of a victim's life are affected.

Women told us about their efforts to reclaim their lives. One woman said simply that the cycle has to be broken. She said that it required a lot of work to reverse the cycle, work that involved learning and understanding how much her low self-esteem was based in sexual abuse; realizing that it wasn't her fault; naming the abuse for what it was; seeing what her habits of survival were and where they'd come from; focusing on the positive things about herself; and beginning to heal. It also required undoing the confusion. It necessitated recognizing her right to set boundaries and limits and learning how to apply them in relationships with family, friends, and lovers in order to get her own needs met.

Diagram II, *Exits: Reclaiming Self*, maps the process of reversing the cycle that women described to us. It reflects the fact that a survivor's goal is awareness and acceptance of herself, rather than an absolute resolution of all the consequences that stem from the abuse. It is a process of recollecting the lost and distorted fragments of her life. It is a process of increasing understanding of her own experience and ever more effectively integrating thoughts and feelings. It is a process of making sense of the various ways a survivor has been affected by the abuse and how she has coped with them.

There is no one road map for everyone to follow in breaking free from the cycle. What is clear from women's accounts is that they reached all the points in the cycle in some order, not necessarily sequentially. What starts a woman on the road to stopping the cycle is usually a problem, but the problems vary. It may be that she feels particularly badly about herself and needs to understand why. It may be that troubling memories of her childhood have come up and she has to deal with them. It may be that one of her survival skills—such as drinking and drugging—is no longer working for her. For children, the road may begin with an adult, likely the child's mother, discovering the abuse and helping the child to find ways to deal with the damage it has done.

However and whenever a woman or child begins the journey, the survivors we interviewed were adamant about the importance of respecting that, in one woman's words, "Healing is done in very different ways and it's important to find your own way to heal." Some want and need to travel alone. Some will benefit from a survivors' support group or a skilled counsellor. Some will try in different ways at different times. As one woman explained, "Maybe when I'm older I'll be able to deal with it again. Right now, I can't do anymore." All survivors need the support and understanding of the people close to them. As one

Diagram 11

Exits: Reclaiming Self

Self-Awareness:
I value and use my thoughts and
    feelings.
I can make mistakes; everyone
    does.
I can learn new things and be
    flexible.
I appreciate myself.

Empowerment:
The abuse was not my fault.
I can shed the guilt and shame:
    they're his not mine.
I did the best I could as a child
    living under those conditions.
I'm remarkable for having
    endured abuse and its
        consequences.

Self-Acceptance:
I know myself.
I like who I am.
I respect myself for having lived
    through the abuse(s) of my
    childhood.
I am strong and able to learn and
    change when I want or need
    to.
I deserve to be loved and respected
    by others.

Clarity:
I was sexually abused.
I can separate out who I am from
    what I've thought and felt
    about myself because of being
    abused.
I have personal rights.
I have the right to set and enforce
    boundaries and limits.
I trust my perceptions.
I am much more than a sexual
    abuse survivor.

Survival Skills:
I can be myself to myself and
    others.
These skills have helped me to
    survive.
Now I can choose which ones to
    keep or change and which to
    put aside.

woman said, "Without it you feel sentenced, damned alone."

It is often a long struggle and one not to be rushed: "Somehow we know what we need; somehow we know when to remember." Several women referred to it as a life-long process. One suggested that it's wise to expect that it's going to take a lifetime for a survivor to go through everything she has to in order to get on with her life and be whole: "If it happens sooner than that, great! But I think there's too much of a rush to fix things."

Survivors found what was helpful and rejected what was not. What was not helpful included "heavy-duty techniques to force stuff on us like hypnosis"; and "all those terrible categories that psychologists and psychiatrists use, like 'victim.'" Survivors realized the importance of really dealing with the issue and not just putting a band-aid on it. They told us of the learning they did; how, as one woman said, "Parts of myself have opened up from my doing my own healing." They claimed their survival "as an act of courage, an act of strength, a way of being alive today." One survivor urged other women to summon up their courage if they can.

> ... That's what it will take to face your pain. You will come out the other side of it. It won't kill you. *Not* facing it, *not* dealing with it will kill you. It's all right to be afraid, but not to let your fears paralyze you.

It is possible, another survivor pointed out, to learn from it rather than avoiding or denying it; to learn to understand your own feelings and values and recognize healthy, nurturing situations for yourself in the world.

It is possible and it is a worthwhile struggle for, through it, women and children reclaim who they are: survivors with courage, self-awareness, and determination to live their own lives beyond child sexual abuse.

Recollecting a Sense of Self

Survivors who have lived for years with the undisclosed trauma of childhood sexual abuse, with haunting partial memories or no recollection of it to speak of, understandably lose a clear and accurate sense of who they really are. If we are all, in effect, the sum of our experiences, self-awareness depends on knowledge and understanding of where we've been and what constitutes our life.

Since so many survivors of child sexual abuse often can't recall or can't face their experiences of abuse, their sense of self is limited. As one woman explained to us, "I forgot about the abuse. I forgot that I had any personal experiences for a period of time. I buried the abuse so I could function, so I could be strong." What this woman and others have had to do is somehow dig up the memories or allow them to surface and integrate the experiences so they can identify why they feel as they do. Recollecting their childhood experiences was a key for many women in understanding or even acknowledging how they felt as adults and why they felt as they did.

The process of uncovering the whole self began for the women we interviewed in various ways. For some, depression and unhappiness with their lives prompted them to try to understand more about their past; for others, bits of memories of their childhoods surfaced, propelling them into more remembering and finding parts of experiences, feelings and beliefs they hadn't known existed.

Unfortunately, blocking memory and knowledge of the abuse, which had served so many women as a survival strategy in childhood and beyond, stood in their way when they wanted and needed to remember and sort out the totality of their experience. One woman, for example, marvelled at "how incredible the human psyche is—it blocks the abuse to protect you as a child and it does that until you're able to remember but even when you're ready to remember, the protection is still there." For her, and for others, remembering is a constant battle. One woman described the process as like "being in a fog bank for a lot of my life and there's something I want beyond the fog but I can't grasp it."

Some women struggled to grasp a memory of ever having been sexually abused at all: it was, until recently, something they

only vaguely sensed and suspected or began to suspect in counselling or therapy as a possible explanation for the problems they
were experiencing in their adult lives. One woman, for example,
recalled going to a marriage counsellor when she was twenty-
one and becoming nervous and upset when the counsellor asked
her about her father. She was so upset that she didn't continue
with counselling but she said that she didn't consciously remember. "I didn't know it was abuse and I didn't know it was him
until a year and a half ago when I got my first memories at age
thirty-six."

Other women had not totally blocked the memory of being
sexually abused but rather lacked memory of specific incidents
or details. They'd carried around a feeling of being flawed, of being bad, of something wrong. One woman told us she turned to
therapy as the answer. Finally, after ten years of being in and out
of therapy, specific memories of the abuse surfaced. Another
woman suggested that she'd used poetry writing as an outlet for
her knowledge of the abuse until recently when she's been able
to deal with it more directly in therapy.

One woman described the memories she had as "snapshots
that used to pop out at me." When she stopped drinking (she
was alcoholic) and was at last beginning to know herself, she
began to understand a lot of the mystery of those snapshots. Another woman's memories emerged in vivid specificity: "I can remember what I did when I was two or three years old. I can chart
it!" Still another survivor described "just not being able to keep
it down any longer." She told us about being at a workshop on
sexual abuse and reacting "to everything on a personal level."
She felt overloaded. She remembered first a bus driver who'd
abused her and then she remembered her father's abuse of her.

Other women seem to have blocked not the specifics of what
was done to them but the emotions it provoked. Because she'd
had no opportunity as a child to think for herself, one woman's
feelings about the abuse are only now coming out. She now experiences anger about having been helpless and screwed up by
the abuse.

Once such memories do surface, some survivors don't see

them ever going away. However, the memories rarely emerge completely, all in one piece. One woman noted that one year of her life—when she was in grade three—is still a blank, but she's confident that when the time is right, she will remember it. Another woman told us she's decided "not to go for more memories at this point. Maybe later I will [but] understanding the effect of the abuse is more important than uncovering all the memories." Instead of pursuing the past—as necessary as she knows that is— she wants to focus on the present. The judgement about how much to pursue memories is not easy, especially when, as one woman said, "The worst times are living *in* the memory of it; the times I feel strongest are living here and now."

Finding this kind of balance between recalling the past in order to understand its effects and getting on with their lives now is made difficult by the lack of control survivors have over the process of remembering. One woman found, for example, that recovering childhood memories takes some similar triggering situation. But it can happen when the survivor is least expecting it to happen and least ready or able to deal with it. Some women's memories were triggered by being touched by friends or lovers; by smells, such as the pipe tobacco the abuser smoked; or by various sounds such as someone walking past the door of their bedroom. Often the memories seemed to sneak up on them but once they were out in the open, women of course had to cope with them.

For one survivor it was the break-up of her relationship with her boyfriend when she was twenty-one that led to remembering the sexual abuse by her father. She recounted being really upset and spending the night at a friend's house.

> I woke up in the middle of the night, crying, upset and tried to tell her about my feeling of powerlessness with men. I told her it had something to do with their eyes and, when I said that, I got a clear image of my father's eyes.

Another woman has found that being in a new relationship is "restimulating" memories. Her lover is also a survivor of child sexual abuse and "We bring up memories for each other; it's only in knowing her that I realize there may be something else I haven't remembered." Realizing that means that she has to find space in her life to deal with her recollections rather than just pressing on.

Several of the mothers we interviewed said that learning about the abuse of their children prompted them to remember their own childhood abuse—and just at the very time they were trying to marshall all their strength to respond to their children's disclosures. One woman said that when her children were in counselling after the disclosure, she started going to a counsellor for herself as well because it's something that she had to work through, she couldn't just bury it.

But whenever and however the memories come, they are critically important in developing a sense of self and an awareness of the effects of the abuse. As one woman pointed out, "Knowing all that stuff is what healing is; it's unraveling the knot" of child sexual abuse.

Realizing "It's Not My Fault"

Getting back memory, finding lost pieces of their lives and realizing they'd been sexually abused was a very painful process for survivors. It turned women's lives upside down and challenged many assumptions they'd long accepted about themselves and their childhoods. But with the pain of realization comes, sooner or later, the liberating discovery that the abuse was not their fault, that they are not bad or wrong or flawed. They see how they'd been tricked, manipulated, controlled—indeed trapped—by the abuser. As one woman put it, "[Because] the effects are really deep and interwoven, it takes a lot of sorting through and it's very convoluted." By sorting it through, however, survivors come to the realization that, in one woman's words, "The bottom line is it really wasn't your fault that this stuff happened to you."

Survivors search back to the source of their sense of shame and guilt. One woman said, "Being abused meant being ashamed of myself, that I wasn't good, that I was at fault, that I'm to blame for it." Wanting not to feel guilty, wanting, for example, to be able to enjoy sex in her adult life without guilt, wanting to make a change, she began finally to talk about her experience and to understand why she felt guilty. She's found that it takes a lot of work to alleviate the guilt. Certainly it takes more than someone telling you not to feel guilty.

> It's fine to tell someone that it's okay but it's not okay... When you tell someone that you've been abused, I wish they'd understand and not say, "oh yeah" with a nice patronizing nod. That makes me feel, "did I do something wrong?"

The problem is, in another survivor's words, "Once a kid is trained by the offender to feel properly guilty, she takes it on without a challenge." It's difficult but necessary for a survivor to "remember that everything you think bad about yourself is mostly from training. It's not true."

The problem is made worse by the way the child's need for affection, combined with the abuser's manipulation, so often creates a sense of complicity in the child. As one woman explained, "You're dealing with guilt and anger" mixed together. "I can say to myself and I can tell you that I loved being abused because it was the first sign of affection in my life and the victim has a love-hate relationship with it." In the same vein, another survivor recalled, "There was some part of me that liked it [the abuse by her father]. I got treated like an adult. He was interested in what I was doing." She struggled to put together her feelings that no one else cared for her in the way he did with her feelings as an adult that it was all a lie. She can no longer believe his caring had to do with her and has concluded her father used her. Some women found it very hard to realize that what they'd grown up believing was a special relationship was, in fact, sexual abuse.

Another woman said listening to other women talk about their experiences, when she was eighteen or nineteen years old and in an Alateen group, helped her to identify some of the abuser's tricks and to alleviate her own guilt: "I learned about me by listening to others talk about their abuse."

One woman described being gang raped by a group of boys

as "like an accident." She said that it was easier to accept than what her father did to her: the gang rape wasn't a betrayal of anything because these were strangers whom she didn't know. It was nothing that she had caused. It was always clear to her that the boys were responsible for the rape but only recently has her father's responsibility for abusing her become clear.

Survivors are extricating themselves from the shame and guilt they'd internalized, seeing the external causes of it, and placing the blame where it belongs—with the abusers. One survivor noted how her father's illness and death impeded the process for her because it was hard to be angry at him—he'd suffered. However, she added, "I resent that he got off and I got left with all this mess and he never had to deal with it in any direct way at all."

Another woman suggested that feeling guilty and different from her friends because she'd been abused got in her way, as did the fact that she blamed herself for not remembering the abuse. "I just had these few things that I really didn't want to look at." Recovering her memories has filled in the gaps in her experience and has helped her to understand why she had no memories. Her father had self-righteously scapegoated her, accusing her of all kinds of sexual activity; she now understands that as a source of her guilt. She is still questioning how her childhood experiences have affected her life, trying to figure out the relative influences of the sexual abuse, her father's alcoholism, and the physical abuse she'd endured.

The abusers' tricks and manipulations were understandably difficult to see through for many survivors. The realization that so much of what they'd taken for truth was a lie, left them lacking confidence to trust their own perceptions. Seeing through the abusers' disguises and tricks, realizing the abuse was not their fault, is a critical step in reversing the cycle of abuse and undoing or dealing with its damage. As one woman explained, until she'd completed her "search for the missing piece—the naming of the abuse"—everything related to the abuse had been *her* problem, she'd been the problem. She reflected many other women's sense of empowerment that came with naming the abuse: "What helped me was the naming: I'm a sexual abuse survivor. It put it out there, not against me."

Sorting Out Survival Skills

Realizing the abuse was not their fault was for many women a key to understanding their own responses to the abuse. They began to see many of the troubling aspects of their behaviour—the memory loss, the intellectualizing, the drinking—as their way of coping with the abuse and not as signs of fundamental flaws in their personalities. For many, getting perspective on their survival strategies also revealed some positive elements in what they'd previously experienced only as negative responses, and it gave them insight into what they could do to stop the cycle of abuse. It marked the end of self-blame and of internalizing the abusers' scapegoating. It marked the beginning of taking responsibility not for everything that had been done to them but for what was rightfully theirs to control. It also became possible to build on those survival skills which served them well and to begin to undo those which did not.

The task was not easy. As one woman explained, "I had learned a lot of games which I've had to unlearn." But it is possible. One survivor's account shows the range of things she's had to sort through, but also the value of doing it. She said:

> I'd developed my intellectual side, I'd put a lot of energy into valuing my thinking. [But] I didn't feel my feelings, didn't know them. I didn't have the capacity to say "no." I didn't know when I was being harmed. For example, I was a battered wife but I didn't know that till after I got out... I had a lot of sexual partners. Saying "yes" was easier than saying "no" and being forced... I was always wanting to be rescued. I had a whole fantasy world about being rescued. I think that's what drew me into getting married at a young age: I got married to get away from home... I was always trying to hurt myself, taking physical risks, hoping I'd break a leg, do something to make it obvious that I was hurt so someone would see it and do something about it. I remember hanging upside down on tree branches because I wanted to fall on my head, but the branches would just never break.

In remembering the abuse she'd experienced and the responses she'd had to it, she said the "negative stuff" undermined her confidence and left her hating herself and feeling powerless, but somehow she found that "something out of that experience was positive." In particular, she's realized that she takes risks and is a courageous woman.

Other women described the process they've been going through. One woman analyzed her struggling to undo the damage as learning to "live around it, like anyone with a handicap or disability." She tries to recognize when the hurt part comes up— "I always cry when it does"—and tries to put the abuse in its time-space. She survived many incidents of abuse the way an animal does—by shuting down, cowering, pulling back, and feeling guilty. Maintaining that "you have to say good-bye" to the abuse and to such negative survival skills, she acknowledged that, when she was a child, "It was not a bad technique, but you can't use it all the time."

Based on her experience, another woman said, "You have to learn to say 'no' before you can say 'yes.' I said 'no' to a lot of things, big and little, [including] alcoholism, cynicism, some of my anger, defensiveness,... being detached." For her it meant progressing from feeling "bitchy and guilty and then comfortable." Saying "yes" led her to keep a food chart of her overeating and exercising to get in touch with her body. She also joined Alcoholics Anonymous. As a result she experienced what she calls "a mini-miracle": she had all kinds of feelings she hadn't allowed to surface before. Although it was very nerve-racking for her, it was worth it. As she sees it, her survival skills started to work against her when she became an adult in a safe place. Accordingly, she had to train herself not to use them: "On a very bad day I could still use my survival skills but now there are fewer places to hide. I have to show my weapons and put them aside."

Many women who identified mind-blocking as a survival skill they had to sort out got help from therapists, counsellors, or support groups. One woman dealt with what she termed a long process of suppression by going to a survivors' support group.

She also went to a psychiatrist for a year and a half and noted that she restored her faith in human nature. And a counsellor, specializing in "body-work," helped her to deal with her detachment from her emotions and to become aware of how she was repressing her feelings. In time, "I gradually became more associated with the abuse and it became part of my thinking," rather than staying suppressed. Another woman told us she sometimes still experiences a "kind of spaciness and a feeling of not being present" that stems from her attempts to protect herself from the abuse as a child. It is an ongoing struggle for her and for other women we interviewed.

A related problem for some survivors is the effect on their adult lives of complying with the abuser's demands on them as children to "keep the secret." For several women, the best ways to avoid telling anyone about the abuse had been to deny it to themselves, to dissociate or to make it a regular practice not to reveal what they were thinking or feeling. One woman found multiple personalities she had developed left as soon as she began to talk about the abuse. The change in her own use of energy was really surprising to her. She is breaking free from the secrets.

Another woman said she still keeps secrets but not to the extent that she goes crazy with her loneliness and isolation. As an adult she's learned, sooner or later, "To blurt it out, whatever it is."

Women also told us they had to sort out how they'd used sexual activity as a survival strategy for dealing with the secrecy and pain of the abuse. For one woman it required awareness of her tendency to measure the success of the relationship according to the frequency of sex; awareness of her difficulty sometimes in staying engaged, as a participant with choices in what goes on sexually between her and her partner; awareness of her tendency to become overly dependent on her partner just as she remembered being dependent on the stepfather who abused her. Another woman described concerns about over-emphasizing sex as a means of communicating love. She has struggled to overcome her view that sexual expression of love isn't real unless it results in a child. She has also worked hard to get clearer about her worth beyond being a "sex object."

One survivor said she had never known what a healthy relationship was. "A lot of my adult energy has been learning to accept and give love in my life." Part of her learning is recognizing the games she plays, such as, "If you really love me, you'll do whatever... " She said, "You're always testing not being able to accept that someone cares for you." Her current relationship with another survivor is working, in part because they can talk, they call the games for each other. One of the lessons she's learned is that she'd had unrealistic expectations of relationships with women as being easier than relationships with men. Instead she's realized, "I've brought the garbage with me and I've got to work it through."

Finding the healthy, positive traits in themselves—skills and talents they could use in place of damaging survival skills—was what made the difference for several survivors. One woman who had long thought she was "stupid," was astonished as an adult to score in the top five percent in all the aptitude tests she took as part of finding a new job. She waited for three days after receiving the results for a telephone call to tell her there'd been some mistake or mix-up. It didn't come. She expressed anger about having had to use her intellect to keep her life together rather than using it to build a life for herself, but realizing that she wasn't stupid put into perspective a lot of frustrations that she'd felt in her life.

Another woman told us about writing poetry as an alternative to the drugs and alcohol she had used to repress her memory of the abuse and her feelings about it. She now finds writing poetry and focusing on her work writing lyrics is a positive way to cope: "I write a lot more poetry, mostly poetry about aspects of child abuse... I'm a writer by nature. It's easy for me to do it and I always get a kick out of reading it." She not only enjoys her work, but it also means "I can be a flaky artist and make enough money to pay my psychologist's bills!"

With encouragement from a social worker, whom she found to be a constant source of wisdom and support, one survivor enrolled in art school. She had been painting and drawing since childhood but was amazed that the social worker figured out that art school could be an answer. Her history had involved trying hard to botch anything she seemed successful in; it was, she believes, a way to support her negative self-image. Although she describes her art work as "frantic, thrashing paintings" with "wild" colours, people surprised her by purchasing them. Furthermore, she experienced one of the most significant triumphs of her life by completing the course and coming first in her class. With justified pride she called the social worker to say: "Guess what? I did it! I'm the best! I came first!"

This woman's story, added to the others we've reported, shows that, with effort and determination, it is possible to build on the positive aspects of survival skills and to replace the negative, damaging ones with positive skills and self-knowledge.

Seeking Clarity

In reversing the cycle of abuse, women and children struggle to undo the confusion they've experienced, to make sense of their lives, and to find their own reality. They work to assert their autonomy and their right to have and to defend boundaries.

Understandably, the earlier the abuse is stopped, the easier it is to interrupt the cycle. The women we interviewed whose children were abused had short-circuited the cycle by stopping the abuse and by validating their children's right to say "no." As a result, several women gave us examples of their children's sense of boundaries. One woman said that while the abuse has justifiably made her daughters distrustful of adults, they can express the distrust and act on it. Another mother thinks her children generally require adults to earn their trust.

One little girl graphically demonstrated the boundary she wanted to establish against someone she considered to be "a bad man" she didn't trust. She was terrified once when a speech pathologist took her into a room and wouldn't let her leave. Later, in the waiting room, her mother recalled that the little girl literally built a fence with toys and said, "Quick, jump! Bad man. Run away!"

An adult survivor said her daughter who had been sexually abused had developed "a sixth sense about men: she can pick out the weird ones." When a man came up to her on her paper route and wanted to show her how to fold newspapers she told him in no uncertain terms to go away. She said, "No, I don't want you to show me how and, if you don't leave now, I'm going to scream." Her mother noted, "When I was a child, I was too scared to scream."

While the damage these children have suffered from the abuse must not be minimized, it is clear that the support and validation they've received from their mothers and others has given them a stronger sense of autonomy than adult survivors had at a comparable age. The longer the abuse goes on and the less validation a child receives, the harder it is for her to know and express her rights and to set and enforce boundaries.

Survivors told us of trying to bridge the gap between how they present themselves to the world and what they feel inside. One woman explained that to deal with her confusion she needs to stand back and distance herself, and said she is trying to learn what's normal. She *is* learning to set limits by refusing to carry on old patterns. She refuses to see her father who had abused her. She also put distance between herself and the abuser by telling her mother about her father's abuse. As a result she, her mother and her brother took different surnames because they didn't want to be associated with the abuser in any way. Still, a phone call from her father can leave her feeling "invaded" and afraid.

Other women described particular confusion regarding their families and the difference between illusion and reality. One woman recalled having "relied a lot" on her illusion that hers was a perfect family, illusions which were shattered as she realized that she had been sexually abused by her father.

For another woman, remembering abuse called into question her sense of the middle class family picture, and she has concluded that it is often not what it appears to be on the surface. Another survivor told us she's struggled with what she feels is too idealistic an idea of relationships. Because her childhood and family life were tragically flawed, she has wanted her adult relationships to be perfect. It has taken her a long time to weigh the ideals and the reality.

Undoing the confusion and coming to a realistic sense of what they want and can achieve was for the women we interviewed most often worked through in relationships with family, friends and lovers. Much of their effort involved learning how and when to say "no" to people. Saying "no" was often cited by women as a prerequisite for saying "yes."

—Abusers

For many survivors, the most significant person to say "no" to was the abuser. Having been powerless in relation to him when they were children, it was critical for them as adults to act on their right to set boundaries to contain the abuser's influence in their lives.

Some survivors have chosen to refuse to have any direct contact with the abuser. One woman explained that, after a couple of visits to her parents' home in Great Britain, she's had no contact with either of them. She found that she was still trying in vain to please them without affirmation from them for her accomplishments or for who she is. She said, "It doesn't even bother me anymore whether they're alive or dead. It's the effect they've had on me I have to concern myself with, not them." She feels particularly angry at her father who sexually abused her, but her realization of the lack of support and validation she received in childhood from both parents has led her to cut them both off. Another woman described her relationship with her mother and abusive father as "very distant." She said she's not yet ready to confront them—though it's something she's been considering. She has discussed it with her husband and believes she'd have strong support from him which would make a confrontation easier for her. In the meantime, keeping her distance seems the wisest course.

Other survivors have come to similar decisions about the need to limit contact with the men who abused them. One woman explained she decided never to see her father again because she can't be herself with him. She said that she can't forget the abuse. Nor would she trust him around her child. Her well-considered decision came after confronting her parents as part of her therapy in a treatment programme. Her father's response to the confrontation was to admit that he now sees he was "bad," but then to suggest that "The devil made me do it." This woman is trying to pursue a relationship with her mother but she sees her outside the family home in what she calls "neutral territory."

Another woman said she won't see her brother who'd sexually abused her because he hasn't changed and wants to continue the sexual relationship. For still another woman, dealing with the abuse has resulted in no direct communication between herself and her father for several years. "When I started dealing with the abuse, I just didn't feel like talking to him and it just carried on—so I've never talked to him. That doesn't mean I don't think about it a lot." She's quite sure her father knows her silence is a consequence of her realizing that he abused her because her brothers told him.

One of the women we interviewed, whose parents abused both herself and her children, said she has admitted to herself that she had long hated her mother and won't pretend otherwise any longer. Remembering the sexual abuse by her father made her realize that he was deceitful and manipulative and not the honest, straightforward man she'd assumed he was. When she confronted her parents, their denials of any wrong-doing re-affirmed her resolve to break off all communication with them.

To check out their own perceptions several survivors thought about confronting the abuser. One woman said when she realized the abuse by a boarder in her family home had not been her fault, part of her wanted to find him, sue him, confront him, but she didn't know his last name. Other women did confront the abusers. One woman told us of writing a letter to her cousin who'd abused her, describing what he'd done. He wrote back and denied everything. He was very defensive. Nevertheless, "Confronting him helped me because I realized that I was looking for validation from him and it had to come from me essentially. Validation did come from me in the end."

Another woman said confronting her father "felt like the hardest thing I ever did in my whole life." She knew he'd deny the abuse but, "What I got out of it was feeling like a survivor for the first time." For her it was an important and empowering step. It's something she'd recommend other survivors consider trying: "I see other women who haven't confronted family and they get sick every time they go home and I wonder if it's that they're compromised and get physically sick." She suggested the compromise may stem from a confusion she senses in survivors, a confusion between forgiving or confronting the abuser.

From her experience and that of other women we interviewed, confrontation empowers not because it elicits validation from the abuser but because it can facilitate survivors' self-validation. It can also help the survivor to see the abuser more clearly for who he is and to break free from him, to experience autonomy previously unknown to her. One woman said that as a result of going with the abuser to therapy, "I now know who the emotional cripple is: he is!" Not only does he not "take up a whole lot of my head or my heart anymore, I've made it all right with myself to have loved him once; that was my one crime." Her conclusion is that "Being in therapy with him was like saying good-bye to him and to his influence and power in my life." It gave her, for the first time, a sense of autonomy.

Whether they confronted the abuser in a formal sense—with the assistance of a counsellor or therapist—or less formally, by speaking or writing to the abuser, most of these women found it to be empowering. It was also helpful in reducing the abuser's influence over them. For some it led to confirmation of his responsibility for the abuse. Some described it as a way of closing the door on the abuser and the period of their lives he had dominated. But whether they confronted the abuser or not, women's accounts indicated that in their own ways and at their own pace they are extricating themselves from the confusion the abuse created. In what is a critically important act of survival, they are recognizing their rights and claiming their authority to set limits and boundaries to protect and affirm themselves.

—Mothers

Survivors are also working to be autonomous in other aspects of their lives. Not surprisingly, a significant struggle is their relationship with their mothers. Many women said they felt betrayed and angry when they thought about their mothers' failure to protect them from childhood sexual abuse. They are dealing with their feelings in a variety of ways.

Several women said they'd attempted to develop a positive mother-daughter relationship but to no avail. One woman, sexually abused by her stepfather, found the major stumbling block was her mother's inability to believe the sexual abuse had actually happened. She recalled her mother calling her a liar and she resents very much that even after the disclosure her mother maintained a closeness with the man who'd abused her. There was a brief period of reconnection when the woman was first married but "When my daughter was born, we'd go there and Mom would say 'let her sit by [the abuser], take a picture of them!' " Fear for her little girl and dismay at her mother's disbelief of her own abuse made it impossible to continue contact. It was a painful decision: her mother doesn't speak to her now and this woman is left wondering, "What do you do? Forget you have a family?" As painful as it is, she sees it's necessary to assert herself in relation to her mother and to maintain her own sense of integrity.

Another survivor told us us she's writing about her relationship with her mother to try to get beyond it and to release the hatred and anger she feels.

For some survivors, only superficial communication with their mothers is possible. They have ambivalent feelings: on the one hand they still love their mothers and want closeness and on the other hand they need to protect themselves by holding back. One survivor said her desire to come out as a lesbian to her mother illustrated that she loved her enough, trusted her enough to be able to talk to her about it. After months of turmoil, she finally said to her mother, "Mom, I think I'm a lesbian." Her mother's well-intentioned but inadequate response—"she hugged me and said, 'No you're not; it'll be all right!' "—

inhibited her from ever talking openly about herself to her mother again. Similarly, another woman is resentful that her mother keeps her lesbianism a secret though it is possible for them to talk about inconsequential things. Their relationship is especially difficult because her mother doesn't believe her husband was abusive. This survivor is struggling to sort out her feelings and to understand her mother.

> Sometimes I think I love her but I don't like her. Sometimes I think she's an adult victim. Damn it, there are more choices! She must know in her psyche that her child was molested and if that doesn't move you, what will? Why waste your life with a pervert? Then I feel guilty and sorry and then I love her again.

One woman said she refrains from telling her mother if she's sick or "something bad has happened" because her mother "blames it on me or acts as if it was my fault." When she told her mother about the sexual abuse she'd experienced at her father's hands her mother seemed to take her daughter's disclosure as just another reason for her to hate her father. She realizes her mother also felt bad, felt she should have known and that she takes it personally that her daughter didn't tell her when the abuse was happening. Her daughter has tried to understand things from her mother's perspective: "Mostly I know she doesn't understand what I understand about the abuse and she won't read books about it." Under the circumstances, trying to balance understanding of her mother while restricting how much she says to her seems the best this survivor can do.

According to several survivors, setting limits on their relationships with their mothers required dealing with the guilt they felt. One woman said, "I feel guilty because I hate her for not believing me." She wanted her mother to save her, protect her. Trying to put her mother's life into perspective she said, "I feel compassion for her. She had to live with the jerk and still does." She wonders if it would have made a difference if her mother had been more economically independent. She now sees her mother as "this little old lady having to live with blindness in order to survive. Rape, wife battering—she can't afford to see it." What

connects her own life and her mother's life is pain: "I feel a fleet-
ing solidarity with her when I feel she worked in her lifetime to
move women in her generation a step forward from the pain of
her mother and I feel like I'm working in my life to move a step
forward from my mother's pain." Recognizing the links between
her mother's life and her own is a way for this survivor to find
her independence and sort out her confused feelings.

Another survivor, who was sexually abused by her father,
told her mother about the abuse. In doing so she realized her
mother hadn't known about it before. She also realized how dependent on each other she and her mother had always been. She
can see that she had spent a lot of time with her mother and her
sisters out of guilt and duty. She is now asserting her right to
choice—which she hadn't had before—and she spends much less
time with them.

It's clear that expiating the guilt or anger they felt towards
their mothers is a difficult but necessary step for many survivors
in defining themselves and their rights. It's important to know
that as problematic as it is to do, it can be done. The stories of
the following two women illustrate the possibility of greater
sympathy and closeness between mothers and their daughters
who've been sexually abused without compromising either's
reality or independence.

In the first case, the adult survivor said, "Since I've come out
and named my own abuse, my mother has named hers and we've
connected through that." It is hard to connect sometimes because the older woman doesn't have the same choices available
to her, and so it seems to her daughter that in some ways she's
staying in the "victim" place. Without pushing her mother to
follow her lead, she can understand her better and identify with
her. "And I don't blame her for not having helped me when I
told her about the abuse because I understand that it just
brought up her pain and she couldn't look at that." This perspective means both generations of survivors benefit: the mother
has been given by her daughter a belated opportunity to reclaim
her own life; the daughter is freeing herself from unproductive
anger and finding new insights into her own and her mother's

experience as well as gaining a new relationship of potential support.

Similarly, a second woman told us that she and her mother are "coming together slowly because I have done work in healing myself and I wanted her to heal as well." Again, there is respect for both the mother's and daughter's pace and rights. As the daughter said of her mother, "In her own time, maybe she'll heal and maybe she won't but I am no longer filled with guilt or anger toward this woman." In what is a clear indication of resources and openness that this survivor had not had before, she said, "Mom deserves my love and compassion and I believe that, to the best of my ability, she is getting just that."

—Friends and Lovers
Developing new relationships and changing old ones often required that survivors sort out survival patterns, created in response to the abuse, and find out how to be close to others in healthier, more positive ways. In friendships, survivors struggle to assert their autonomy while respecting their friends' limits. One woman said that friendship is one of the hardest things she's dealt with in working through the sexual abuse. She needs to be open about the fact that she is a sexual abuse survivor, she needs to talk about her experience and have her friends' support. At the same time she has to be aware of her friends' feelings and to get them to define their needs around it. She's found, in telling her friends about the abuse, that it brings up a lot of fear in people. "A few have admitted it—they say they can't be around me much." For example, one friend got angry at her for not doing political work and disappeared from her life. Such responses have made her feel more isolated from some friends but, "On the good side, a couple of people feel more trusting and closer." She is finding a balance between recognizing her friends' difficulties and drawing on the supports that *are* there for her.

Another survivor told us of developing a greater appreciation for her good friends and the effort that people around her make. As a child growing up in one of the only Roman Catholic families in a Protestant community, she had some close friends but felt "different" from them. That experience, plus coming to terms with the sexual abuse she'd suffered, has given her tolerance for the lifestyles people have. "I try not to stereotype people."

Other survivors told us of having to learn not to "sexualize" their friendships and to recognize the distinctions between sexual attraction and being drawn to someone as a friend. Their experience of abuse had taught them their real value in the world was as sexual objects. It was, therefore, difficult for many survivors to recognize or accept affection or attention that didn't have a sexual element, that valued them for all of who they are and not just in sexual terms.

Some women described themselves as suspicious of people who seemed interested in them, afraid the interest was only sexual. Others said they were unable to accept that people were sexually attracted to them because the abuse had made them ashamed of their bodies and uncomfortable with their sexuality. One woman said the abuse caused her to internalize a lot of self-hatred, especially around herself as a woman and as a sexual woman. Another woman talked about having a negative body image. She recalled recently being in a sexuality workshop and having to make an image of herself: "I drew myself without breasts. Whew! That is strange—it really shows how I see myself." She has become very accomplished in karate which has helped improve her image of her body but she says she still has trouble validating her positive attributes, physical and otherwise.

To develop positive sexual relationships, survivors not only have to overcome the negative self-image that abuse has instilled in them, they also have to define what they want sexually and then assert their right to get it. This is not an easy task for any woman in a society dominated by men's definitions of sexual pleasure. For survivors of childhood sexual abuse it is especially difficult. Their sense of their sexuality, their definition of what is good or bad sex has been determined by what the abusers liked and wanted. As women who were sexually abused in childhood, sexual violation dominates their experience. In the absence of positive, respectful sexual experiences based on mutual pleasure, it is hard for women to define what good sex feels like or to understand their own sexuality. One woman explained that, as a result of the abuse, she knows she has pain and pleasure mixed up. Though she wouldn't say painful sex is "easier," she has had to learn to enjoy sex that is gentle and caring: "Painful sex is more familiar."

Another woman understands now that she'd used pornography in her sexual relationships because it was another form of abusing herself which she learned from being abused as a child. Pornography reminded one woman of the humiliation and arousal connection she'd experienced as a child when her father abused her. She used pornography for a time in her relationships with men but it always left her feeling terrible and angry. She contended, "Pornography removes consent: your body responds and you get trapped somehow," just as a child's body often responds against her will to the abuser's manipulations. She emphasized that it's her *experience* not just her intellect that tells her pornography takes your power. Although at the time "It feels like it gives you power," she believes it doesn't, it traps you. This woman, like other survivors, is trying to understand her sexual responses in order to find positive alternatives.

One woman talked about trying to find out where the center of her own sexuality comes from, searching for her own sexual self-definition. She wants to know because if her sense of her sexuality comes from the abuse, she wants to change it. Noting, "I'm still at odds as to how to do that," this woman is working it through in her relationship with her husband and in therapy.

Another woman referred to real trouble with feeling she deserves pleasure. And several women said a major hurdle is trusting their sexual partners enough to say what they want. In relationships with men one woman said, "I had a good cover and men live on a different planet anyway so I didn't expect to share the same things with men." With women, however, she has had to confront the hiding and protection because she finds there's a greater potential for closeness with women. Another woman said she's been closed for years and is just now starting to open up with her female lover of two and a half years: "That's a good indication of how hard it's been to develop trust." She believes that keeping some distance between herself and her lovers was a necessary step, part of her way of saying "no." She finds that some effects of the abuse are lessening and though she's never had an orgasm, she does now have pleasure.

Several survivors told us they find it's easier to define what they don't want or like sexually than to say what they do like. One woman said that when she began dealing with the abuse her interest in sex left and it's only now coming back. With her current partner, the sexual relationship is "fairly okay. It's the best I've had." But for her, intercourse is not possible. She described an oppressive sense, "A feeling that I have a penis inside me—it really makes sexual relationships difficult, like a trial." She is trying to discuss sex with her boyfriend, to tell him what she feels, what she likes and doesn't like, but sometimes she finds the words get stuck and she can't get them out. She needs to be cuddled and she needs her boyfriend to wait for her "to come out of the stages when I get grossed out." Though she is not totally satisfied with their sexual relationship and says she'd be very happy if she could ever have intercourse that's satisfactory, she is learning ways to assert her right to define what is and what is not acceptable or pleasurable sexual activity for her.

For many survivors clarifying their sexual needs involves specifying sexual activities that remind them of the abuse and which parts of their bodies they don't want touched or stimulated. One woman has written about what she calls sexual limits connected to sexual abuse. She has listed what feels safe and "what raises incest triggers." Her list of safe experiences includes activities in which she is being treated gently and respectfully and can retain some control. The triggering list includes activities that may seem innocuous to others—such as holding hands while walking and kissing—but obviously have negative associations for her. Also on this list are things which suggest lack of control: "Being on the bottom, pinned down; hearing aroused breathing; fingers inside; arm over shoulders; and being in closed spaces." She noted that the lists change: the more work she does around the incest the more open she can be. By starting to figure out how to say "no," " I feel a much deeper eroticism than I knew was possible." And she is also learning how to move through the connection she's long felt between shame, humiliation and arousal.

Other survivors also talked about the importance of taking control (which they'd never been allowed before), to define the sexual activity they want to engage in. In so doing they can become clearer about their needs and gain in their relationships both the trust and the sense of respect for their rights that are prerequisites for more openness. They are working to undo the confusion the abuse created in their lives, particularly in their sexual lives. As one woman concluded, letting go of the pain and anger that's been eating away at her means feeling powerful and it means she can get on with her life. She's realized that "every day I hold on to it or close up with my lover sexually, I not only deny myself sexually, I also continue to be sexually abused by the abusers."

Another woman's account also shows how important it has been for her to sort out the confusion the abuse created, and to validate her right to set her own limits in her relationships. She described a progression in her marriage from initially being satisfied simply because her husband made her feel "so special, so important" to being clearer about what she needs. She realized that she'd also felt special and important to her stepfather who'd abused her and she began to look more critically at her husband's behaviour and at her own feelings. She saw her husband was "dominant and interested in his own pleasures and I ended up feeling left out and alone." He also had a bad temper and was explosive. She decided to assert herself: "I stated what I wanted and if I didn't get it, I was leaving." As a result the relationship is "getting better,. . . he's trying now."

By setting boundaries, by declaring their rights, survivors are reversing the cycle of childhood sexual abuse. They are claiming an authority and self-determination the abuser denied them. While their experience shows that no woman or child can be totally safe, they are making themselves less vulnerable to the next abuser who might come along. They are recovering pieces of their childhood and belatedly asserting the right of every child to fulfill her basic needs for love, affection, and autonomy. As one survivor summed up her long journey to understand and undo the effects of the abuse: "I'm moving towards wholeness."

Self-Acceptance

Exiting the cycle of child sexual abuse is for survivors essentially a process of putting their lives back together—of recollecting and reclaiming pieces of their experience that the abuse had damaged or distorted or displaced. As we've seen from women's accounts, remembering their childhood experiences, recognizing the abuser's responsibility for the abuse, and realizing how they survived all contribute to survivors' building a clearer sense of who they are and can be. Many women also told us an essential part of dealing with the self-alienation that had plagued them from childhood was accepting the various aspects of themselves they'd discovered, and integrating these pieces into their sense of self.

This acceptance requires awareness of the bad feelings as well as the good, awareness of where the feelings came from and how they inform survivors' thoughts and influence their lives now. Acceptance does *not* mean minimizing the abuse or excusing the abuser or denying the hurt and pain they've experienced. It means accepting that, as one woman said, "It happened; it shouldn't have but it did." She has resisted the inclination to try to undo what happened in favour of understanding the consequences of the abuse as best she can and accepting herself, thereby trying to limit the effects of the abuse on the rest of her life.

Another woman said, "The obvious thing is not to blame yourself [but] to learn to understand your own feelings and values,... to learn from the abuse rather than avoiding and denying it... It's important not to cut yourself off." She made a commitment to herself to be healthy and to survive and she sought alternative ways of fulfilling herself and exploring her creativity. Self-acceptance also involved recognizing how the abuse affected her, being aware of her feelings about herself and taking responsibility—not for the abuse—but for dealing with its effects.

> I think what happened is that based on the sexual abuse and the denial, I lost touch with myself as a creative person. I lost touch with my heart... I'm aware of the patterns and those feelings. I still have to be responsible and aware now and responsible for my own feelings of negativity which may arise.

She realizes that her negative feelings can be directed at herself or directed outwardly. She is determined to live with some dignity and gentleness towards herself and others and to make choices based on these values rather than self-negation. By trying to use her experience of abuse as a tool for self-knowledge, she sees the profound effect it's had on her ability to move in the world and fulfill her own goals. As a result, she said, "I feel more accepting of myself; I have a level of acceptance in terms of owning my memories and not denying my own personal strength" in coping with the abuse.

This woman's account illustrates the rewards that come from dealing with even the most painful emotions and sense of alienation. Other women described similar struggles and accomplishments. For many, the first hurdle was reconnecting with painful feelings the abuse had provoked, feelings they had repressed and would rather not have to face again. For some women, remembering their feelings of shame, guilt, of being wrong or bad was especially difficult. For some, it was hardest to recall their feelings of betrayal. For other women, especially those who'd prided themselves on being in control, it was hard to realize how little control they'd actually had over the abuser, how powerless and helpless they had been. It's been a struggle also to acknowledge and express their thoughts and feelings.

One woman said she has found it liberating to learn to recognize her emotions. She'd blocked her feelings and began to sort out her experiences intellectually. Eventually, "Emotionally, I started to click into the intellectual feminism I'd learned—ideas about patriarchy, sexual abuse, heterosexism, wife battering, al-

coholism... One day I felt lonely and that was good." As a result, she's able to integrate emotion and thought as well as physical sensations. In the relationship she has with another woman
she feels young inside again because she's emotionally, sexually
and mentally stimulated at the same time.

Another woman noted that she still has a lot to work on in
terms of learning to assert herself against denials of her rights
which began with abuse in her childhood and continued through
her adult relationships with men who assaulted her. Nevertheless, she has over the years come to value herself more and has
left relationships with violent men because, as she said, "I realized my life was worth more."

The means women found useful in coming to greater self-
acceptance and self-esteem included individual counselling, support groups for survivors, learning about feminism, and developing an awareness of their spiritual needs. For most women it was
a combination of things that helped. One woman explained that
"Raising my political consciousness helped open up my spiritual,
feminine awareness. And, off and on, I've participated in
women's groups and talked about women's issues."

Learning relaxation techniques was important for one
woman who also recommended doing something pleasurable for
yourself once a day on a consistent basis so you see there is
something positive in life. She remarked as well on the need to be
aware of patterns in your life and to try not to repeat the negative, self-defeating ones. In addition, she said it is necessary to
find something on which to build a sense of competence and
accomplishment—"Whatever it is, knitting, karate, go for it!"

Therapy has made it possible for another woman to free herself from uncontrolled flashbacks to her childhood and to the
abuse. It's not that she's forgotten or denied her experience,
rather she's come to terms with it. She said it's like having "echo
chambers that echo the new, the good and not the bad." In a
statement that reflects the experience of many women we interviewed she described a progression from mourning all that she'd
lost to a valuable self-awareness. By dealing with her experience,
"Now I feel grateful that I've got a depth of understanding and

wisdom which I couldn't have got any other way."

Self-acceptance acquired through the process of healing prompted one survivor to say that she can see even the abuse itself in positive terms: "I wouldn't wish it on anyone. But because I have been hurt so deeply I have also healed to the point that I can never lose myself again. That doesn't mean that I don't lose myself sometimes but I'm becoming aware of when I do and what I can do to stop it." Through her struggles to know who she really is, she has developed a real love of herself. The ability of women to triumph over what abusers had done to them is an encouraging testament to their determination. It must not, however, be taken as an indication that it's easy to survive child sexual abuse. In fact, the triumph is all the greater because it is so difficult. As one woman angrily declared, "I gained nothing from it. I got short-changed. It was not fair. I'm angry about it." She takes justifiable pride in saying, "I had to survive and I did survive!" She said, "I bumbled my way through it," and, "It's only out of instinct, gut instinct, survival instinct that I've made it. I've done a damn good job. I'm proud of what I've done for myself."

The struggle is also, as many women told us, a long one with sometimes small but significant incremental gains. One woman said she is finally at the point where she can imagine things to live for, but it's still not easy. Another woman is overcoming her uneasiness of having "something weird inside me" which meant "I couldn't let people know me or they'd find out something terrible about me." She's also working through her tendency to avoid thinking about herself by focusing on other people and her desire to be perfect in order to get approval and validation from other people. She has come to an understanding and acceptance of herself: "I feel like I made some kind of decision to love myself." Still another woman, by dealing with the sexual abuse of her children as well as the abuse she'd experienced as a child, has come out of it all with a clear sense of herself as a much stronger, more confident and assertive person.

These women's accomplishments are the result of recollecting feelings and pieces of their experience they'd lost for a time.

While they do not minimize the toll the abuse has taken, neither do they deny their experience of it and the place it will always have in their lives. As one woman declared, "It's so much a part of me. It's my identity. Do I want that taken away from me? It's made me this fantastic person." In gaining self-awareness, self-acceptance, and a self-esteem they'd never before known, survivors have gained new ground to build on in living their lives beyond child sexual abuse.

V

Beyond Survival

Women do resist, persistently and tenaciously, the effects of male violence. Women are survivors. They have done so for hundreds and hundreds of years. Many have developed scar tissue, but survive they do and continue to struggle for autonomy. Women are not, as some would have us believe, masochistic, addicted to violence, prone to seeking it out, or in any way defeated by violence directed toward them. Our survival is our strength, our experiences the reminders that there is much more work to do. (Stanko 1985:19)

ELIZABETH Stanko's statement reflects the accounts of the women we interviewed. Women *and* children *do* resist. They do survive. They do find exits from the cycle of child sexual abuse. They are getting on with their lives.

But the women we interviewed did not talk about their survival in dramatic terms. One woman described it all very simply as a progression from being a victim, to being a survivor, to beginning to live her life on her own terms. In another woman's words it amounts to this: "I have some peace of mind. I have a few simple tools. And I know how to cope." She cited laughter—regaining her sense of humour—as a very special sign of health for her. She noted that as a child, she never laughed.

233

This woman and others indicated they are keenly aware of how far they've had to come, but they are also aware of the strength they have developed, which will serve them for rest of their lives.

> I think I've fought with the abuse and come to terms with it, for all the emotional damage done to me... If you can fix your self-image, your self-respect, your belief in yourself, you get to breathe a sigh of relief and life is not so threatening, not a life sentence. You can start to enjoy life.

Similarly, a woman who is herself a survivor and whose children had been sexually abused said, "It's been a long haul and it will be a long haul yet," but through their struggle she and her children have gained a lot that's healthy.

> In retrospect I guess I'm very happy with how it's turned out—the kids are doing beautifully and I'm doing beautifully. It's a trite clinical assertion that it's possible to heal, but it's really true. I wouldn't wish sexual abuse on a flea but given that it happened, we're all better for having gone through it as we have.

Life is not easy, of course. Sometimes, women told us, it feels like they're taking three steps forward and two steps back. For one mother the daily living is hard, the stress and pain she's been through with her children makes her wonder if they wouldn't be better off with what she calls "an intact family, one that could 'take it' better" than she can. As difficult a decision as it would be for her to give up her children, she said, "It helps, knowing I can make that choice." Her children—though often unhappy and unpredictable—none the less are improving: sleeping better, not running away from home, not running in front of cars.

Another woman said she feels "anxious, like I don't have any control." She's afraid that if her ex-husband gets psychological help the courts will award him some kind of access to the daughter he abused, and the mother's efforts to protect and help her daughter will have been in vain. Nevertheless, it's clear that she will be an even more formidable protector in the future. This woman, who fought with tenacity and determination through a long court battle to limit her ex-husband's access to their child, described herself as stronger now because she stood up to him for the first time. She has also decided to return to school to get a para-professional certificate in social work so she can help other mothers like herself.

Another mother told us she still gets angry with herself for not realizing sooner that her children were being abused. She's worried about her children in the future, knowing that mothers can't totally protect their children. Her anger at herself and her worries are balanced, however, by a recognition of how much she and her children have accomplished.

> I feel good about what I've done with my children... I feel good about myself, that I have turned this family around... I'm sorry that [the sexual abuse] happened at all, that they had to go through that. But I feel proud of them because they're growing people. Even my oldest daughter who has blocked it out is still taking steps to deal with her environment, which is pretty good for such an introverted child.

In spite of the hard times, the worries and fears, most mothers we interviewed have gained confidence: they are less confused and worried, less self-blaming than before, and they see their children gaining confidence, doing better in school, getting along better with their brothers and sisters. Like adult survivors, they try to maintain perspective, including recognizing that for both them and their children, the process of healing is a long one. Though they hope that their children represent the last generation who will know sexual abuse, they are realistic in recognizing the obstacles which must be overcome for this crime to be eradicated. They have seen changes in their own lifetimes, and anticipate more in their children's, especially the growing understanding of the effects of child sexual abuse and ways to deal with them. Yet their experience reminds them that, as Elizabeth Stanko says, there is much more work to do.

The stories of women's and children's struggles described throughout this book contain many lessons for those of us trying to survive and those of us trying to help. When we asked women what advice they would give to others, they specified some of the most important things they had learned from their experience, as well as some of the tasks that face us all.

First and foremost, they spoke directly to children and adult survivors and mothers. They also made recommendations for counsellors and therapists. And they offered their views of a society that has allowed child sexual abuse to go on virtually un-checked for hundreds of years.

Speaking to Women and Children

To survivors, young or old, women said "keep telling," "talk about it," "don't keep the secret." From their own experience they know that's not a simple matter but they also know, as one woman said, "The more we talk, the more we learn." They told us of the need to find and make "safe places" for children and adult survivors to talk about what's been done to them. They cited support groups, self-help groups and talking with other women who've had similar experiences as especially helpful. For children, they said something less structured than a support group may be needed, but that the opportunity to play and talk together informally with other child survivors is important for overcoming the isolation children feel.

Women also spoke of the importance of encouraging all kinds of talking and expression of all the feelings children, mothers, and adult survivors have—aggression, insecurity, nega-tivity, anger, as well as countless questions children especially need to ask. One woman contended that we must help children and adults to build a language to describe what's really happen-ing, to speak about their experience and their feelings. She and other women reminded us of the difficulty children have finding the words to express their experience of abuse in ways grown-ups can understand. One woman cited her own experience with visual arts as evidence of the need to encourage children in vari-ous forms of expression, not just verbal forms. She challenged us to find ways to ask children questions about abuse rather than leaving the onus on the child to tell.

The women we interviewed also emphasized the importance

of respecting survivors' differences, their need to deal with what comes up about their experience in their own ways, to heal at their own pace, in their own time. This is the lesson one woman learned in the course of her own children's disclosures of child sexual abuse. She understands why a child may initially deny being sexually abused.

> You think it's obvious she's been abused but you ask her and she says "no"; *not* because she's weak and *not* because she hasn't been sexually abused. It's just that she's not ready to deal with it at that moment for whatever reason.

Accordingly it's essential to listen carefully, to be patient, to make it safe for a child to talk when she's ready and to be prepared for things to get worse right after the disclosure. "Though it's hard to believe it when you're going through it, it does get better later on."

For it to get better, for a survivor to feel safe, much depends on the response she receives. Women stated unequivocally that the responses a survivor needs and deserves are "I believe you" and "It's not your fault." Over and over again women cited these two responses as central to their own and their children's needs. One woman said simply that believing her daughter was the key to stopping the abuse.

An adult survivor explained that belief in the truth of a child's disclosure is critical, especially a mother's belief.

> It's hard enough for children—the offender makes them feel it's their fault. It's hard enough to tell. Believe them! I'd take my daughter's word over my husband's any day. Be there for them, support them. It's not their fault. Give them a sense of security.

This woman is reluctant to sue her stepfather for the damages his abuse caused her because she is unwilling ever again to risk being disbelieved as she was in childhood.

Similarly, an adult survivor who now works with abused children told us, "One of the things I reiterate over and over is that it's never, ever, ever their fault!" If her own children disclosed to her she said, "I would attempt in whatever way possible to let them know they are lovable persons and try to give them all the love and comfort I could." Another woman said, "As a survivor myself, I realize the importance of really dealing with the issue and not just putting a band-aid on it." She advised other survivors "to find someone they're comfortable with and talk about it and go through it. It's a pretty scary thing... if they were someone I was close to, I'd want to offer as much support as I could give." If her own children had been sexually abused she said, "I'd find out as much as I could and do everything that I could to cut off the abuse entirely. I'd want my children to feel that I was completely on their side and that I was there to support them and to really go through it with them." One survivor summed up her advice to other women and children this way:

> Tell someone you trust. Don't blame yourself. Get away from it as soon as you can. Remember that you're okay.

Some survivors spoke of the guilt they assume they'd feel if their children were abused and the importance, therefore, of mothers receiving support.

Women whose children have been sexually abused confirmed that, as mothers they indeed need support. Some found reading books about sexual abuse helped them at least initially to understand their own and their children's feelings, and to learn, as one woman said, that "There is a way out and [there are] answers to those questions you've kept hidden." Some women found working with counsellors or therapists facilitated the recognition that "Whatever your reactions are, they're normal reactions," and that mothers can't "expect themselves to be perfect." "Just learning how to talk about the abuse and about other things as well, as a family unit" was the benefit one woman derived from counselling. The professional help she received, as well as talking with friends, helped her to uncover how she felt about the abuse.

Since the majority of the mothers we interviewed are adult survivors of sexual abuse themselves, they recognized the particular difficulties survivors face in dealing with their children's experience of abuse. They spoke of the enormity of the task of coming to terms with memories of their own abuse and realizing its effects while struggling to be strong in support of their children. They maintained that a mother must confront—not suppress or deny—her own feelings if she is to be an effective supporter and advocate for her children. Based on her experience, one woman suggested that survivors share their feelings and emotions around their own abuse with their children. She advised women to share what they can about how they're feeling, but cautioned that it's not details children need as much as assurance that their mother's experience enables her to understand and relate to what they are going through.

When they tell friends, family or systems personnel of their children's experience of abuse, mothers, like survivors, need to know they are believed and that the abuse isn't their fault. As we've noted, several mothers faced disbelief, denial, mother-blaming, and even accusations that they were lying about the abuse of their children when they sought help. Such reactions not only cast unfair and unwarranted aspersions on the mothers' characters, but also exacerbated the difficulties these women had to confront as advocates for their children. Accordingly, it's not surprising one woman advised other mothers to find a counsellor skilled in working with sexually abused children who will hear the child's disclosure. She acknowledged that "Telling Mom wasn't enough," to get the abuse stopped. The counsellor her daughter saw was instrumental in accomplishing that, for without her testimony in court, this mother believes her child's father would still have access to their little girl. Other women said that as well as needing professional backing in standing up to the abuser in the courts, parents also need assistance in helping their children to heal. Citing her own parents' ineffectiveness in helping her to deal with the sexual abuse by her uncle, one survivor urged parents to recognize their limitations and enlist professional help for their children.

Many women maintained that the key thing for mothers is to "Trust your feelings, trust your child." Crucial as that is, the reality is that a mother's word or a child's word is rarely accepted on its own merit by institutions such as the courts, and certainly not by abusers. For mothers to hold on to their trust in their feelings and in their children, support from family and friends and from counsellors often is essential. As well, counsellors, in their role as "professionals," often provide much-needed validation of a child's disclosure.

What Is Helpful

Most of the women we interviewed had turned to counsellors or therapists for support for themselves or their children. Based on their experiences of what's helpful and what's not, they offered advice to counsellors and therapists as well as advice to women making the decision to seek professional support.

Respect and sensitivity are the cornerstones of effective support and counselling. Survivors and mothers said counsellors must follow the lead of the women and children they're working with rather than pushing them. As one woman explained it, that requires sensitivity, good judgement, and recognition of the survivor's right to take responsibility, especially if she blocks or distances herself from the abuse.

> Let the person lead. Remember there are no "wrong" answers. If the survivor has "spaced," try what you think is best but make sure she takes responsibility for being there in phases. It's her life; she's in control of it.

This survivor recalled telling her counsellor that at times she would probably block or "slough off," but that she would be adamant if she didn't want to work on herself and the counsellor would have to listen to that and respect it.

This woman and others learned how to assert their right to have a say in the counselling process. Their assertiveness and the counsellors' respect for it were particularly important in light of survivors' history of having abusers run roughshod over their rights. Too often, the women we interviewed weren't consulted in their therapy. Instead, as one woman described it, she and her daughters were labelled sexual abuse victims, a term she sees as limiting and damaging. Having affixed the label, therapists then determined what would be good for them to do in therapy and pushed them into the victim mold one more time. Her sense is that their accounts weren't seen as valid in the therapy and that she and her children were regarded as "manipulative, lying people who'd somehow manipulated the therapist." She also encountered therapists who believed (disrespectfully, in her opinion) that they could heal their clients, rather than assisting survivors to heal themselves.

Other women told us of bad experiences with counsellors and therapists who were ill-equipped to deal with childhood sexual abuse. One woman was greatly relieved when she finally found a counsellor who felt safe to her because she wasn't shocked by the survivor's disclosure of abuse. Her previous encounters with counsellors had led her to conclude that they were either shocked by sexual abuse or that those who have been doing counselling for too long "lose genuine interest and you're a theory to them, not a person." Still other survivors had perceived a victim-blaming attitude from some therapists as well as a tendency to excuse abusers. Some therapists' simplistic admonitions to "Love yourself," and their inclination to find quick fixes, presented serious difficulties for survivors struggling to understand the complexities of their past.

Having made the rounds searching for skilled, sensitive counsellors, the women we interviewed found that the best help is between women. They said a feminist counsellor is less likely to protect the abuser or make excuses for him, and it's wise to be very careful to choose a counsellor based on referrals from other women and from women's groups.

Women's advice to counsellors, or to anyone who wants to help survivors, focused on sensitivity and an ability to relate to the experience of sexual abuse. Several women acknowledged there's a fine line to walk. On the one hand it's important to recognize that child sexual abuse is a specific form of violence with particular consequences that are not experienced in the same way by every survivor. On the other hand, it's important to realize that all women in our society are vulnerable to sexual violence and survivors are not different or other or bad.

The key, according to several women, is to relate your own experience, to work "from your heart," and not let your personal fears distance you or make you deny the abuse. But don't assume you know what the survivor has been through. One woman put it this way:

> Don't make assumptions. Take people seriously when they say what it was like and don't assume that you know. Be very careful of not victimizing or making incest survivors feel "different." Realize that, as a woman—even if you think you're not an incest survivor—you can still have a lot in common with this woman or child you're dealing with.

She noted, "I'd feel better about a therapist who shared her own experience and made herself vulnerable too."

For survivors, the abusers' betrayal of their trust means, as one woman said, "Trust issues are paramount" in counselling. A counsellor's ability to relate her own experience helps to foster a feeling of trust. However, one woman cautioned against assuming that if you're a survivor yourself you'll be trusted automatically. It's not that simple because, as another woman pointed out, "You can't assume your abuse is the same as hers." She urged helpers to relate but to keep their experiences separate if they can. In her view, anyone who wants to help women or children who've been abused must be very respectful.

> Be patient. Give a lot of caring but also give a lot of space—physical space. Let the person come to you or ask for things. Don't assume anything. Also be somewhat confrontative in a caring way. Push the person a little bit, but don't shove.

Of course, respect for survivors' physical boundaries is particularly important. As one woman stated, a counsellor must never be sexual with a client and counsellors must be especially careful in how they use touch.

Counsellors or therapists who have not been sexually abused themselves were advised by one woman to avoid assumptions: "Don't read theory books and think you know it all." Further, they must guard against treating survivors like victims by "feeling sorry for them or feeling guilty because they haven't been abused themselves."

Two cardinal rules for counsellors were summed up as follows: "Take your cues from survivors, and be honest." Just as self-knowledge and self-acceptance are critically important for survivors in reversing the cycle of abuse, so are they central to a counsellor's effectiveness. As one woman said, if you're a counsellor who isn't "at least semi-comfortable with yourself, don't get into working with people who've been sexually abused." Anyone thinking about working with survivors should, in another woman's opinion, "really think about why they're wanting to do the work and sort out their own stuff first."

Changes Needed in the System

Though there's clearly room for improvement on the part of many counsellors and therapists, the women we interviewed were able to offer constructive suggestions in large measure because most of them had some positive counselling experiences to use as a guide. They'd encountered bad counsellors and therapists but it was the good experiences they were able to draw on in recommending better approaches. Unfortunately, this was not so with the various systems they'd dealt with. In particular, they found the social welfare and criminal justice systems to be fundamentally flawed.

What women wanted and needed from the systems is very simple: they wanted them to stop the abuse. But adult survivors were typically ignored or abandoned by the agencies which could have and should have intervened. In their day, sexual abuse was so hidden, their mothers so powerless, and the family so sacrosanct that turning to an institution for help was not an effective option for children or their mothers. As we've seen in the previous chapter, women whose children were sexually abused in recent years turned to the criminal justice system primarily, and secondarily to the social welfare system, in their efforts to stop the abuse and to protect and support their children. With rare exceptions what both adult survivors and mothers of today experienced was disregard for women and children's rights and safety, and the distinct impression that the systems' real purpose is to uphold men's primacy and abusers' rights.

Women have concluded that drastic measures are required. One adult survivor said, "Society is based on some pretty sick premises and, unless we change those, no amount of programmes and resources will help." Another woman said institutions and agencies "need to be torn apart and built all over again. They're not doing any good; they're doing a lot of damage." The sick premises and damage these women referred to are reflected in the tendency among institutional personnel to excuse abusers' behaviour and to blame the victim.

Repeatedly adult survivors and mothers stressed the importance of removing the abusers' opportunity to abuse. They said: "Get away, take the child out of the situation"; "get the abuser out of the picture"; "don't let him lay eyes on the kid"; "kids need to feel *safe!*" But women who tried to accomplish those goals learned it was impossible unless they had access to sufficient financial resources or happened to find an advocate or a sympathetic police officer, social worker or prosecutor.

All of the mothers we interviewed found ways to help their children—most often drawing on support from counsellors in private practice or a community-based rape crisis centre or child sexual abuse group. The systems set up to protect children and prosecute offenders did neither. As a result, protection was left in the hands of the women.

The women tried to understand why they were met with such indifference. One woman said:

> I have very little faith in the system. I always get the impression from the police that they don't want to deal with child sexual abuse. And personally I don't think people in the social services department know enough about it to even be tackling the problem... And there's a lot of mother-blaming going on.

She wondered if things might be different if government funding for social services hadn't been cut back and if there were teams of workers to deal specifically with child abuse. Another woman questioned the lack of assistance afforded her by government social services personnel. One woman tried to understand the difficulties social workers face with impossibly heavy case loads and pressure to "patch things up so they can put that case on the shelf and feel they're at rest with that particular case." She thinks they should "work to rule" to show the system that social workers can't do it all themselves.

Some women thought of improvements that could be made, such as laws that could be changed to respect a child's right not to see the abuser, and more accessible information about how to get money from Criminal Injury Compensation. Some focused on prevention: more pre-school programmes for children to alert them to child sexual abuse; improved teacher education to enable teachers to detect abuse and better support children; more television programmes and public service announcements to increase awareness of the problem; more toll-free "help-lines" children can call to disclose abuse and get help. Some suggested workshops and support groups to help more women become aware of the effects of abuse, and to let them know they're not alone.

But even the most positive of these suggestions have limitations. For example, what good are "help-lines" or workshops without a comprehensive infrastructure of quality services to back them up? Women's accounts make it clear those services were not available to them. Isn't there also a serious danger of leaving children or adults in the lurch by helping them to disclose without having follow-up mechanisms in place? How do we deal with the dangerous assumption that public education programmes can prevent child sexual abuse when, as one woman pointed out, their real value is in encouraging some children to take the first step of disclosing? As essential as that is, the question remains: what is there for them then? How do we ensure that any new laws (and those already on the books) are implemented and clearly give abusers the message that society will not tolerate the sexual abuse of children?

Obviously, no single strategy will eradicate child sexual abuse. An integrated, co-ordinated, multi-faceted approach is required. Unfortunately there are few signs of that happening. In the interim the onus rests with women and children themselves.

The Work We Have to Do

The tasks they face, the tasks we all face in trying to stop child sexual abuse, are onerous. According to the women we interviewed the key is stopping the abusers. As one woman declared: "The abuse won't stop until the abusers are stopped."

And what does that entail? Some women suggested that it's a matter of breaking the cycle or changing it. To them it means refusing to accept that people can't change. One woman articulated her concern about the myth that exists in society that "once a victim, always a victim." Not only is it untrue, she said, but "There's a connotation that goes with it that you are irreparably damaged, that no matter what you do you'll never be totally healthy. I think it *is* possible to become emotionally healthy." She worries that this myth about victims and the companion notion that "once an offender always an offender" set up a situation "where society can't change. It just becomes a re-creation of a pattern over and over." Furthermore, "It takes away the offender's responsibility to change what he's doing." What's the point in trying to change, she asked, if you're always going to be an offender or a victim? Similarly another woman commented on the common view of a generational cycle of abuse which suggests that if someone has been sexually abused, "they're going to grow up to be an abuser." Not only does the theory of a generational cycle scare her because of its emphasis on "negative expectations," it is also overly simplistic. It denies the reality that girls who are sexually abused rarely become sexually abusive adults, and that not all sexually abusive men were abused as children.

But women were not in agreement on the question of how people change and, in particular, whether abusers can change at all. One woman contended that jail is not the way to deal with offenders: "There should be a choice between treatment or jail." Another woman would make therapy mandatory for abusers. Several women, however, were adamant that the priority, society's central responsibility, must be to protect the child and give her a sense of security and safety by keeping the abuser away from her, which offender treatment programmes rarely do, at least not on a permanent basis. Furthermore, one woman—who was in therapy with the stepfather who abused her—insisted that "therapy doesn't work for offenders because there's a place inside the offender that can never be reached." Offenders, she said, "have no conscience. It's like societal rules don't apply to them; an offender's reality is so distorted."

For other women the problem is that society gives men permission to sexually abuse. The criminal justice system has been extremely reluctant to interfere with the sanctity of the family, and laws on the books do not translate into real restraint of abusers. Neither abusers nor their victims are given clear messages that sexual abuse is against the rules. As we noted previously, none of the abusers discussed in our interviews were prosecuted by the state. Instead, society seems to look for reasons to excuse the abuser's violence. This tendency prompted one woman to argue passionately against ever "accepting any excuses from the offender."

> I really feel strongly about that. Maybe it's because I've tended to look for answers or reasons for things. But once you find the reason, you tend to excuse what he's done. Forget it!

To convey the message to abusers that no excuse is acceptable, that child sexual abuse is wrong and has consequences for offenders too, some women recommended civil suits to exact damages and make abusers pay the costs of survivors' therapy or counselling. Other women, however, despaired of ever having any effect on abusers. In their opinion the only solution is to keep abusers away from children and to focus on empowering women and children. One woman said she thinks teaching women and children self-defence won't help in dealing with an

abuser, "because the abuser uses trust." Nevertheless, she thinks
the psychological assertiveness of self-defence is "good for giving
women and kids a sense of the power and physical control that
men have always had." Another woman emphasized the importance of making children aware of their bodies, aware they don't
have to share their bodies, even with their parents, and aware of
how to say "no." Children in a society that sanctions sexual
abuse have to be taught assertiveness; they can't afford, in her
telling words, "to have innocent eyes."

The conclusion many women have reached is that women
and children must protect themselves. That possibility and the
chance that talking about sexual abuse, exposing it for what it is
might prevent it from continuing, is what one woman identified
as her only source of optimism. She doubts the effectiveness of
anything else because she thinks "If someone wants to sexually
abuse, they'll do it." The powerlessness of children, particularly
female children, must also be addressed. One woman summed
up her understanding of why sexual abuse happens.

> It happens because kids don't have power, because society won't
> recognize the humiliation of childhood. Parents are always sup-
> ported; kids don't get seen as people.

An additional factor is the sexual objectification of women.
She said, "Every time I see the objectification of women, I see
that it's permission to abuse less powerful people. It's part of
sexual violence." The more powerful people in society—men—
have control and the weapons to enforce it. Men make the rules
and they have the authority to define what sexuality is, what acceptable sexual practice is, and what sexual violence is. They
define women and children and use violence—wife assault, rape,
child sexual abuse—or representations of it—pornography—to
"teach" us their definitions.

One woman's analysis summarized the lessons inherent in all
the accounts women gave us of childhood sexual abuse.

> I think that men have been conditioned to believe that they are sup-
> posed to be the ones in control. With regards to their sexuality, dif-
> ferent men have different ideas of when they have lost control.

When they feel they've lost control they try to find a reason for it or they get angry and become abusive and blame it on their victim. The more experienced a man is at keeping control sexually, the more weapons he has and the more likely he is to be able to foresee when to use those weapons and which weapons to use in order to keep control.

No doubt some would like to dismiss such conclusions as bitter or negative or man-hating. No doubt some would hasten to remind us that women can be abusive too. But to dismiss women's experience or to divert attention from the fact of male dominance and its controlling influence over all women and children is to avert our eyes from the truth.

The truth of childhood sexual abuse is horrifying, but it also provides hope. For the attendant truth is that women and children do survive the violation. "Our survival is our strength," as Elizabeth Stanko says. In facing the truth about what women and children must overcome in order to survive, we see how remarkable is their accomplishment. In remembering *how* they did it and *that* they did it, we see it is possible for all of us.

What women and children need is not much to ask. It's belief not blame. It's the right to self-determination and inviolable boundaries. It's love, caring, affection—without strings and distortion. It's a chance to learn, to play, to speak out, to laugh, to find our strengths. It's the right to struggle for autonomy. It's the chance to risk loving others without fear of victimization or the threat of an abuser around every corner. It's freedom from sexual terrorism.

To get what we need we must do what survivors have done. We must listen to each other and believe what we hear. We must see the patterns in our lives and question why we've experienced what we have. We must support each other. We must recollect and learn from our lives what changes to make individually and collectively. We must and we can go beyond survival.

We have much work to do but it is work women have done for hundreds of years. Taking our cue from the women and children in this book, there's no sign of stopping now.

References

Stanko, E. A. 1985. *Intimate Intrusions: Women's Experience of Male Violence*. London: Routledge & Kegan Paul.

Child Sexual Abuse Research Project
Women's Research Centre 1985

Assumptions

1. Sexual abuse of children is wrong.
2. Being sexually abused distorts one's own experience of one's sexuality.
3. Sexual victimization means a total invasion to the core of one's being and it is personalized rather than generalized.
4. It is primarily female children who are sexually abused.
5. Male victims of child sexual abuse are female surrogates (as in pornography) and male adult survivors deal with it differently than female adult survivors.
6. Sexual abuse of children crosses racial and class lines.
7. There is no classic family profile in child sexual abuse.
8. Children in our society are considered *not* to have rights.
9. Sexually abused children *do* tell others about their sexual abuse.
10. Children's behaviour is used as a rationalization for sexualizing them and for sexually abusing them.
11. The sexualizing of children in the media is a projection of male desires on children and creates the expectation for children to meet them.
12. A child who is sexually abused is seen as an adult; she is held responsible for the sexual abuse and treated as other than a child.
13. Sexually abused children are assumed to have sexual knowledge beyond their years and therefore are perceived as sexual adults.
14. There aren't enough effective services for sexually abused children and adult survivors, and government cutbacks, economic restraint, etc. have had a negative impact on service delivery.
15. There is a difference between males and females who sexually abuse children, especially in terms of frequency, intensity and dynamics of the abuse.
16. There is a relationship (training) between the sexual abuse of children, wife battering, prostitution, pornography, rape, male sexuality and the heterosexual imperative.
17. There is social permission for the sexual abuse of children by men.

18. With few exceptions, it is men who sexually abuse children.
19. Sexual abuse of children will be stopped only when the subordination of women ends.
20. The more sexual abuse of children is uncovered, the more threat it poses to the ideology of the Right and the more attempts will be made to cover it up and cut off services.
21. There is no safe place from sexual abuse; men have power to take the private world of the home/family and do with it what they want, including making it even more private.

Interview Guide for
Child Sexual Abuse Research:
Adult Survivors

Introduction

[Note to interviewer: Begin by explaining why we're doing the research, that is, to obtain women's descriptions of their experience of childhood sexual abuse and use them as the basis for developing an analysis of the issue from women's perspective. Outline who the Women's Research Centre is, similar work the Centre has done before, and that our aim is to do research that will be useful to women and lead to action. Explain that interviews are strictly confidential, that the identity of the women interviewed will be known only to WRC researchers and will be protected in any research report, book, or use we make of the research.]

In these interviews we're asking women to describe their experience to us so we can understand, and help others to understand, what sexual abuse really is. So we're going to ask you to tell us what your experience is, what happened to you, how sexual abuse affected you, and what you think could be done to help other women.

To begin we want to get some background information by asking you to tell us a bit about what your family and what your life was like generally.

Description of what life was like generally, when you were a child:

A. How would you describe your family? number of boys and girls in the family? were the girls and boys expected to behave differently, do different chores, etc.? what was your mother and father's relationship like, how did they talk about each other? what was your relationship like with your mother, father, brothers and sisters? did your mother work/have a job outside the home? who else lived with you? which people in your family were close to each other? what does "close" mean—for example: talking together? where did your family live? what was your family's economic situation?

B. Were members of your family affectionate with each other? what was their attitude about touching? was it all right to be seen naked? what impression or understanding did your family give about sex? did anyone in the family use pornography? how?

C. Did you have close friends your own age? how were their lives similar or different than yours? were there women you looked up to or admired? why—what did you admire about them?

D. What did you want to be when you grew up? did you like school? why/why not?

Description of sexual abuse:

We want to ask you now to describe, in your own words, your experience(s) of being sexually abused in order to help us and others to understand better what sexual abuse is from the point of view of women who have experienced it.

A. What happened to you? who abused you? was it one person or more than one? [*Note to interviewer: From here on use the woman's term for the abuser(s) in asking the questions.*] how often did it happen? how old were you when it began? when would it happen? under what circumstances? what did he do to you?

B. How did you think about it—about what was happening? how did you realize it was "abuse," rather than something that happened to everyone? at the time, *why* did you think it was happening?

C. What did he [the abuser] say to you about what he was doing to you? how did he talk about it? what other messages did you get from him about the abuse—for example: threats, explanations? did he use pornography? do you think he abused others too?

D. What was he like otherwise, when he wasn't abusing you? how was he with other people—inside and outside the family? what did/does he do for a living? [*Note to interviewer: Refer back to woman's answers to the questions regarding "Description of what life was like." If more that one offender/abuser, ask about any differences the woman experienced.*]

Effects of sexual abuse:

A. How did the abuse make you feel? did your feelings change over time? how? how did being sexually abused affect you? [*Note to interviewer: Not just in sexual terms.*] what did you do, how did you behave as a result of being sexually abused? Some women have said they "trained" themselves not to remember what happened to them; others have said they used drugs or alcohol as an escape. How did your seeing the abuse—what was happening to you—as "wrong"/not okay make you feel about yourself? about him? about your family? how did it affect your relationship with your friends?

B. How did the abuse make you feel, in general about your sexuality? about your sense of yourself sexually? about your expectations of relationships? of sexual relationships, in particular? about men? about yourself in relation to men? about women? about yourself in relation to women? Some women have said that because they are lesbians/bi-sexuals they were particularly affected by being sexually abused, for example, in how they accepted their sexuality/lesbianism. What particular effects, if any, did the abuse result in for you because you're a lesbian/bi-sexual?

Trying to stop the abuse:

When did the abuse stop? how? did you tell anyone you were being abused? for example: family, friends, professionals such as social workers, doctors, etc.? if "no," what do you think stopped you from telling anyone? if "yes," who did you tell? what made you choose that person? or people? what did you say? how did you talk about it? how did they respond? what did they say/do? why do you think they responded that way? Some women have said that they tried to let the offender/abuser know they didn't like it, didn't want it to continue, by crying or avoiding him. Others said they couldn't do anything to stop the abuser from abusing them. What was your experience? what did you want someone to say or do (to help you)? was there someone in particular you hoped would help? what would have helped (to stop the abuse)? [*Note to interviewer: Be sure to note fully any "mother-blaming" comments that come up here.*]

Your life, now:

What are your feelings now about what happened to you? about the abuse you experienced? about why it happened? how does being a survivor of sexual abuse affect your life today? your relationship with your mother? with your brothers and sisters? with your friends? with the abuser? as an adult, have you talked with the abuser about the abuse? We realize that it's often hard for women generally to talk about sex and sexual relationships but we understand that being a survivor of sexual abuse can affect the survivor's sexual life. Some women, for example, have said they don't like certain parts of their bodies to be touched or they don't like to be hugged, and so on. So we need to ask you about that. How does being a survivor of sexual abuse affect your current sexual life? your sexual relationships? your sexual life with the person you're involved with now? what about pornography—does your lover use porn or have any of your lovers used porn?

Advice to others / what you've learned from your experience:

What advice would you give, what would you say to other women or children who've been sexually abused? if your own child was being abused what could you do to protect her/him? what would you tell people who want to help women and children who've been sexually abused?

[Note to interviewer: Ending the interview.] Is there anything you want to tell us that we haven't asked about? how are you feeling now after this interview? [Note to interviewer: Indicate whom she can call if she needs to talk, if there's more she wants to say.]

Interview Guide for Child Sexual Abuse Research: Mothers of Sexual Abuse Survivors

Introduction

[Note to interviewer: Begin by explaining why we're doing the research that is, to obtain women's descriptions of their experience of childhood sexual abuse and use them as the basis for developing an analysis of the issue from women's perspective. Outline who the Women's Research Centre is, similar work the Centre has done before, and that our aim is to do research that will be useful to women and lead to action. Explain that interviews are strictly confidential, that the identity of the women interviewed will be known only to WRC researchers and will be protected in any research report, book, or use we make of the research.]

We're interviewing mothers of children who have been sexually abused because we want to understand, and help others to understand, mothers' perspective/experience of sexual abuse. So, we're going to ask you to tell us what your experience is, what you know of what happened to your child/children, what has happened in your family since the abuse was disclosed, how the sexual abuse has affected you and your child/children, and what you think could be done to help other mothers and children.

Background:

A. First I want to ask you to talk about your own life: do you work outside the home? did you ever? when? at what jobs? your friends, social life, now? what was your childhood like? were you abused as a child? *[Note to interviewer: Ask if it's all right to ask more questions about it; if so, continue.]* how old were you? who abused you? what happened? what did he do to you? how did he talk about it? *[Note to interviewer: Use the woman's own term/words for the abuser.]* when did the abuse stop? how/what stopped it? what was the response of professionals and agencies you talked with/dealt with? I'm going to go on now to other kinds of questions but if there are ways your being abused as a child affects your answers to these questions or reminds you of other things you want to say, please tell me.

What were your expectations or hopes about marriage? about having a family? about what your life would be like? how does the way your life has worked out so far fit with your expectations or hopes—specifically, regarding: marriage, work, children? have you experienced any kind of abuse as an adult—for example, battering? sexual assault? when? by whom? what happened?

B. Let's talk now about your own family, you and your child/children. How would you describe your family, that is the family you are the head of? [Note to interviewer: Verb tense in these questions will depend on when the child sexual abuse took place—i.e. recently or long ago.] how did/do members of the family talk about each other? how are boys and girls in the family treated regarding responsibilities, chores, expectations, schooling? differently? the same? are/were members of the family affectionate with each other? how do they get along together? what is/was the social life of the family? did/do you all do things together? what kinds of things? who else is/was around—for example, friends of yours, of your child/children's, of your husband's? or social workers, etc?

C. What was/is the attitude in your family around sexuality? touching? being naked? did anyone in the family use pornography? did any of your friends or other friends of family members use porn? who? how is this different from the family you grew up in?

Description of child sexual abuse:

[Note to interviewer: If more than one child was abused be sure to be clear in your notes who's who.] How did you learn about the sexual abuse? which child/children? who told you? when? how were you told? what was said? how would you describe your child/children who were sexually abused? who abused your child/children? how old was he [the abuser]? how old was the child? when did it happen? what did the abuse consist of? in what circumstances? what do you know about how it happened? what differences, if any, did you notice in your child/children's behaviour? how would you describe the abuser? how did you feel about him prior to knowing he abused your child/children? how had he treated you?

how had he treated the child/children? what was he like with "outsiders?"

Disclosure of child sexual abuse:

A. What had you known or thought about child sexual abuse *before* you knew your child/children was/were abused?

B. What were your reactions/feelings when you learned your child/children had been abused? did you believe it? have doubts? did you have difficulty knowing how to talk with her/them about it? who outside the family did you tell or talk to about the abuse? what was their response? were you made to feel guilty?

C. What was the offender/abuser's response to the disclosure? what happened to the offender as a result of the disclosure? did you tell him you knew? what did he say about it? about the child/children? did you believe him? did others (outsiders, the professionals, etc.) believe him? what was the effect of the disclosure on your relationship with him? what was the effect on the abuser's relationship with the child/children he'd abused?

D. What was your child's/children's response to the disclosure? how was your relationship with the child/children (who was/were abused) affected? what was the effect on the other children in the family? on your relationship with them?

E. Describe how the agencies or institutions you and your child/children dealt with responded to the disclosure.

F. [*Note to interviewer: If the woman was herself sexually abused as a child ask the following question.*] What differences, if any, do you see in how you were treated compared to how your child was treated—regarding disclosure?

Effects of child sexual abuse:

What are the things you see now as "signs" of abuse that you didn't see before the disclosure? how do you think being sexually abused has affected your child/children? how has her/their behaviour changed? what does she/do they say are the effects? what, if any,

260 Recollecting Our Lives

long-term problems do you foresee in your relationship with your child/children as a result of the abuse?

Your feelings, now:

What are your feelings now about yourself? the child/children? the abuser? the institutions or agencies that were involved or that you went to for help?

Advice to others / what you've learned from your experience:

What advice would you give to other people about how to deal with child sexual abuse? who or what helped you to deal with it? how? what/who helped your child/children to deal with it? to stop it? what in your opinion was the key thing in stopping the abuse? what would you tell other people/mothers who've had the kind of experience you've had?

[*Note to interviewer: Ending the interview.*] Is there anything you want to tell us that we haven't asked about? How are you feeling now, after this interview? [*Note to interviewer: Indicate whom she can call if she needs to talk, if there's more she wants to say.*]

Bibliography

Abel, Gene G., Judith V. Becker, William D. Murphy, and Barry Flanagan. "Identifying Dangerous Child Molesters." Paper presented at 11th Banff International Conference on Behaviour Modification, March 1979.

Aries, Phillippe. *Centuries of Childhood*. New York: Knopf, 1962.

Armstrong, Louise. *Kiss Daddy Goodnight: A Speak Out on Incest*. New York: Pocket Books, 1978.

——. "Making an Issue of Incest." *Northeast Magazine* (3 February 1985):10-29.

Barry, Kathleen. *Female Sexual Slavery*. New York: Avon Books, 1979.

Bass, Ellen, and Laura Davis. *I Never Told Anyone: Writings by Women Survivors of Child Sexual Abuse*. New York: Harper & Row, 1983.

——. *The Courage to Heal: A Guide for Women Survivors of Child Sexual Abuse*. New York: Harper & Row, 1988.

Brickman, Julie. "Examining the Myths: A Feminist View of Incest." *Kinesis* (June 1982):8-9, 15.

——. "Feminist, Nonsexist, and Traditional Models of Therapy: Implications for Working with Incest." *Women and Therapy* 3 No. 1 (Spring 1984):49-67.

Briere, John. "The Effects of Childhood Sexual Abuse on Later Psychological Functioning: Defining a Post-Sexual-Abuse Syndrome." Paper presented at the Third National Conference on Sexual Victimization of Children, Children's Hospital National Medical Centre, Washington, D.C., April 1984.

Burgess, Ann W., and Lynda L. Holmstrom. "Sexual Trauma of Children and Adolescents: Pressure, Sex and Secrecy." *Nursing Clinics of North America* 10 No. 3 (September 1975):551-63.

Butler, Sandra. *Conspiracy of Silence: The Trauma of Incest*. San Francisco: New Glide Publications, 1978.

——. "Incest: whose reality, whose theory." *Aegis* (Summer/Autumn 1980):48-55.

Carter, Betty. "A Feminist Perspective on the Badgley Report, Sexual Offences Against Children." *Occasional Papers in Social Policy Analysis* No. 10. Toronto: O.I.S.E., 1985.

Clark, Lorenne. "Beyond Badgley: A Critical Review." *Canadian Human Rights Advocate* 1 No. 4 (April 1985):7-9.

Cole, Susan G. "Incest: Conflicting Interests." *Broadside* (February 1987):8-9.

Courtois, Christine A. "Victims of Rape and Incest." *The Counselling Psychologist* 8 No. 7 (1979):1, 38-40.

——. "Studying and Counselling Women With Past Incest Experience." *Victimology: An International Journal* 5 Nos. 1,2 (1982):322-34

Danica, Elly. *Don't: A Woman's Word*. Charlottetown: gynergy books, 1988.

Dawson, Ross. "Fathers Anonymous—A Group Treatment Program for Sexual Offenders." In *Sexual Abuse of Children in the 1980s*, edited by Benjamin Schlesinger. Toronto: University of Toronto Press, 1986.

Dietz, Christine A., and John L. Craft. "Family Dynamics of Incest: A New Perspective." *Social Casework* 61 (December 1980):602-9.

Donaldson, Mary Ann. *Incest, Years After: Putting the Pain to Rest*. Fargo, ND: Village Family Service Centre, 1983.

Dreiblatt, Irwin S. "Issues in the Evaluation of the Sex Offender." Paper presented to Washington State Psychological Association Meetings, May 1982.

Dunwoody, Ellen. "Sexual Abuse of Children: A Serious Widespread Problem." *Response* 5 No. 4 (July/August 1982):1-2, 13-14.

Finklehor, David. *Child Sexual Abuse: New Theory and Research*. New York: The Free Press, 1984.

Ford, Ann R. "Breach of Trust: Unmasking the Incest Advocates." *Healthsharing* (Fall 1982):10-13.

Forward, Susan, and Craig Buck. *Betrayal of Innocence: Incest and its Devastation*. New York: Penguin Books, 1979.

Fritz, Gregory S., Kim Stoll, and Nathaniel N. Wagner. "A Comparison of Males and Females Who Were Sexually Molested as Children." *Journal of Sex and Marital Therapy* 7 (Spring 1981):54-9.

Geiser, Robert L. *Hidden Victims: The Sexual Abuse of Children*. Boston: Beacon Press, 1979.

Gelinas, D.J. "The Persisting Negative Effects of Incest." *Psychiatry* 46 No. 4 (November 1983):312-32.

Gil, Elina. *Outgrowing the Pain*. San Francisco: Launch Press, 1983.

Grescoe, Audrey. "Nowhere to Run." *Homemaker's Magazine* (April 1981):26-44.

Groth, A. Nicholas. "Guidelines for the Assessment and Management of the Offender." In *Sexual Assault of Children and Adolescents*, edited by Ann W. Burgess, A. Nicholas Groth, Lynda L. Holmstrom and Suzanne Sgroi, Toronto: Lexington Books, 1978.

Hamblin, Angela, and Romi Bowen. "Sexual Abuse of Children." *Spare Rib* (May 1981):6-8,31.

Herman, Judith. *Father/Daughter Incest*. Cambridge: Harvard University Press, 1981.

Jones, Margaret J. "Psychotherapy with children who have been sexually assaulted: some general principles." Paper presented at the workshop Sexual Abuse of Children: A Feminist Perspective, sponsored by Feminist Counselling Association and the Justice Institute of B.C., Sept. 12, 1982.

Lahey, Kathleen A. "Research on Child Abuse in Liberal Patriarchy." In *Taking Sex Into Account: The Police Consequences of Sexist Research*, edited by Jill M. Vickers. Ottawa: Carleton University Press, 1984.

Lystad, Mary. "Child Sexual Abuse: When it Happens in the Family." *Response 5* No. 2 (March/April 1982):5-7.

Martens, Tony, Brenda Daily, and Maggie Hodgson. *The Spirit Weeps: Characteristics and Dynamics of Incest and Child Sexual Abuse with a Native Perspective*. Edmonton: Nechi Institute, 1988.

Maynard, Fredelle. "The Girl Child as Sex Object." *Chatelaine* (June 1982):49, 84-89.

McIntyre, Kevin. "Role of Mothers in Father-Daughter Incest: A Feminist Analysis." *Social Work* (November 1981):462-6.

McLaughlin, Laurie. "Some Missing Pieces: New Books on Incest." *Aegis* No. 36 (Autumn 1982):61-4.

Miller, Alice. *The Drama of the Gifted Child*. New York: Basic Books, 1981.

———. *Thou Shalt Not Be Aware: Society's Betrayal of the Child*. New York: New American Library, 1984.

Mitchell, Alanna. "Child Sexual Assault." In *No Safe Place: Violence Against Women and Children*, edited by Connie Guberman and Margie Wolfe. Toronto: Women's Press, 1985.

Penfold, P. Susan, and Gillian A. Walker. *Women and the Psychiatric Paradox*. Montreal: Eden Press, 1983.

Rankel, Marlene D. "Dealing With Incest." *Resource News* 6 No. 5 (February 1982):25-6.

Rush, Florence. *The Best Kept Secret: Sexual Abuse of Children*. Englewood Cliffs: Prentice Hall, 1980.

Russell, Diana E. *The Secret Trauma: Incest in the Lives of Girls and Women*. New York: Basic Books, 1986.

Russell, Watson. "A Hidden Epidemic." *Newsweek* (May 14, 1984):30-6.

Sanford, Linda T. *The Silent Children: A Parent's Guide to the Prevention of Child Sexual Abuse*. New York: McGraw Hill, 1982.

Scott, Darlene. *A Blueprint for Action: The Report of the Working Group on Child Sexual Abuse*. St. John's: Community Services Council, 1986.

Sigurdson, Eric, and Malcom Strang. "The Role of a Rural Team in Preventing Sexual Abuse of Children." *Canadian Family Physician* 30 (February 1984):440-4.

Snowdon, Rich. "Working With Incest Offenders: Excuses, Excuses, Excuses." *Aegis* No. 35 (Summer 1982):56-63.

Stanko, Elizabeth A. *Intimate Intrusions: Women's Experience of Male Violence*. London: Routledge & Kegan Paul, 1985.

Tingle, David, George W. Barnard, Lynn Robbins, Gustave Newman, and David Hutchinson. "Childhood and Adolescent Characteristics of Pedophiles and Rapists." *International Journal of Law and Psychiatry* 9 (1986):103-116.

Ward, Elizabeth. *Father Daughter Rape*. London: The Women's Press, 1984.

Weber, Ellen. "Sexual Abuse Begins at Home." *MS* No. 5 (April 1977):64-7, 105.

West, Lois A. "Sexually Abused Children and Teen-Age Prostitution." *Response* 3 No. 9 (May 1980):2.

White, Sue, Gerald A. Strom, Gail Santilli, and Bruce M. Halpin. "Interviewing Young Sexual Abuse Victims With Anatomically Correct Dolls." *Child Abuse and Neglect* 10 (1986):519-29.

Index

The Women's Research Centre is a community-based, feminist organization focused on research which makes visible women's experience and facilitates action on women's issues. We have conducted research and produced publications on violence against women and economic issues such as pay equity, and have published guides for women's groups on action research and evaluation methods. We also assist groups in developing their own projects. A complete list of our publications is available from the Centre.

We are a non-profit, charitable organization funded by government grants and contracts and by donations. (Tax receipts will be issued on request.)

We would appreciate receiving feedback from the readers of *Recollecting Our Lives*. Please send your comments on the book—how it is useful, how it could be improved, suggestions for further work in the area—to the Women's Research Centre, 101-2245 West Broadway, Vancouver, B.C. V6K 2E4.

Press Gang Publishers is a feminist collective committed to publishing works by women who are often made invisible and whose voices go unheard.

For a free listing of our books in print, write to:
    Press Gang Publishers
    603 Powell Street
    Vancouver, B.C. V6A 1H2 Canada

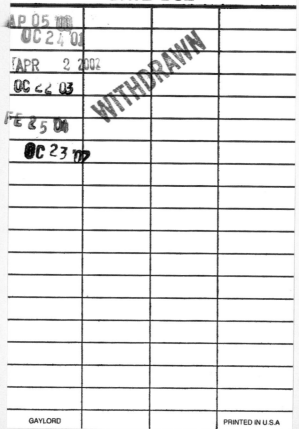